T0339815

RED STATES, BLUE STATES

RED STATES, BLUE STATES

and the Coming Sharecropper Society

Stephen D. Cummings

Algora Publishing
New York

Library of Congress Cataloging-in-Publication Data —

Cummings, Stephen D., 1947-
    Red states, blue states, and the coming sharecropper society / Stephen D.
Cummings.
        p. cm.
    Includes bibliographical references and index.
    ISBN 978-0-87586-627-7 (trade paper: alk. paper) — ISBN 978-0-87586-628-4 (case
laminate: alk. paper) — ISBN 978-0-87586-629-1 (ebook) 1. United States—Politics and
government—20th century. 2. Political parties—United States. I. Title.
    JK2316.C766 2008
    324.2736—dc22
                            2008010421

Front Cover: © Joseph Sohm/Visions of America/Corbis

Printed in the United States

For Mitzi, Squeaky,
and the other denizens of
Lime Avenue

For Noah, Adeline, and Zaden,
and the nation
they will inherit

TABLE OF CONTENTS

Democrats have been frustrated not only by the lack of a clear message by the party leadership in the 2000, 2002, and 2004 campaigns but also by the lack of courage in articulating such a message. This book started as an answer to that persistent weakness, particularly for those of us in the California Democratic Party who, in campaign after campaign, have seen national candidates and their consultants paralyzed by polling data and focus groups, and acting as if they were afraid of their own shadow—doing their best not to offend anyone. In the process they ended up not only alienating everyone but looking weak and confused, to boot. We have seen them position their campaigns in this direction or that, trying to gain the support of disparate voting blocs. We have seen them attempt to appear strong on defense, when in fact their convictionless mush made them look the opposite—regardless of what they said or did. We have seen them attempt to position themselves on an issue such as "choice," or express their religious beliefs, and throw around the word "values" like a new found toy; most of these attempts have not been very convincing. And while all of this was going on, we saw the activist base that we depend on abandoning the Democratic Party, in many cases because they were fed up with manufactured campaigns promoted without conviction. On top of this the ground-level activists felt that they already had been abandoned for big money–big media campaigns.

These activists said time after time that the candidates had no backbone or, in the political parlance of the Vietnam War era, lacked the courage of their convictions. Many activists were alienated by the fact that candidates would run away from their basic principles and political reference points, even running away from words such as "liberal," as if basic political principles can be re-invented through the right media relations campaign. In an attempt to make the Democratic Party more effective, we have seen a number of new initiatives, such as George Lakoff's work on framing issues. We are also seeing the California Democratic Party embark on its new "faith and values" initiative across the state, certainly a valuable project, worth doing.

But what these efforts and responses lack is a fundamental justification for why the average American should take any of this seriously; there has been no attempt in recent times to justify why anyone should be a liberal or follow a liberal progressive agenda. In fact, much of the effort has been to show why Democrats are NOT liberals, and why they can be trusted because they are not that much different from the other guys.

That was not the case forty years ago. Anyone watching the 1964 Democratic Convention on television knew exactly where the Democratic Party stood. They were liberals and proud of it. And they took no prisoners when it came to excoriating the Republicans at their convention that year. Vietnam and subsequent political events changed all that. But the most important loss was the separation of the Democratic Party from its mid-century liberal New Deal roots. The subsequent Democratic Party editions as represented by the Carter and Clinton administrations have been pale reproductions of the original and not all that convincing. When one realizes that George W. Bush managed to get over 50% of the vote in 2004 with an administration that will go down as one of the worst that this country has endured (rivaling James Buchanan's administrative drift into the crisis of the Civil War), one can only begin to grapple with the magnitude of the weakness of the Democratic Party message.

What the Democratic Party lacks today is a theoretical justification, historic, economic, and social, for its liberal policies. Without such a justification, its policies and its platform positions have lacked the cohesion and conviction necessary to compete in, let alone win, the ideological battle with the Republicans and conservatives who have been working on that message since their defeat in 1964. In a sense the victories that the Republicans have achieved can now be seen to have been accomplished by default, because they had no real competition. And despite such lack of competition and with complete command of the ideological platform, as well as the media vehicles to deliver it, the Republicans have failed spectacularly. The day-to-day soap opera of incompetence that is the George W. Bush Administration is graphic evidence of that failure. And yet this administration has survived because there has been no credible alternative to them and there is no answer to the question of why a liberal–progressive orientated administration would do any better.

These are the questions that this book seeks to answer: What are the historical and economic roots of what we now call liberal–progressive thought; and why could it and its political vehicle, which is currently the Democratic Party, succeed where the Republicans have failed? An initial response to that question was made in the first part of my 1998 book, *The Dixification of America: The American Odyssey into the Conservative Economic Trap.* In that book, an attempt was made to split the US into two economic models that had their origins in the economies of the Northeast and the South. It was observed that the liberal model of the Northeast was more successful than the conservative model of the South, but that the political dynamics of the country following Richard Nixon's Southern Strategy allowed a nationalized version of the Southern model to become US economic policy over the next four decades, and with it, the long-term economic dangers of that model.

Today these questions take on new urgency. First and foremost, even without the Iraq War and subsequent occupation, the George W. Bush Administration has become the new standard of economic failure. The budget deficits, the financial crises in the real estate and securities markets, the dependency on foreign funds and central banks, the destruction from Hurricane Katrina and the bungled "recovery" efforts in New Orleans and the Gulf Coast, and the virtual abandonment of domestic needs and priorities all point out the risks I outlined in 1998.

Second, a whole list of terms has been coined in the last decade to enable political discourse on general problems like those outlined in my earlier book. High on that list are the terms "Red state" and "Blue state". On the night of the 2000 election, as states won by Bush (red) and Al Gore (blue) were posted on the election night board shown to TV viewers, the geographic pattern created by the red and blue blocs of color created a whole new political lexicon and a new reference for discussion. The Red states were clustered in the states of the Old Confederacy, connected to the states on the High Plains and the Rocky Mountains. Those states plus some key Midwest states and New Hampshire gave Bush an electoral college victory while losing the popular vote. Gore's Blue states were clustered in the Northeast, the upper Midwest and the Pacific. Beyond being places on a map, the red and blue areas seemed to convey a larger meaning. As a general statement, the Red states were more rural, culturally more conservative and poorer. The Blue states were more urban, culturally liberal, and richer.

Since the 2000 election, many a political article has referenced "red states" and "blue states," and we have further variations of the color scheme of light and dark red and blue, purple, and everything else in between. We have seen it applied to counties, to cities, and just about every political construct you can think of in this country. And we have also seen this color system integrated by political analysts in many different ways. This book was not written for the purpose of defining or clarifying such terminology; in fact, it will no doubt add to the confusion. It will not attempt to define what is a red or blue state, which states or regions they comprise and which election they refer to (although the 2004 election is used as a reference point for discussion and to simplify the geographic anomalies of earlier elections), whether they are Democratic or Republican, or even to some degree liberal or conservative. Those factors change over time in each state. And certainly within a state or political jurisdiction there will be exceptions. But Red states and Blue states have general economic and political characteristics and this book will present a discussion of historical patterns regarding those characteristics that have long term economic consequences. Some of the current impacts can be seen in the statistical charts in this book. In this regard, the Red state–Blue state discussion in this book is an extension of the argument made in *The Dixification of America* ten years ago.

Today, the political dialogue is dominated by those states that elected George W. Bush—the Red states. At the core of the Red states were the old ante-bellum slaves states which symbolized four centuries of worker exploitation, from indentured servants to slaves to sharecroppers to factory workers, and along with their compatriot Red states they represent today's abandoned workers as America has been put up for sale and jobs leave for overseas. It is the people in these Red states and their counterparts else-where that investment guru Warren Buffett was referring to when he noted in his March 5, 2005, annual letter to his Berkshire Hathaway investors that, far from becoming George W. Bush's "Ownership Society," America was turning into the new "Sharecropper Society" — a place where people are virtual tenant workers for foreign masters in what is tantamount to a quasi economic vassal state. Like the Old South, whose economic fortunes were in the hands of New York and London banks, twenty-first century America finds itself at the economic mercy of Asian central banks.

As historian Paul Kennedy pointed out, when you run any organization (not to mention a country) on other people's money, bad things are bound to happen. For Britain, two world wars brought virtual bankruptcy and al-lowed the United States to surpass it as the dominant global power. Now the US finds itself having to borrow several billion dollars a day to finance the war in Iraq. Thus we have an amazing situation: China, the country con-sidered by many to be the greatest threat to America's super power status, is lending billions of dollars each day to finance our war, just as we lent bil-lions to Britain and its allies to fight World War I. Needless to say, it is a parallel that most Americans find very uncomfortable. And when the market value of the European stock markets exceeded US stock markets for the first time since World War I (first quarter 2007 report by Thomson Financial/ Datastream), the parallels are even more ominous.

This book will show that since the founding of this country, two eco-nomic models have guided this nation, one that evolved into the economic activity of what we now call the Blue states, and one for what we now call the Red states. One of them expanded economic opportunity; one stifled that opportunity through economic exploitation. One made the United States a global economic power; the other became an economic colony for the rest of the nation. One was an agent of innovation; the other was an agent of reac-tion. One represented change and reform. The other clung to the status quo. It is this division that has powered the American experience. Through much of that period, when the values exemplified by the Blues states have predom-inated, the nation has prospered. Likewise, the discouraging performance of the current Red-state dominated culture reinforces the case for Blue-state economic and social policies.

However, while this book extensively discusses American economic development in terms of seventeenth- through twentieth-century geography, it is important to understand that this is not a book about economics or social behavior. It is not an intellectual discussion over some economic or social point. At its core this book is about politics—twenty-first century American politics in general and Democratic Party politics in particular. Some readers will be disappointed that the potential political discussion about Red states and Blue states is cut short. But I have found in my years in Democratic Party politics that fine sounding discussions and political repartee do not do a whole lot of good if you lose the election. The voters have the final say, and if you can't convince them, it doesn't matter who else you can convince. This book is not about noble political debate; it is about how to influence the elections in 2008 and thereafter, and how to run the country.

This book provides Democratic Party leaders with a theoretical and philosophical basis from a historical, economic, and social point of view to advance those ideas that were so successful for the Democratic Party from 1930 to 1964. Many things have changed over time, but it is my belief that the core values embodied in those years by the Democratic Party (and those that they borrowed from earlier periods) are as important today as they were then. In fact, I would argue that the polls showing that the overwhelming majority of Americans feel that the country is heading in the wrong track clearly show that the values subscribed by the Democratic Party of 1930–1964 have a ready American audience waiting to hear them if the party would adapt them for use in the 2008 election.

And so, based on the above, this book is divided into two parts. The first part begins by outlining the problems this country faces after forty years of conservative economic policy and the vicissitudes of the George W. Bush Administration. As this section points out, the United States has descended into a quasi-bankrupt vassal state of China and the Asian central banks, deep in debt to foreign interests. The next chapter goes on to outline the historical economic forces that have divided this country, their consolidation into what can be called Red-state and Blue-state culture, and their long-term economic impact on the country. The third chapter presents a set of statistical charts divided by Red states and Blue states based on the 2004 election. They note various economic characteristics in the current economic data. The fourth chapter of the first section discusses the economic implications of the Red-state culture, which has dominated the last 40 years.

The second half of this book deals with the Democratic Party response to what is laid out in the first half of the book. The first chapter of this section is a general political discussion of the party and recent events. The final three chapters, an overview of the Democrats in the 1920s, the speeches of William Jennings Bryan, and a brief discussion of the 1932 campaign and the early organization of the New Deal, are presented to bring to modern-day Democrats some of the historical background with regard to the making of the Democratic Party up to 1932. This provides Democrats a model by which to make the Democratic Party a majority party once again. The last portion of the final chapter is an attempt to put together a modern-day Democratic Party platform outline based on the methods used in putting together the New Deal in 1932–33.

While there are no doubt other avenues that this book could have taken, it is my belief that the most critical need of our time is to change political direction in 2008. And as inadequate as it has been in recent times (the Iraq funding vote in May 2007 is a chilling reminder), the only realistic option is the Democratic Party—a Democratic Party that knows what it wants and has the historical, economic and philosophical tools to get there. It is only by making major changes that we have any hope of escaping the Sharecropper Society.

My thanks to Algora Publishing for making this book possible.

Stephen Cummings
Ventura, California

Part I

The American Landscape
Past and Present

1. America Today

When the Berlin Wall came down, and later when the Soviet Union disintegrated, there was great rejoicing in conservative America. These events, which signified the end of the Cold War, were viewed as the tangible proof of the triumph of American Capitalism. Indeed, John Hopkins Professor Francis Fukuyama proclaimed this triumph as "the end of history"[1] in which the ideological conflict between Capitalism and Communism, which had been posited as the basis of conflict for the prior half-century, no longer existed. But in the chronological scale of things, such celebration has been misplaced, as the dry rot of conservative economic thought has undermined the economic structure of this country to an extent not seen since the American Revolutionary War. This is a stunning achievement of epic economic mismanagement. Indeed, in March 2006 US Senator Harry Reid labeled the Bush Administration "dangerously incompetent."[2] The ongoing financial crisis and the bailout of America's most prominent commercial and investment banks by Asian and Middle Eastern sovereign wealth funds at the end of 2007 graphically illustrates the scale of that incompetence.[3]

---

1   Francis Fukuyama, *The End of History and the Last Man* (New York: The Free Press, 1992).
2   Associated Press, "Reid: 'Dangerously Incompetent,'" *CBS News*, March 23, 2006, http://www.cbsnews.com/stories/2006/03/23/politics/main1432159.shtml.
3   David Wighton, "Morgan Stanley taps China for $5bn," *FT.com*, December 19, 2007, http://www.ft.com/cms/s/0/294ed78a-ae3a-11dc-97aa-0000779fd2ac.html.

This mismanagement has been twofold. The most obvious aspect of this mismanagement visible to most Americans has been in defense and foreign policy, in particular the war in Iraq. Iraq is degenerating into civil war, with the populace either fleeing the country by the millions or aligning itself in different camps and with death squads from each segment of the society roaming the countryside in search of confronting and eliminating the opposition. All the while there are limited supplies of food and gasoline, only limited electricity and a much reduced supply of oil from one of the largest oil reserves in the world. The budding civil war has the potential of turning into a regional war, creating a situation in which the US will not only be unable to stop escalating conflict but may very well find itself in the crossfire. While Iraq is being torn apart, both the Iraqi and United States treasuries are being systematically looted through dodgy accounting and bogus no-bid contracts. In additional to their adverse military and financial impact, these policies have also had the effect of alienating governments and people around the world from the United States.

But even more dangerous has been the mismanagement that most Americans do not see, or have only recently begun to see — that is the erosion of the financial security of our country. A number of policies and activities have characterized this. The first set of policies has been an extension of initiatives that began in the Reagan Administration, namely, tax cuts. In the 1980s the Reagan Administration initiated a series of tax cuts at the same time that defense spending received a major boost (which followed up on more modest increases begun during the Carter Administration) and some significant cuts were made in domestic programs. These policies, dubbed supply-side economics by supporters and voodoo economics by detractors, were supposed to augment economic growth and generate enormous revenues for the US treasury. In fact, they generated huge budget deficits and the Reagan Administration was later forced to pass a series of tax increases to offset this deficit. The situation would not be resolved until the newly-inaugurated Clinton Administration passed another modest tax increase which got the budget under control and allowed for a lowering of interest rates to boost growth (or set off the stock market dot.com bubble—take your pick), which generated the budget surplus. This was the scenario at the time of the 2000 election.

During that election, candidate George W. Bush reopened the Reagan playbook advocating lower taxes and higher defense spending, and covering the difference with another round of phantom supply-side growth. When then-Vice President Al Gore challenged him on this issue, Bush accused him of using "fuzzy math."[4] In fact, we now know that Bush's plan was voodoo economics déjà vu.

Pounded by the 2001 tax cut and subsequent tax cuts, the books of the federal government have been blown to smithereens. After the budget surplus of the Clinton years, we now have massive budget deficits. In 2005, the budget deficit grew to $760 billion,[5] not including the Iraq War and other items that by 2008 were pushing it toward an annual figure of $1 trillion. The cumulative on-book national debt is now over $9 trillion.[6] When you add off-book unfunded obligations such as Social Security, Medicare and the various government pension programs, that number exceeds $50 trillion, several times the Gross Domestic Product (GDP).[7] This accounts for only the debt of the US government. It does not include the obligations of the states and local jurisdictions.

But the existing public debt is only the tip of a gigantic financial quasi-pyramid game. Part and parcel to the budget deficit is the trade deficit. The 2007 trade deficit was $711.6 billion, down from $758.5 billion in 2006, but still over 5% of GDP.[8] According to the *Economist*, economists at ABN AMRO believe that the trade deficit will be running at 12% of GDP by the end of the decade.[9] These are numbers that one would expect to find from third world countries undergoing restructuring by the International Monetary Fund (IMF). Hardly what one would expect from what is supposed to be the world's sole super power. As these percentages increase, the risks to the economy also increase—as was shown in the spring of 2006 when the

4   CNN, "First Bush-Gore Debate Alternates Between Issues, Attacks," *CNN.com*, October 3, 2000, http://archives.cnn.com/2000/ALLPOLITICS/stories/10/03/debate.wrap/.

5   U.S. Treasury Department, *Financial Statements of the United States Government. Statement of Operations and Changes of Net Position* (Washington DC, 2006), http://fms.treas.gov/fr/06Frusg/06stmt.pdf.

6   U.S. Treasury Department, "Debt to the Penny and who Holds It," *Treasury Direct*, http://www.treasusrydirect.gov/NP/BPDLogin?application=np.

7   Republican Study Committee, "Highlights from the 2007 Social Security and Medicare Trustees Report" (Washington DC 2007), http://www.house.gov/hensarling/rsc/doc/PB_042407_SSMedicareTrustees.doc. See also 2007 Social Security Trustees Report, Table IV.B6 and 2007 Medicare Trustees Report, Tables III.B10, B11, C23.

8   Bureau of Economic Analysis, *Trade in Goods and Services, December 2007*, http://bea.gov/newsreleases/international/trade/2008/trad1207.htm..

9   "The Yen Also Rises," *The Economist*, March 18, 2006, 69.

country of Iceland, with a deficit of 16% of GDP, saw a major fall in its currency value and its stock markets.[10]

But the situation gets dicier on the global level when you start looking at how the US trade and budget deficit is financed and who is financing it. Today these deficits are financed in various parts of the world, some in Europe, some in the Gulf States, but the greater portion is in Asia, particularly Japan and China. Both countries hold massive amounts of dollars as well as US securities. These Asians countries, primarily through their central banks, are in effect lending the US $2.5 billion a day just to keep America's accounts in balance. They purchase US Treasuries and other securities with the proceeds they receive from the sale of goods to the US. Indeed, two thirds of the trade surpluses in the rest of the world are financing the US trade deficit.[11] In addition to securities, foreign countries are also purchasing assets in the US.

The question of course is just how long will foreign governments be willing to accept US paper assets in exchange for real assets; and how long will these foreign governments be willing to purchase US assets priced in overvalued dollars. These are political as well as economic questions because they come at the meeting point of international finance and global power politics. Some say that the US can continue this way indefinitely because other nations are so heavily invested in US dollars directly or indirectly through US assets that they cannot remove their investment without taking heavy losses. But others are mindful of the old banking rule: when banks start to realize that they are deeply exposed in a check-kiting scheme (and US economic policy today closely resembles check kiting), the first bank to pull the plug usually gets out with the least damage. Already foreign governments and foreign banks are employing strategies to minimize their dollar holdings. They are also aware of another banking rule, which is that economies that get this far out of balance invariably come down hard. And that hard landing could include damage to the banking system, which will be unable to replenish the day-to-day funding from Chinese and other foreign money sources that keeps it afloat. Or if funds are found, it is at astronomical interest rates that shut down large sectors of the economy anyway. In either event, a severe economic contraction results, on the scale of the Great Depression of the

---

10 "Still Waiting for the Big One," *The Economist*, April 8, 2006, 19.
11 "Trade, Exchange Rates, Budget Balances and Interest Rates," *The Economist*, March 24, 2007, 110.

1930s, with a crushing level of debt not seen since the American Revolutionary War. Altogether, not a pretty picture.

Still, there is a third viewpoint on this situation that says that a creditor like China gets the value of its investment not by pulling the plug on a debtor government like the United States but by threatening to pull the plug. It is highly instructive to watch the George W. Bush Administration bully a country like Iraq while it steers clear of a North Korea bristling with nuclear weapons or negotiates with a far more dangerous rival in Russia. US actions regarding China in recent years have been limited to trade policies intended to encourage appreciation of China's currency vis-à-vis the dollar. But even this effort has been hollow because, while raising the prices of China's products would help US products compete, reducing the influx of cheap imports would cause a drop in America's standard of living. China, in fact, can just about do what it likes economically, militarily and diplomatically as long as it maintains the creditor's grip.

But holding America's IOUs is not the only means that China has to advance its agenda with regard to the US. An April 20, 2006 article in Asia Times Online by Victor Corpus delineated a whole laundry list of actions and options that the Chinese have at their disposal. On the economic growth front China has had an annual 9.4% GDP growth rate for 25 years. On the financial front in 2004 China had $61 billion in direct investment and foreign trade of $851 billion. It also held $252 billion in US Treasury bonds with Hong Kong holding a $48 billion for a grand total of $300 billion. According to a November 19, 2005 Wall Street Journal report, China has about $1 trillion in personal savings with a personal savings rate of 50% while the US has $158 billion (recent reports indicate that the savings rate in the US has now negative, with consumption financed by debt outpacing savings). The report also pointed out that on the construction front, Shanghai has twice as many skyscrapers as New York City, 4,000 to 2,000, and that the Chinese are building a city in the north of China as big as New York City. On the education front, China is annually producing nearly eight times as many engineers as America at the same time that we are now reading stories about American engineers seeing their jobs outsourced overseas.

All of this has lead to a remarkable outpouring of Chinese production that has become increasingly sophisticated over time. Corpus's China list shows that output per capita has increased by a factor of five over the twenty years up to 2002 and that they are building on average about 20,000 manu-facturing plants a year. And it has not all been for the production of trinkets. China moved into first place in the export of technology wares in 2004 that included a $34 billion trade surplus in advanced technology products with the US. One of the critiques of US policy has been that US neoliberal trade ideology has allowed foreign nations in general and the Chinese in particular to acquire American technology on the cheap and allow foreigners to de-velop competing products, part of the "America is up for sale" critique heard in many quarters. Other nations like Japan have been far more possessive about their technological secrets and in the case of Japan, the Japanese have not allowed their production facilities to leave the country.

Just as important is the fact that not all of this production is going over-seas. Consumption in China has now surpassed the US in the key areas of grain, meat, coal, and steel. The Chinese also now buy more TV sets, refrig-erators and mobile phones than Americans do. Ten years ago the US had six times as many cell phones as the Chinese; now the Chinese have more cell phones than the US has people. Given the fact that China sells the lion's share of TV's in America, the fact that their own consumption of TV is much larger than they export is astonishing.[12]

All of the above shows that the China commands important levers against the US in a number of key economic areas. The idea that China is somehow dependent on the US economy in order to prop up its own is naïve. A collapse of the US economy, including its banking and securities markets would be a worldwide catastrophe and the Chinese would not be immune. But unlike the developed world, China has massive undeveloped markets in its interior that it could develop in order to keep its economy afloat. America's debtor status is a far more precarious situation than China's creditor status.

In this way through its debt binge under the Bush Administration, Amer-ica has become a vassal state of the Chinese and China's emerging satellite countries in Asia. Not only has US military options vis-à-vis China been blunted, but the US is now obliged, both in the public and private sector, to offer a form of quasi-tribute to the Chinese in order to protect its standard of living, such as it is. The ongoing stream of Treasury and other private securi-ties, along with a host of private real, financial and other assets is ongoing

12   Victor N. Corpus, "If It Comes to a Shooting War," *Asia Times Online*, April 20, 2006, http://atimes01.atimes.com/atimes/China/HD20Ad03 .html.

testament that high-tech feudalism is alive and well in the twenty-first century. And the Chinese, who have played this political and diplomatic game for centuries in Asia, know a vassal state when they see one.

But while China and Asia has been the focal point of America's economic concerns in recent times, it is not the only concern. In 2005, Toyota Motors announced that it would build its next North American plant not in the United States, but in Woodstock, Ontario, Canada, starting in 2008. The Canadian bid was accepted even though many US states offered subsidies that were double what Canada offered. But Canada's lower health care costs and better skilled workforce (requiring less training) carried the day. US car manufacturers have also been shifting existing production to Ontario for the same reason. And in the recent announced General Motors production cutbacks, American plants were hit substantially harder than Canadian plants. This example along with the ongoing stories of trials and tribulations of the US auto industry shows that America is losing ground to nations in the G7 developed world as well as the developing nations of Asia.

Another statistic confirming the erosion of American high tech comes in the list of the world's 100 largest corporations. For generations, American companies dominated that list. But even in the recent era of NAFTA and the virtually non-existent anti-trust laws under the Clinton and Bush administrations, the number of US firms on UNCTAD's list of the top 100 non-financial transnational corporations showed 27 US firms and 59 European firms.[13] Given the expected decline of the US dollar versus the Euro and other currencies, one could only expect the current trend to continue. In a similar vein, the World Economic Forum's 2006 ranking of global competitiveness has shown the US falling from the top ranking to number six, falling behind Singapore, Iceland and a cluster of European countries.[14]

This is the prospect that the United States faces in maintaining its domestic economy. But that domestic economy has its own problems. For starters, the distortions exhibited in our budget and trade deficits are mirrored by equally large distortions on the domestic front. Not surprisingly, these governmental and trade distortions interact with the domestic ones.

---

13   UNCTAD, *World Investment Report 2006*, http://www.unctad.org/sections/dite_dir/docs/wir2006top100_en.pdf.

14   World Economic Forum, *Global Competitiveness Report*, http://www.weforum.org/en/initiatives/gcp/Global%20Competitiveness%20Report/index.htm.

The most visible of the domestic distortions is the extreme level of income inequality. The gap between the rich and the poor in this country has reached levels not seen since the 1920s or what is now called the Gilded Age, the period of the late nineteenth century. The share of national income going to wages and salaries is the lowest since government records began in 1947 while the share going to corporate after-tax profits is the highest since the 1960s.[15] Depending on which income barometer you use, real wages have basically stagnated since 1973. Average real incomes after inflation fell after 2001 offsetting the dot.com bubble expansion of the 1990s.[16] And it isn't just outsourceable workers on the shop floor. Since 2000, the inflation-adjusted wages of college workers has fallen. Net worth has also shown the same characteristics. From 2001 to 2004, the top 10% of household had a 6.1% increase in net worth (in spite of a falling stock market) while the bottom 25 percent saw their net worth shrink.[17]

Along with the shrinkage in income, there has been an increase in poverty. After falling in the 1990s, the percentage of those living in poverty has started to rise again. It is now 12.3% in 2006 after peaking at 12.6% in 2005, the first drop of the decade. The same U.S. Census report that showed a drop in poverty also showed an increase in the number of people without health insurance from 44.8 million (15.3%) in 2005 to 47 million (15.8%) in 2006.[18] The poverty rate is the highest percentage in the developed world, and one of the highest anywhere. All told, 36.5 million Americans live in poverty with some 5 million slipping below the poverty line since 2001. Most of these people have jobs. Many have more than one just trying to keep afloat. Just about all of these people are part of the 40 million-plus Americans that don't have health care. They are also part of the group of people that give the US an infant mortality rate closer to that of a third world country. Not surprisingly, such figures also reflect a large homeless problem that is in all parts of

15 Steven Greenhouse and David Leonhardt, "Real Wages Fail to Match Rise in Productivity," *New York Times*, August 28, 2006.

16 Thomas Piketty and Emmanuel Saez, "Income Inequality in the United States 1913–1998," *NBER Working Paper no. 8467* (September 2001); cited in David Cay Johnston, *Perfectly Legal: The Covert Campaign to Rig Our Tax System to Benefit the Super Rich—and Cheat Everybody Else* (New York: Portfolio 2003), 30–33.

17 Martin Crutsinger, "Family Income Falling," *Associated Press*, February 23, 2006, http://pqasb.pqarchiver.com/ap/access/996677531.html.

18 U.S. Census, *Current Population Survey 2006*, http://www.census.gov/Press-Release/www/releases/income_wealth/010583.html.

the country. In Los Angeles, the figure is close to 100,000.[19] And again, these are not all derelicts.

A recent story by *Washington Post* staff writer Neil Irwin on the median American household as laid out by the Federal Reserve Board's Survey of Consumer Finances illustrates the point. In Irwin's story, the average family has about $3,800 in the bank and no Individual Retirement Accounts. The more affluent neighbors of this family have about $35,000 in IRAs. This average family has no other liquid investments. They have a house worth $160,000 with a $95,000 mortgage. They make $49,000 a year but can't pay off $2,200 in credit cards. Basically a family that is treading water, making the mortgage, but propped up by debt that they can't pay off and are one setback (a hospital bill, an accident) away from a serious financial crisis.[20]

While this is going on, income for the well off is sharply increasing. Where thirty years ago the income of CEOs was roughly thirty times that of his workers, today it is in the range of 1000 times (this, given the fact that that there are many studies out there that indicate that company performance has nowhere near kept up with CEO pay). But even this trend doesn't capture the full picture. In a research paper entitled "Where Did the Productivity Growth Go?," Northwestern University professors Ian Dew-Becker and Robert Gordon note that in the final three decades of the twentieth century income earners in the top 10 percent, saw their income rise by only 1 percent a year. But income doubled for those roughly in the top 1 percent and went up nearly six-fold for the top 0.01 percent.[21]

Since 2001, the well to do have been given a boost by the many tax cuts of the Bush administration. These tax cuts have been especially beneficial to non-earned income such as capital gains and the inheritance tax, areas of the economy that are almost the exclusive preserve of the very wealthy. Warren Buffett has stated that he pays a lower percentage of income in tax than his secretary does.[22] Not surprisingly, America has the highest number of billionaires in the world, many of whom have benefited enormously by these tax cuts.

---

19 Paul Harris, "37 Million Poor Hidden in the Land of Plenty," *Observer (London)*, February 19, 2006.

20 Neil Irwin, "Family Savings Look Scary Across the Board," *Washington Post*, March 5, 2006.

21 Paul Krugman, "Graduates versus Oligarchs," *New York Times*, February 27, 2006.

22 Tom Bawden, "Buffett Blasts System That Lets Him Pay Less Tax Than Secretary," *Times Online (London)*, June 28, 2007, http://business.timesonline.co.uk/tol/business/money/tax/article1996735.ece.

The idea of course was that these tax breaks would boost investment and stimulate the economy. In fact, they have either gone into investments overseas or into the pockets of the wealthy. The economic "recovery" has been virtually nonexistent for most people. In fact, it is the second slowest recovery of the post-World War II era. Only the "jobless recovery" of the early 1990s was weaker. Interestingly, both "recoveries" occurred during a Bush Administration. In the first eighteen months of this current recovery, which supposedly began in late 2001, employment shrank by over 1 million jobs, an unheard of event at that point in the business cycle. Jobs have been created since then, but in most months since, job growth has been pretty tepid. In April 2006, some 5 years into the recovery, jobs grew by 144,000,[23] and 200,000 new jobs in a month is considered a roaring success. In comparison, the average monthly job growth since World War II has been around 300,000 jobs.[24] With the release of the January 2008 employment numbers showing a loss of 17,000 non-farm jobs, the first such loss in nearly five years, the job picture now appears to be deteriorating under the pressure of the current financial crisis.[25] So clearly, the tax cuts have done little for economic or job growth. But they have done wonders to make the deficits grow.

It is no small wonder that in his 2005 annual letter to investors of his Berkshire Hathaway firm, Warren Buffett noted that the company underperformed in 2004 because he had been unable to find suitable investments. As a result, Buffett found himself holding $43 billion in cash and cash securities. When someone with $43 billion has no place to spend it, it should be no surprise that less aggressive wealthy people are pocketing their tax cuts.[26]

And what is not going overseas or into people's pockets went into the new investment vehicle of choice—housing. Since the dot.com debacle, there has been a virtual feeding frenzy in the housing market. Although the housing bubble has been international in scope, in this country it began during the dot.com bubble in California's Silicon Valley. This featured an extraordinary drama in which the prices of nondescript ranch-style tract houses went from something like $15,000 when new to some $60,000–$100,000 as the bubble

23 Bureau of Labor Statistics, *Employment, Hours, and Earnings from the Current Employment Statistics Survey (National)*, http://data.bls.gov/cgi-bin/surveymost.

24 *Left Business Observer* No. 107, 6.

25 Bureau of Labor Statistics, *Employment Situation Summary, January 2008*. http://www.bls.gov/news.release/empsit.nr0.htm.

26 Simon Bowers, "Buffett Attacks American Spending Junkies," *Guardian (UK)*, March 7, 2005.

began to expand, and ultimately inflated to $500,000. They were purchased by the Silicon Valley nouveau riches who were getting money thrown at them by venture capitalists and investment groupies, and had no idea what to do with it.

When the dot.com bubble burst and the Silicon Valley nouveau riches became the Silicon Valley nouveau unemployed, the bottom fell out of the Bay area housing market. But fear not—those investors who survived began throwing money into the rest of the housing market, and the game was on. The game was not new. Several areas of the country, notably in Southern California and Boston, housing markets had been tight and prices had hit the stratosphere. Nor was it a peculiar American phenomenon. Overheated housing markets have been simmering around the globe, particularly in Europe. What occurred after 2001 was the spread of this activity to others parts of the country and the increasing risk of the transactions. In a special report on the global housing boom in its June 18, 2005 issue, the *Economist* magazine noted the residential housing bubble in developed economies appeared, from all objective calculations, to be the biggest bubble in history, surpassing the dot.com bubble and the American stock market bubble and crash of the late 1920s. In the US, the bubble spread most notably to the states of Florida, Hawaii, Maryland, and Nevada, as well as Washington, DC, where prices rose by 20% in the first quarter of 2005.

But it was not just the scale of the overheated housing activity. Having people lining up to bid on new housing tracts, bidding on them by lottery, or bidding over the asking price of existing housing was nothing new. It was the kind of housing that was being bought and the way that it was being financed that set off flashing red lights that alarmed financial analysts. The *Economist* cited a National Association of Realtors report which said that 23% of all homes bought in the US in 2004 were for investment, not home ownership, and another 13% were bought as second homes. Thus housing market demand was being inflated by a substantial amount of speculative activity in which people were buying homes for resale in an overheated market, and either renting them out at a loss or living in them on a secondary basis until they were sold. In some cases, the housing properties were bought and resold before they were even built, a sort of housing futures market.

Compounding the speculative buying was the way that the housing market was being financed. The traditional 80 percent financing with 20 percent down has become, like the spotted owl, an endangered species. If it exists at all, it is purely by accident in the brave new world of housing finance.

According to the National Association of Realtors report, 42 percent of first-time buyers and 25 percent of all buyers made no down payment at all. The 105% loan covering loan costs and other goodies—the siren song of many a prior housing bubble in the always-volatile California housing market—has now become commonplace elsewhere. But the frontier of creative financing as gone well beyond this form of tame lending. Not only have adjustable-rate mortgages (ARMs) become a staple of the housing market, but it has been joined by the interest-only and the negative-amortization loan. Not only are people not paying any principle on the interest-only loan, in the case of the negative-amortization loan, they are not even paying the interest, just adding it to the balance of the loan. As usual, California leads the way in this brand of looney-toon financing. Interest-only and negative-amortization loans in California have risen from 8 percent of total loans in 2002 to over 60 percent in 2005. Most of these loans are ARMs, and ARMs form a significant portion of the market.[27]

The popularity of ARMs is due to another facet of the American economy of recent years—the policies of the Federal Reserve and its chairman Alan Greenspan. Virtually since the beginning of his tenure in 1987 when he was immediately confronted by the short but savage stock market crash of September 1987, Greenspan's answer to most crises was to literally throw money at the problem, thereby lubricating the market and dropping interest rates. This was clear in the Asian Crisis on 1996–97, and the Russian default triggering the insolvency of the Long Term Capital Management hedge fund shortly thereafter. In both cases Greenspan drove US interest rates down sharply to diffuse the crisis. The same thing occurred when the dot. com bubble burst. The net result was that short-term crises were avoided at the expense of risking a larger crisis later on. One of the by-products of this policy was to create artificially low interest rates, which then subsequently reduced by the rate discount used to entice people to take ARMs, made the entry price of an ARM almost impossible to turn down. Add to that an interest-only or negative-amortization feature, and you had millions of additional marginal buyers who never could have bought in a normal housing market, thus fueling the housing market frenzy.

---

27   "In Comes the Waves," *The Economist*, June 18, 2005, 66–68.

The buying and selling of housing was not the only thing heating up housing finance. Equity financing was another part of this disoriented market. Those who had tapped out on their credit cards or wanted a cheaper, interest deducible way to spend money that they didn't have, started plundering the equity in their houses. Also as interest rates fell after the dot.com bust, housing refinance added to the equity market. And what a rich vein of cash they found. Between 2001 and 2005 it is estimated that Americans converted over $700 billion in real estate equity into cash and replaced that cash with loans. That was equivalent to roughly 40 percent in the growth of personal spending during the period.[28] With borrowing on that scale, it is easy to see how the economy continued to grow and consumption kept roaring along despite the minor handicap that this economy was not creating any jobs, and the jobs it was creating did not pay the income level of the jobs that were replaced.

But by the spring of 2006, the consequences of the artificially low interest rates and the booming housing markets came home to roost. The Federal Reserve finally had to ratchet up interest rates as the deficits continued to surge. Those rising interest rates put a drag on the housing market and burst the housing bubble. The net result in late 2007 is that delinquent real estate loans and housing foreclosures have exploded, resulting in falling housing prices and a financial crisis across the international banking system, the likes of which has not been seen in decades. The losses, which are estimated in the hundreds of billions (and possibly into the trillions) of dollars, are part of a collateral base supporting several times its nominal value in loans. And the entire structure is so complicated and opaque that not only are there serious questions as to the value of these pyramiding tiers of loans, but with the buying, selling and repackaging of these loans there is some question as to who are the actual holders. Whether significant parts of the banking system will survive is now an open question.

All of the above risks to the economy, the growing deficits, the mountains of debts, the risks inherent in the banking system (this discussion hasn't even touched upon the potential lethal risks in the financial derivative markets) and the housing market, are but background noise to the 800-pound gorilla in the middle of the national living room—oil prices. As the price of gasoline has soared past three dollars a gallon, while oil pipelines continued

---

28   Doug Henwood, "Leaking Bubble," *The Nation*, March 27, 2006, 6–7.

to be sabotaged in Iraq and the saber rattling of the Bush Administration unnerves oil commodity traders, millions of Americans find themselves spending money that they don't have just to keep on the road. The escalation of the price of oil drains even more income from people who already are running the first negative savings rate since the Great Depression.[29] Further increases in the price of oil for any reason could bleed the whole economy right down the drain.

Finally, the militaristic nature of our current imperialist foreign policy is revealing to Americans the fact that not only such a policy makes us less safe militarily, but it undermines our economic security as well. Before September 11, little or no thought had been directed toward terrorism, even though the outgoing Clinton Administration had told the incoming Bush transition team that it was one the Clinton's highest security priorities. The result of course was that potential events like September 11 were not on the Bush radar. At the same time, great focus was put on those activities that could enrich the defense contractors who were clients of both the Administration and the Congress.

The after-effects of September 11 augmented aspects of military expenditure as a numbed Congress voted for appropriation after appropriation. But as was the case in the domestic economy, the military appropriations went to the defense elite like Lockheed-Martin, and gangster operations like Halliburton were allowed to loot the treasury with no-bid contracts while the servicemen fighting in Iraq were sent there without adequate amour, adequate equipment and tainted food and water. The price tag of the war will top a trillion dollars, maybe several trillion dollars. At the same time the Bush Administration is building in Iraq the largest embassy in the world, housing a small city of at least 5,000 employees. That is assuming that the ongoing civil war doesn't wipe out the US presence altogether, just like it did in South Vietnam. The embassy will merely add to the permanent military bases now in the country, in addition to the hundreds of military bases around the globe. All of which, we are supposed to believe, will be gladly financed by the Chinese along with all the other activities they are financing in this country. Somehow, the idea of our national security being dependent on China makes you wonder just what the Bush Administration is really protecting.

29   Bureau of Economic Analysis, *Personal Income, and Outlays, December 2006, Table 2*, http://www. bea.gov/bea/newsrelarchive/2007/pi1206.htm; "U.S. Savings Rate Hits Lowest Level Since 1933," *Associated Press*, January 30, 2006, http://www.msnbc.msn.com/id/11098797/.

All the while that we are pouring money down the Iraqi rat hole, billions of dollars of domestic needs are going unmet. Hurricane Katrina highlighted some of the problems for Americans. But the disaster on the Gulf Coast after Katrina is merely the poster child for what is occurring across this country. Quite simply, America is falling apart and is threatening to turn into one gigantic pothole. While trillions are thrown away in the Department of Defense, roads are falling apart, bridges and dams are crumbling (there are communities below some aging dams that would make September 11 look like a non-event if the dam collapsed). Schools, libraries and other public buildings are rotting away. Sewers, waterlines and a whole host of infrastructural items are being ignored. Meanwhile, cargo and port security are neglected while airports merely implement cosmetic "security screening" programs that fail to keep guns from being carried onto airplanes, as various investigative reporters have demonstrated..

The result is that we still have not adequately secured our facilities from violent criminal and political action, and we are allowing the country itself to go to pieces in every sense. We have opened ourselves up to both military and economic blackmail.

Needless to say, the financial options for the average American are becoming fewer and less palatable day by day. In addition to the enormous economic risk posed by debt, financial asset speculation, and high oil prices, the specter of social crisis looms behind the financial crisis. In an economy of growing inequality which is unable to create new jobs in the middle and upper class professions and services as well as manufacturing, in an economy where a college education is no longer a guarantee to obtaining those upper middle class jobs, the future of a viable middle class is clearly in doubt. In such an economic environment, the middle class gets squeezed and ultimately joins a mushrooming lower class. We are seeing that phenomenon unfold as this chapter is written.

America is losing its capacity to provide upward social mobility. According to the Bureau of Labor Statistics 10-year jobs forecast in 2005, the majority of jobs created in that period will be for domestic services that do not require a college education.[30] In December 2004, the *Economist* issued a special report on income inequality in the United States. It talked about a

---

30 Norman C. Saunders, "A Summary of BLS Projections to 2014," *Monthly Labor Review Online*, November 2005, Vol. 128, No. 11.

public educational system starved of funds, which denies a quality educa-tion to Americans of lower income in poor school districts. It talked about a higher educational system increasingly magnifying educational inequalities as poorer students are required to pay soaring tuition costs at public and private colleges and universities and coming out of the process loaded down with heavy debt burdens before they began earning a decent income. That of course assumes that they can find a job commensurate with their educa-tional skills, which itself is becoming more difficult. With the hollowing out of whole industries and disappearing layers of middle management, these same workers are finding it harder stay with one company, let alone to start at the bottom and move up the corporate ladder through hard work and self-improvement. *The Economist* concluded that the US runs the risk of fossilizing into a class-based society similar to that of imperial Britain.[31] At the same time the Wall Street Journal, reporting on American income inequality, not-ed that a poor child's chances of rising to wealth and a rich child's chances of falling into the middle class are fairly fixed. And despite the widespread be-lief that the US is a more mobile society than Europe, poor children born in Europe or Canada have a better chance of finding economic security than do American poor children.[32] That opinion is re-enforced by an article entitled "Goodbye, Horatio Alger" by Jeff Madrick in the February 5, 2007 issue of *The Nation*, based on research by a group of economists led by Bhashkar Mazum-der of the Federal Reserve Bank of Chicago which states that 60 percent of a son's income is determined by his father's income. The article goes on to list the growing handicaps from health care and education costs to the shrinking governmental programs which are making it increasingly impossible for mil-lions of working poor to better their lives. This plus the mountains of debts that they must incur to keep themselves afloat all suggests that we are not far off from Warren Buffett's Sharecropper Society.[33]

What these articles are saying is that if the Horatio Alger story was ever really true in this country, it is rapidly becoming a myth. Depending on your point of view, the American Dream is either disappearing or turn-ing into a nightmare. With an economy built upon the shakiest of financial

---

31 "Ever Higher Society, Even Harder to Ascend," *Economist.com*, December 29, 2004, http://www.economist.com/world/na/displayStory.cfm.
32 David Wessel, "As Rich-Poor Gap Widens in U.S., Class Mobility Stalls," *Wall Street Journal*, May 13, 2005.
33 Jeff Madrick, "Goodbye, Horatio Alger," *The Nation*, February 5, 2007, 20–24.

structures and with economic opportunity fossilizing into stone, it is clear that America risks major political, social, and economic crises if the present trends continue.

But as depressing as the above description may seem, the truth is that it is nothing new for America. For much of today's scenario could have just as easily been discussed in the late 1920s. Then as now there were great extremes of wealth. Indeed, most of the economists and financial analysts that discuss income inequality today invariably have to make comparisons with the peak year 1929, as earlier periods don't have as reliable data. Then as now there were large segments of the economy (in the 1920s, the agricultural community) which did not participate in what was passed off as economic prosperity. Then as now, the economy was sustained by massive infusions of debt (in late 1920s terms, a pittance by today's standards) and speculative real estate behavior. In fact the 1920s and the early twenty-first century have a great deal in common.

In the late 1920s, the economic distortions produced by these policies were "resolved" by the Great Depression of the 1930s. The issue posed by today's economic adventures is whether a financial collapse on a scale like that of the 1930s is in the offing. Economist and Nobel Laureate James Tobin postulated one analytical answer in his quantification of the stock-value index "Q." Tobin's "Q" is the ratio of the stock market value of a corporation divided by the assets of the corporation. If the Q index is less than 1.0, then the value of underlying assets are greater than the stock value and the stock values will rise. If Q is greater than 1.0, then the stock value is greater than the underlying asset value and the stock price will fall. As of 2002, Q was the highest value since the 1920s, and historically, Q values of substantially greater than 1.0 fell back to market levels only after a severe economic contraction. So the prospects of avoiding a Great Depression-scale crash is not as good as one would like, although it is not a sure thing either.[34]

What is worse than the 1920s is the level of debt in the economy. The federal government ran at a surplus through the 1920s. Indeed, the famed Mellon tax cuts were possible because of those budget surpluses. America was the world's largest creditor nation, with most European nations owing the US money after World War I. Today, the federal government is run-

---

34 Alan Newman, "The Importance of 'Qs,'" *Crosscurrents*, November 6, 2004, http://crosscurrents.net/archives/nov04.htm.

ning massive deficits. In the private sector in the 1920s corporations were so profitable that many could generate enough capital internally without having to access banks loans.[35] Today, corporate lending is such that, at times, junk bonds have become fashionable. Personal lending in the 1920s was in its infancy. In addition to short-term mortgages, individuals could get short term installment loans cars and appliances. But lending based on a person's monthly income had only just started and was very crude. Today of course families are burdened with huge credit card, mortgage and equity finance loans, with terms on these loans stretching 30 to 40 years, not just out to 5 years, as was the case in the 1920s. The debt situation, then, is a major difference from the 1920s and is the one major negative item not present eighty years ago.

The most important similarities of 1920s and now was that conservative Republican businessmen whose policies were responsible for economic distortions that occurred then and that we see now ran the federal government in both eras. In both eras supposedly smart businessmen who knew how to run organizations and whom the general public had great confidence in blindly stumbled into economic crises which not only set back the country for years, but also discredited the business community and its friends in the Republican Party for decades. The late Louis Rukeyser on the show Wall Street Week would periodically ask the question: How was it that, historically, the stock market did better under Democrats than it did under Republicans, the supposed party of business? That question most certainly must be on the lips of stockholders around the country who made money in the market during the Democratic Clinton Administration, but saw those gains disappear or stagnate under the Republican George W. Bush.

This brings up the larger question: What is it in conservative economic and social policy that brings on these disasters and how is it that the supposed financial amateurs in the Democratic Party seem to have done better. A recent article in *The Nation* points out the fact the best Republican minds can't afford government salaries, which may be true. But the stock market reversals are also a reflection of decisions made in the private sector by high-priced help. One would think, though, that Democrat policy people would consider the Federal pay scale more to their liking. Another viewpoint that

---

35 Simon Kuznets, *National Income and its Composition 1919–1938* (New York: National Bureau of Economic Research, 1941), 316; cited in George Soule, *Prosperity Decade from War to Depression 1917–1929* (1947; reprint New York: Harper and Row, 1968), 122.

has been propounded for years by columnist George Will is that people whose political philosophy is fundamentally against government are not particularly adept at running government.

But a more practical reason of why conservatives seem to do so badly can be found in basic macroeconomics. Conservative, and more particularly Republican, economic policy has a tendency to emphasize supply over demand and investment over consumption. This was most demonstrably stated in the early Reagan Administration focus on supply-side economics. In general, this policy supports cutting taxes and reducing or removing regulations—benefits to the suppliers of goods and services (business) and to investors. At the same time conservative economic policy tends to reduce or eliminate government expenditures on social programs, which in turn reduces consumption and demand in the economy. The excess of supply over demand tends to be deflationary and results in the fall of prices and a contraction of the economy. If the deflation goes too far, you have the kind of deflationary spiral that can trigger a financial crisis like the Great Depression. Democratic policy, however, has tended to emphasize more government expenditure and more money going to lower income people. Since people with lower incomes are more likely to spend the money they get, they tend to boost demand and consumption more. Thus Democratic economic policy tends to emphasize demand over supply, and as such, tends to be inflationary. While excessive or hyperinflation can be damaging to an economy, low levels of inflation are helpful in making the economy grow. So the ideal economic policy is one with small amounts of inflation, and as such, a Democratic economic policy is more favorable for the economy than a Republican one. What this means is that stock markets do better in Democratic administrations because Democratic economic policies tend to be more successful.

Beyond the macroeconomic issues, however, are the social issues. Conservative economic policies tend to benefit a small, wealthy elite; Democratic economic policies tend to benefit a much larger segment of the population. The sheer numbers of people that benefit from Democratic policies are able to drive larger sectors of the economy. That in turn makes it easier to move forward the economy as a whole. Stock market technical analysts refer to it by the term "breadth of the market." When the market has wider breadth, it is it easier to sustain an upward move in the market because large numbers of buyers are driving the market up. When a market has narrow breath it means that there are fewer people with larger amounts of cash (or larger amounts of loans) buying into the market and driving it up. This corresponds to the kind of activity we see in the US economy today. But market technicians also note that rising markets with narrow breath tend to come at the end of bull markets or large upward moves in the market. So do market technical analyses coincide with economic reality? That remains to be seen. But as previously noted, the situation does not look good, and the plunging poll numbers of the Bush Administration would seem to confirm that point.

So, is what we are seeing the primrose path to decline and will America follow the path of the USSR, Britain and other empires of yore? It doesn't necessarily have to do so, and in fact, none of what we are experiencing is really new. Shades of what we are experiencing today can be seen right back to the founding of the American colonies in the early seventeenth century and their subsequent economic development. They can also been seen in the debate between Thomas Jefferson and Alexander Hamilton more than two hundred years ago. Further clues can be found in the debate over slavery in the years leading up to the Civil War and also a number of issues such as homesteading, the reform in the banking system, and the land grant colleges which were propelled forward with the onset of the war. There are further signs with the beginning of the early environmental movement, the establishment of the national park system, and the Progressive movement of the late nineteenth century.

All of the economic forces that shaped these eras can be found today in the political, cultural, and social behavior that we define as Red-state and Blue-state activity. The list of states may have changed over time, but the activity that defines these two kinds of economies has remained surprisingly consistent. The economic characteristics of these two economies hold the key as to whether or not we can escape the path that led to our current situation. Therefore, in order to understand the economic situation today we need to go back to the founding of this country to understand the choices that we have, and how they affect the political and economic landscape, in order to proceed on from this point.

2. THE GREAT AMERICAN DIVIDE—RED STATES VERSUS BLUE STATES

One of the things that is different in discussing the early history of what became the United States is that we know so much more about the beginnings of the European settlement of this area as opposed to the older cultures of Europe and Asia. Of course there were cultures in the New World at the time of Columbus, but the Europeans and their descendants saw to it in their own savage way that they would have a clean slate (that is, continent) to work with when they started to develop their communities. Since that development occurred after the invention of the Gutenberg Press in Europe, we know much more about how America developed than we could ever possibly know about the founding of earlier nations where the survival of written histories of the era were much more problematical.

For instance, we know that Jamestown was founded on May 14, 1607; that the Mayflower Compact was signed on November 21, 1620 before the landing at Plymouth. And we know from the beginning what kind environmental challenges these early settlers faced. To a remarkable degree, many of those early activities can be observed in what was originally known as the North and the South, and what we now call Red states and Blue states today.[36]

---

36   For a more detailed discussion on the historical data in this chapter, please refer to Stephen D. Cummings, *The Dixification of America: The American Odyssey into the Conservative Economic Trap*, (Westport , CT.: Praeger, 1998), Chapters 3,4,5, and 6.

The first major difference of course was the topography of the Atlantic coast of North America. In the North, the northern extension of the Appalachian Mountains hug much closer to the coast, and as a result, there is very little flat land, and most of the land is rocky and forested. This was not very conducive to farming. Someone wanting to farm such land would first have to clear the trees and the boulders. Then the farmer would have to limit the kind of crops he wanted to grow because of the short growing season. Finally, he would have to endure the bitter New England winter. This was not altogether the most appealing prospect for someone who wanted to settle in the New World.

On the other hand, the lands in the southern parts of the British portion of the American east coast would have appeared much more enticing. The Appalachians fell away from the coastlines, allowing for broad fertile flatlands to the Atlantic. In addition, temperatures were much warmer in the southern part of the colonies with a longer growing season, making settlement there much more attractive. And of course, the initial Spanish and British settlements were in the southern part of the continent at Saint Augustine, Jamestown, and Santa Fe.

Logic would have said that given those advantages, the southern part of the country would have been the more prosperous. But as is the case in many instances, logic did not seem to win out. In this case, as is true in many situations, natural advantages are helpful, but the key to successful operation for most organizations is how they are managed. Business case studies show that the primary cause of failure for most businesses is poor management and lack of capital. The corollary is also true: in less than promising situations, organizations can excel by superior management. The early years of the northern American colonies proved that point.

The colonists in New England may have lacked the agricultural advantages of Virginia, but they compensated for it in other ways. First, they were near the abundant fisheries of Newfoundland, and the New England colonialists exploited this resource to great advantage. They developed a highly successful fishing industry that would be a major force in the New England economy for over two centuries, and the ports of Salem and Marblehead (Massachusetts), not to mention Boston, would be known throughout the world. Building a world class fishing industry requires world class hard-ware—specifically, ships. And New England built some of the finest any-where. The Yankee clipper ships would remain among the premier ocean go-ing vessels until the advent of steam-powered ships and still actively carried cargo throughout the nineteenth century.[37]

Behind the fishing and boat construction industries was one of New Eng-land's two major natural assets—lumber. While the trees and forests in New England were a major impediment to farming, the vast scale of the forests offered a priceless commodity for any kind of construction, especially ship construction. Ships require large pieces of wood for masts, beams, siding, and other specialty applications. Large vessels like the clipper ships required exceptionally large pieces of wood. With European sources rapidly disap-pearing, the new sources in New England were especially valuable. Even today, lumber is an important part of the economy in the state of Maine, al-though it has declined significantly in other parts of New England.

Wood resources were complemented by that other great natural asset—waterpower. The same northern Appalachian mountain range that practi-cally fills up entire states and leaves very little flat land also provided the topography for the abundant waterfalls, rapids, and fast flowing streams that became the basis for a huge hydropower industry. Water-driven mills of every kind honeycombed New England. Water powered the mills that processed trees into lumber, and the mills that processed wheat into flour, and other mills that drove all kinds of early manufacturing activity. Water-power in New England was abundant and cheap. Industries powered by wa-ter were extremely competitive in the colonial period. In the New World, water-powered mills and factories were still able to compete right into the middle of the nineteenth century, when more advanced steam-power plants had been in use in England for roughly a century.[38]

The net result of all this was that the New England colonies, far from be-coming and economic backwater on the Atlantic became the most dynamic economy in British North America. The focal point was the states of Mas-sachusetts and Connecticut. The wealth produced by these areas naturally attracted other potential colonists, so that by 1660, this area had over half of

---

37   Ross M. Robertson and Gary M. Walton, *History of the American Economy*, 4th ed. (New York: Harcourt, Brace Jovanovich, 1979), 66; Martin L. Primack and James F. Willis, *An Economic History of the United States*, (Menlo Park, Ca.: Benjamin Cummings, 1980), 14.

38   Robertson and Walton, *History of the American Economy*, 196.

the population of the American colonies.[39] New England would eventually see major manufacturing rivals in New York and Pennsylvania, and at the time of the American Revolution, Virginia would be the most populous state. But New England's economic impact was, and still is, a significant factor.

The Southern colonies in contrast were established from entirely different perspective. Today when we speak of family, cultural, or moral values, we think of the states of the South. But in fact, the early landing at Jamestown brought none of that. Unlike the religiously driven Puritans who sought salvation in the New World, for the colonists at Jamestown and their backers in England, this was purely a business venture. For the British monarch, the aristocracy, and Parliament, colonies meant the development of resources unavailable at home. Being an island nation with limited resources, the British had always needed to obtain goods from a not always friendly mainland Europe. So there was always a commercial rationale for the British colonies. This was in contrast to the Spanish, who saw their colonies as a means of plundering the wealth of the region, without investing in the infrastructure and economic development that made the British colonies so much more economically viable.

The colonists of Jamestown pursued farming, and Virginia and the rest of the South established themselves as a major agricultural area. The first crop that proved a commercial success was a native plant that had long been grown by the Native Americans in the region—tobacco. It would be followed by rice and indigo and still later by cotton, the crop that would come to dominate the region.

By becoming an agriculturally based economy, the Southern colonies diverged in many significant ways from the New England and middle colonies. The Southern colonies didn't develop the urban areas of the North. Charleston was the only significant city in the South, whereas Boston, New York, Philadelphia, and Baltimore were the core of urban centers that included many towns and villages in close proximity, plus smaller urban centers. The farms and the plantations of the Southern colonies were large and the population dispersed.

The rural nature of the Southern colonies also had different needs for economic inputs. Specifically, they were much more labor-intensive than the capital-intensive North. The Southern economy required more physical

---

39   Primack and Willis, *Economic History of the United States*, 14.

brawn and less entrepreneurial innovation. All they had to do on the planta-tion was grow what was already there; they didn't have to create an entirely new product from a limited set of resources as was being done in the North-ern cities. The Southern farmers required a greater number of agricultural workers than Britain or the rest of Europe could provide. And so the logical option was to introduce the practice of slavery, which had been going on in the Caribbean and South American agricultural areas for some time. The first slaves were introduced into Virginia in 1619. Slaves were used through-out the American colonies and slavery persisted in the North into the early nineteenth century, but it never was as effective or on such a wide of scale in the North as it was in the South. The large manpower needs and the division of labor made slavery much more practical on a large farm than in a sawmill or small shop.

Even so, slavery was dying out in the South as well as the North until a New England inventor by the name of Eli Whitney came south and devel-oped the cotton gin, which revolutionized the production of cotton fiber, jumped-started the short-staple cotton industry in the South. This in turn called for huge labor demands on the Southern farms and plantations which could only be filled by the expansion of slavery. This established slavery in the Southern states and ultimately led to the virulent domestic debate on the issue.

While the story of the cotton gin and its ultimate economic and political effects is well known, the story also illustrates another point that has only been partly developed. Of course, many have been struck by the irony that it was a Northerner who rejuvenated the Southern economy and its peculiar institution. But it also points out that it was the innovative skills developed in the North that were largely lacking in the South that made the economic transformation possible. This economic characteristic not only defined the North and South up to 1861, but also has strong carryover effects right into our own time. It is in fact the basis for what could be called The Great Amer-ican Divide.

The Great American Divide can be viewed in many ways. The traditional way has been to view it in its most simplistic terms—the division between the North and the South over slavery. Even in the 1860s, the issue was not that simple. Others looked at slavery as the key issue in the larger issue of states right versus the Federal government. But even that issue was muddled, and the contradictions were best defined in Lincoln's early statement that he did not wish to repeal slavery from where it was established, only to limit its expansion. The eventual war itself involved other issues such as the Southern states' insistence that any new territory annexed in the future should be brought in as slave states (as had been done with Texas and proposed with Cuba, in the Ostend Manifesto).[40]

But in economic terms, the Great American Divide means something much broader than the issues that embroiled the 1850s and 1860s. Many issues of that time ended with the surrender at Appomattox. But the issues involving The Great American Divide, while highlighted by slavery and the Civil War, were there before the slaves landed in Virginia and have continued right through the present day. They center on a series of issues and policies which have been defined as liberal and conservative, progressive and reactionary, but which in fact deal with the way people have lived and have developed this country.

In the beginning, The Great American Divide was marked by how the American colonies developed. Out of that period came a set of characteristics. In the North, the need to find solutions to the harsh environment and make innovative adaptations led to a culture that readily accepted change. The less demanding environment in the South fostered a more rigid society, one that was more resistant to change. People farmed there the same way they had in Europe, only on a much larger scale. Centuries of feudal laws and the fragmentation of the land through inheritance had limited the average European's opportunity to acquire vast land holdings. The American South provided the early colonists the opportunity to be large land owners. Thus, while some adaptation was made to account for the environmental change from Europe to the New World, there was not the compelling need to find innovative solutions to the environment in the Southern colonies like there was in New England. Thus began the initial divisions between liberal (which by definition is a philosophy that accepts change) and conservative (which tends to remain the same) economics and cultures in America.

---

40   John Mason, Pierre Soulé, and James Buchanan, "The Ostend Manifesto" cited in *The Annals of America* (Chicago: Encyclopaedia Britannica, 1968) 8:289–293.

In New England, and later the Middle Atlantic colonies and the Middle West, the drive for innovation required the development of a body of information, which could be used to foster further innovation. The need for information led to the development of a system for fostering education. Higher education was still primarily the province of the clergy and the well-to-do young man who wanted the education of a well-rounded gentleman (there are still vestiges of this today in the elite prep schools and colleges). But for the community in general and the business community in particular, a strong general education base was necessary in order to develop innovative products and ideas for the local economy, and also to have a workforce with the skills to develop those ideas. From this need eventually came the establishment of the American public education system.

It is fashionable among conservative thinkers today to dismiss the public education system in this country as a bloated, bureaucratic monstrosity that should be privatized and put out of its misery. And there are certainly troubled school districts that fit that description. Any organization, public or private, can be susceptible to bureaucratic hardening of the arteries. But in the eighteenth century when the American colonies first developed their public education system, it was revolutionary. Public education wasn't entirely new; there had been limited attempts in Europe. But class-based societies like those in Europe were not the ideal environment for such an idea. It was the wide-scale adoption of public education in America that was so revolutionary. Education was no longer for the elite. It was open for everyone.[41] In New England and the Middle Atlantic colonies, it provided a vast pool of talented young workers who filled the factories, the mills the workshops and merchant houses in developing the economic might of the North. When the first factory was set up in Pawtucket, Rhode Island in 1790,[42] the combination of the public education system and the factory system were joined in American industry.

The combination of the innovativeness and the educational system of the North spilled out into the rapid development of technology. It was common for American manufacturers to build products with short lifetimes for the simple reason that these products would be rapidly superseded by a more sophisticated version of the same product. Older products were dismantled

---

41   Stuart Bruchey, *Growth of the Modern American Economy* (New York: Dodd, Mead, 1975) pp.43–44.

42   Robertson and Walton, *History of the American Economy*, 201.

or simply thrown away, characteristics that we see in electronic products today. Out of this activity came the technology and products of early American industry.[43] While high tariff barriers for most of the nineteenth century would protect these new industries, these were the products and ideas that would build the American manufacturing base. In addition to the cotton gin, there was the development of the textile industry and the associated development of factories and weaving technology. The development of interchangeable parts was pioneered at this time, too, which first gave a boost to the firearms industry, but was later incorporated into numerous other manufactured goods. This concept, also the work of Eli Whitney, laid the foundation for the mass production of durable goods. From it came the mass productions of clocks, tools and a host of other hard goods that made the Northern states the workshop of the nation.

Two other factors came into play as the industries of the North developed. The first was that the urban, industrialized North developed its economy on a workforce made of relatively high wages. Even in Colonial times, the American economy was the second or third largest economy in the world, behind only England, and by some measures, the Netherlands.[44] America presented the exact opposite of economic inputs when compared to Europe. In Europe, land was limited; therefore, it was valuable. The owners of this land in Europe were the aristocracy of the various countries. In contrast, workers were plentiful and therefore cheap. In America land was abundant, and from the colonist standpoint, practically free (although the Native Americans had other ideas about of how "free" this land was). All one had to do was move out beyond the current line of settlement and start a new farm. Later, people had to cross the country to do this, but in the beginning, it was relatively easy to do. But because America was nowhere nearly as densely populated as Europe, free labor was relatively scarce, and consequently wages were much higher in America than in Europe.[45] The high wages also led to technological development of products that could save labor costs, which in turn spurred the North's industrial base. The high wages required a more productive and skilled workforce, also requiring a highly effective public education system that could develop the skills of all able-bodied workers, not just the elite few that could afford a private education.

---

43   Michael Perelman, *The Pathology of the U.S. Economy: The Costs of a Low Wage System* (Houndmills, England: Macmillan, 1993), pp. 202–204.

44   Robertson and Walton, *History of the American Economy*, 100–101.

45   Ibid., 21–22.

The public education system as developed in the North also points out the second key factor that accelerated the Northern economy—the fact that the states of the North were willing to fund the economy through government expenditures. While government funding of institutions was commonplace in Europe, that was not the case in America. As colonies of Great Britain, government resources were limited and government's role was limited in scope. Even so, Americans took a dim view of what little government there was. With independence, of course, there was the great debate about the role of government as expounded by people like Jefferson and Hamilton, but even the Federalists' idea of government was to limit it more than any European country had done. In America, the government was intended to be smaller in scale and government budgets balanced; any government expenditure was an exceptional event. That being said, the Northern colonies and later states were still more prepared to fund activities from government sources than the Southern colonies were. Eventually, the government commitment spread from schools to infrastructure projects like roads, canals and later railroads. The most famous of these projects was the Erie Canal, which was funded by $7 million from the state of New York in 1817.[46] These infrastructure projects drove down the cost of transport and other business costs while at the same time opening up the interior to rapid development.

The net result of these various initiatives was that the North grew rapidly in population and in wealth. But there was an important side effect in democratizing the whole region. Politically, the core of the region was Federalist New England and the Federalist party of Alexander Hamilton in New York. People like Hamilton, John Adams and his son John Quincy Adams were supporters of a strong federal government, the merchant and manufacturing class, and a central bank, as opposed to Thomas Jefferson's yeoman farmer and Andrew Jackson's common man. But while the views of Federalists may have favored the merchant and manufacturing ownership class, they paradoxically opened up the economy to a greater number of people. Government investment in education, in transportation infrastructure, and other services of the time, made it possible for people of lesser means to get ahead in the American economy. It also provided opportunity for smaller businesses and farms to thrive in that kind of an environment. When the country expanded into the Middle West, the policies that had been devel-

---

46   *Encyclopaedia Britannica*, 15th ed., s.v. "Erie Canal."

oped in the Northern states transferred over to the new region and allowed that part of the country to develop rapidly as well. Although primarily a farming economy like the South, the Middle West was dominated by numerous small family farms rather than a few large plantations.[47] The education system of the North came as well and paved the way for the development of farming technology such as Cyrus McCormick's reaper, which revolutionized farming production in the Middle West.

The democratizing of the Northern economy democratized the politics as well. It was from the Northern states that the abolitionist movement, the suffrage movement, and the labor movement began. These political movements and others like them were made possible because of the development of a freewheeling society where individuals could make a difference.

The situation in the South could not have been more different. Southern society took on the characteristics of a landed aristocracy very early. As stated before, Southern farming was very labor intensive, but to get that labor required either paying wages sufficient to attract such labor or acquiring slaves. The colonies had begun with the concept of indentured servitude in which people who could not pay their own way across the Atlantic came to the colonies as indentured servants and worked off their obligation to their masters. When the debt was paid, they were free men. The early days of the colonies also saw the importation of convicts, particularly to the Carolinas, who also came as indentured servants. But these were supposed to be temporary economic situations. The establishment of slavery in the colonies made them permanent. How the South would have developed if it had not relied on slavery is open to question. But there is no question that once the South chose that route, it was on an economic path which has hindered the region's growth ever since.

The divergence of the Northern and Southern colonies in their early period offers an interesting managerial question. As stated at the beginning of this chapter, one would have assumed that, given the environmental situation, the Southern colonies would have been the more economically successful. In the event, the Northern colonies accumulated greater wealth and it was the New York and London merchants who financed the plantations of the South.[48] Necessity is indeed the mother of invention, and the environ-

---

47   Primack and Willis, *Economic History of the United States*, 159–162.
48   Harvey C. Bunke, *A Primer on American Economic History* (New York: Random House, 1969), 38; Fred A. Shannon, *The Farmer's Last Frontier: Agriculture 1860–1897* (Armonk, NY: M.E.

mental challenges forced the Northern colonies to be inventive. The need to overcome severe challenges forced them to think "outside the box." It also meant creating both public and private institutions to foster such thinking. Ultimately, it is the foundation for liberal political, economic, and social policy.

There was no such urgency in the South; they could create an agricultural society without much fear of the elements and no compelling need to change. That in turn bred a conservatism into the culture. The conservative culture then intended to reinforce the status quo, and the status quo was the landowning elite of the large plantations. Some farmers acquired very large holdings of arable land that were simply not possible to obtain in the Middle Atlantic colonies and certainly not in New England. These large plantation owners formed the tip of the landed aristocracy pyramid. They were not interested in having a lot of freemen competing with them for resources.[49] Likewise, they didn't want to pay them as laborers.

Acquiring a slave seemed to be a more cost-effective solution. It was, in effect, the easy way out. Indeed, a lot of conservative thinking is not based on reverence for the tried and true solution; it is based on doing things the easiest way possible in the short run, regardless of the long-term costs. This is what traps and ultimately destroys these societies.

As for the profitability of slavery at the large plantations, for a long time there was no question. The division of labor made slavery and these plantations more profitable as they acquired more slaves. Slavery really paid, however, where at least 50 slaves were held.[50] Below that number, the economics were much less attractive. Thus, the large plantations had the strongest interest in keeping the status quo, politically and socially as well as economically.

This kind of a conservative economic and social system leads to several handicaps that dogged the region and still present problems today. The first of these was that, since the large plantations had no interest in hiring workers, potential workers had no interest in the Southern states. Any free man coming to America from overseas was more likely to find gainful employment

---

Sharpe, 1989), 99–100.

49 James C. Cobb, *Industrialization, and Southern Society* (Lexington, Kentucky: The University Press of Kentucky, 1984), 7–9, 80–81, 25.

50 Robert W. Fogel and Stanley L. Engerman, "Explaining the Relative Efficiency of Slave Agriculture in the Antebellum South," *American Economic Review* 67, no. 3 (June 1977), 285 Table 7; also cited in Robertson and Walton, *History of the American Economy*, 232.

in the North. That, plus the fact that salaries were already high by European standards, made the North more attractive.[51] Needless to say the population of the Northern states grew more rapidly than the Southern. Virginia, which was the most populous state in the 1790 census, fell behind a number of other states, especially New York and Pennsylvania, in the censuses of the early nineteenth century.

Second, the plantations did not want competition from a free labor force, and they also did not want competition from other businesses. Industry was discouraged in the South. Likewise, education was discouraged because it could bring in dangerous new ideas that could upset the status quo. Education would have been necessary to upgrade the skill level for industry workers, so discouraging education also discouraged the development of industry.[52] Thus discouraging education provided the double "benefit" of keeping a lid on competing workers and competing industries.

Education wasn't completely ignored. The sons of the elite attended private colleges, and there were some enlightened moves, such as the establishment of the University of North Carolina at Chapel Hill in 1793, the first public institution for higher learning in the country. But it was the exception, not the rule.

With the discouragement of public education came a general discouragement of public infrastructure projects, because large projects tended to need government funding. As a result the South also fell behind in the development of roads, canals and railroads. In general, the size and the scope of government were limited. This may have suited the Jacksonian and Jeffersonian types, but it had severe economic consequences for the region.

The combination of all these policies created massive inequality, discouraged entrepreneurial activity, and stifled economic development in the South. On the income side, estimates of wealth for the period just before the Civil War showed that white free men (i.e., the plantation owners) in the South had the highest levels of wealth in the country. But when the slaves were added in, the overall wealth of the region was severely behind that of the North.[53] By 1860, the North led by just about any statistical measure. The

---

51 Ibid., 204.
52 Cobb, *Industrialization and Southern Society*, 16–18, 24–25, 80–81
53 Fogel and Engerman, "The Economics of Slavery," in *The Reinterpretation of American History*, (New York: Harper and Row, 1971) 335, Table 8; cited in Primack and Willis, *Economic History of the United States*, 155 and Robertson and Walton, *History of the American Economy*, 244. Bruchey, *Growth of the American Economy*, 46.

population of the North was 31 million to the South's 9 million. In the production of various commodities, in the miles of railroad track, in the amount of bank deposits, it was no contest. The merchants in the North were lending money to the farms in the South, not the other way around. On the eve of the Civil War, the states that would become part of the Confederacy were rapidly falling behind the rest of the country.

By then, of course, the expanding Middle West was gravitating to the North's orbit. The North's economic and social policies were much more amenable to the settlers carving out the Middle West. Economically, the transportation of crops, the developing of farming technology (particularly for Midwestern crops like wheat and corn) and other industries were more easily accomplished by access to the Northern transportation infrastructure. Socially, there was greater opportunity to develop by emulating Northern-style institutions. By the middle of the nineteenth century, these trends in the Middle West would lead to the support of the Homestead Act and the land-grant college, both of which were opposed by the South for the same reasons that it had opposed other earlier initiatives that found support in the North.

The only economic policy promoted by the South that by today's standards would be considered liberal was the South's support of free trade as opposed to the American Plan of high tariffs supported by Henry Clay and the North. The South was a massive exporter of cotton goods to England and the rest of Europe. As the seller of a dominant, mature product, naturally they would want the lowest tariffs possible to be able to sell their goods without restriction. The North, on the other hand, was trying to develop new products in competition with the British and the rest of Europe. Northern business people had plenty of domestic markets to sell to and did not need to sell overseas. They also had higher wages than Europe that would offset any transportation cost advantage. Northern business interests wanted high tariffs to protect those industries. Throughout most of the nineteenth century, tariffs were the primary source of revenue for the federal government. This allowed the federal government to avoid imposing direct taxation. Direct taxes like the income tax would not come along until the late nineteenth century. Now, in the early twenty-first century, when the economic byword is globalization, nineteenth-century Southern trade policy seems forward-looking by contrast, although some third world countries might disagree.

The net result of all this is that on the eve of the Civil War in 1861, the South was in a very vulnerable position in terms of economic wealth and manpower. Only the incompetence of the Northern generals in the early part of the war allowed the South to hold out as long as it did. By the end of the war, the South was an economic ruin.

The economic trajectories of the North and South continued after 1865. Although the radical Reconstructionists in Congress sought to impose fundamental changes in the South after the war, resistance to those changes continued until the pullout of federal troops in 1877, when the status quo returned and a severely diminished plantation elite regained control. Sharecropping replaced slavery, but the same factors that had made the South an economic backwater before the war continued after the war, with the difference that Southern cotton's global dominance had been challenged in places like Egypt and India, where the British had begun developing alternative sources for its mills when access to Southern cotton was blockaded by the North during the war. Then the boll weevil devastated cotton crops at the turn of the twentieth century. Although they got hand-me-down textile plants from an aging New England industry, essentially the Southern economy remained that of an imperial colony until the 1930s, when massive federal investments through New Deal agricultural programs and the construction triggered by World War II transformed the economy. Yet even today, the South is still the poorest region in the country, is heavily dependent on defense expenditures and agricultural subsidies in many of its states, and is a net receiver of federal funds.[54]

In contrast, the states that fought for the Union continued to build from strength to strength. During the war, the absence of Southern legislators made it possible for several reform measures to pass the Congress, including the aforementioned Homestead Act and the Morrill Act for the land-grant colleges. Legislation also established the national banking system. Shortly afterwards came the establishment of Yellowstone National Park, the National Parks System, and the beginning of the environmental movement. Later would come other movements: the Progressive Movement, women's suffrage, anti-trust legislation, and the early regulatory agencies. All of these programs had at their core the late nineteenth century progressive Republican base (the Democrats would become a factor at the end of the century),

---

54   See Appendix A.2a.

centered in the Northern states with allies in the Middle West and Far West. Economically, these states were the engine that eventually made it possible for the United States to surpass the United Kingdom as the largest economy in the world. Today these states (primary the Northeast, the area around the Great Lakes, and the Pacific Coast) are still the core of the US economy and a net provider of funds to the federal government.[55]

The above discussion illustrates the Great American Divide in historical terms. But its effects can also be seen in our own time, particularly when one looks at the 2000 and 2004 elections. At the core of the Red States are Southern states of the old Confederacy. All of those states without exception voted for George W. Bush in both elections. At the core of the Blue states are the states of the Northeast. With New Hampshire (a Red state in 2000) voting for John Kerry in 2004, all of the New England states voted for him as did New York and Pennsylvania. The record was mixed in the Midwestern States with the states splitting evenly for both candidates. But with the notable exception of Ohio and Indiana, the industrial Midwest around the Great Lakes voted for Kerry in 2004 while the rural Midwest voted for Bush. The Western states are a more recent part of the picture and are not part of the early historical record. But the wealthier states of California, Oregon, and Washington clearly showed strong "blue" characteristics in both elections.

The results of those elections clearly favored Bush's policies and those of the Red states. And given the economic and political history of the Red states in the form of their Southern/Confederate ancestors, it should come as no surprise that their history mirrors many of the problems that we see today. The extreme inequality that we see between CEOs and their workers today? Even greater inequality occurred between plantation owners and their slaves. An economy that substantially favors business over labor? Again, one only has to look at the ante-bellum South. Companies with union contracts discouraged from locating in a right-to-work area? Look no further than an American industrial sector discouraged from locating amongst the plantations. Lack of infrastructure to attract a desirable auto plant? No different than in the nineteenth century when immigrants and new businesses went to the Midwest rather than the South because of its extensive railroad system, and why the railroad hub of Chicago, not Saint Louis or New Orleans,

---

55   See Appendix A.2b.

became a dominant city in the middle of the country. A natural disaster on the Gulf Coast due to lack of maintenance of the levee system? Same thing on the lower Mississippi River in 1927. Red state economies dependent on the Federal government? Southern economies have been the poor section of the country for two centuries and dependant on outside funds. A nation heavily in debt and at the economic mercy of China? Southern plantation owners were at the mercy of New York and London bankers.[56] Indeed, just about everywhere you to turn today, you can find eerie parallels of the policies that dogged the precursors of the Red states right from the beginning.

Given the unpleasant parallels above, the question of how the current economic situation evolved is a long and detailed one. Many pundits have issued glib statements about cultural values, the sophisticated manner in which Republicans have developed their issues, and the inept response by the Democrats, all of which is true to some degree. However, the historical record shows that while Republicans made significant gains in the South with Richard Nixon's Southern Strategy in the late 1960s, the Republicans had slowly gained ground fifty years before that, starting with the Democratic Party problems with Prohibition in the 1920s, followed by the Dixiecrats in 1948, and Eisenhower's gains in the 1950s. Nixon's move was a logical extension of that activity. But it also allowed for Southern economic policy, heretofore a regional issue under the control of Southern Democrats, to be linked up with conservative Republican economics that resulted in the national economic policies of Ronald Reagan and George W. Bush—thus the Red-state dominated politics that we have today.

Ultimately the question is whether the Great American Divide can be bridged and merged in a new Democratic and liberal vision, and whether the values of the Blue states can succeed where the values of the Red states have been found wanting. In order to answer that, it will first be necessary to review those areas of the country that constitute the Red states and the Blues States to see what economic indicators provide the clues to answer some key questions: namely, what are the differences between the Red states and the Blue states and how these structural differences affect us today.

---

56   See note 47.

3. Red State–Blue State Demographics

While the labeling of the states into Red and Blue occurred during the 2000 election, it was the 2004 election that clearly defined the labels on the map. That is because of the two geographic anomalies of that election, New Hampshire and New Mexico, switched to the dominant colors of their regions—the Blue of New England and the Red of the Mountain states. Iowa also switched to Red, but since the Midwest was already a mixed area, Iowa was a wash from an analytical standpoint.

The Red States

In the 2004 election, the Red states won by George W. Bush totaled 31 of the 50 states [Table 3.1A, Column 1]. Of those 31 states, thirteen may be considered Southern: the eleven states of the old Confederacy (Alabama, Arkansas, Florida, Georgia, Louisiana, Mississippi, North Carolina, South Carolina, Tennessee, Texas, and Virginia) and two border states (Kentucky and West Virginia). All are south of the Ohio River and only two are completely west of the Mississippi River. Added to this total are nine of the thirteen Western states, eight Mountain states (Arizona, Colorado, Idaho, Montana, Nevada, New Mexico, Utah and Wyoming), and Alaska, which has many of the characteristics of the Mountain states. Finally, rounding out the Red states there are nine of the thirteen Midwest states. These include Ohio, Indiana, and seven states west of Illinois (Iowa, Kansas, Missouri, Nebraska, North Dakota, Oklahoma, and South Dakota).

THE BLUE STATES

In the 2004 election, the Blue states won by John Kerry consisted of 19 states and the District of Columbia [Table 3.1B, Column]. Since the District carried the same number of electoral votes as the smallest states in the union (some of which are smaller in population than the District), DC will be treated as a state for the purpose of this analysis, making 20 Blue states. Of those 20 states, twelve are located in the Northeast: the six New England states (Connecticut, Maine, Massachusetts, New Hampshire, Rhode Island and Vermont), three Middle Atlantic states (New Jersey, New York and Pennsylvania), and three border states (Delaware, DC, and Maryland). Like the Southern states, this group is a unified geographic bloc with no Red states in its region. In addition to the Northeast states, two other blocs form the Blue states, both of which have Red state neighbors. The Western Blue states, which could also be called the Pacific states, consists of four of the thirteen Western states—California, Hawaii, Oregon and Washington State. The other Blue states are four of the thirteen Midwest states, from the upper Midwest and Great Lakes—Illinois, Michigan, Minnesota and Wisconsin. Both the Western (unified through the Pacific Ocean) and Midwestern Blue states consist of unified blocs without other political entities (Red states or Canada) in the way. This is in contrast to the Western and Midwestern Red states, where Alaska, Indiana and Ohio are isolated from the other Red states. Particularly in Midwestern Red states, this means that there is much less homogeneity among the states than there is in other blocs.

POPULATION AND ELECTORAL VOTES

In looking at the Red states, the first thing that needs to be analyzed is the comparative data, and that starts with the population and the electoral votes. In the 2000 US census, the United States had 281 million people. Of that 281 million, the Red states had 144 million or just over half. The regional breakdown was 90 million in the South, 19 million in the West and 35 million in the Midwest [Table 3.1A, Column 1]. The Blue states had 137 million people, 60 million in the Northeast, 44 million in the West, and 33 million in the Midwest [Table 3.1B, Column 1].

Accompanying the populations were the electoral votes. The Red states had 286 of the 538 electoral votes, a slightly larger percentage of electoral votes than the Red state population to the total population [Table 3.1A, Column 2]. This is because the average Red state population of 4.6 million is smaller than the average Blue state population of 6.9 million. Since electoral votes are not based exclusively on population but the size of a state's delegation in Congress, both House and Senate, and since the less populous states have equal representation in the Senate, they have a slightly higher representation in the Electoral College and the large states have a slightly smaller representation. The Red states' 286 electoral votes are broken into 166 from the South, 47 from the West and 73 from the Midwest [Table 3.1A, Column 2]. The Blue states' 252 electoral votes are broken down into 117 from the Northeast, 77 from the West, and 58 from the Midwest [Table 3.1B, Column 2].

As can be seen from the population and the electoral votes, the Southern states are the foundation of the Red-state bloc. This bloc has been fairly cohesive throughout most of its history. For starters, all of these states were slave states and voted consistently together to maintain their position in the Senate prior to the Civil War. After the end of Reconstruction in 1877, the eleven Confederate states of the bloc were known as the "Solid South" because of their consistent voting for the Democratic Party in opposition to the Union and Pro-Reconstruction dominated Republican Party. The bloc began to fall away from the Democrats, first in the 1920s, then with the Dixiecrats in 1948, some votes for Eisenhower in the 1950s, and ultimately over time shifted to the Republican Party starting with Nixon's Southern Strategy in the 1968 election. They are now the foundation of Republican's national election strategy.

The Western and Midwestern blocs have been much more fluid in their political alignment, but at their core have come from a historically Republican base. Only Missouri was an actual slave state before the Civil War, but there was strong sympathy for the Southern states in the southern portions of Ohio, Indiana and Illinois, as many of those residents had come from slave state Virginia, and there were violent battles over slavery in the Kansas Territory. The western portion of the Midwest and all of the Western Red states were not admitted to the Union before the outbreak of hostilities in 1861, and several of these states had only been part of the United States a little more than ten years at the time. In the Southwest territories, the influence of Mexico remained strong. (In Ventura, California on July 4, 1865, the Declaration of Independence was read in Spanish on the steps of the San Buenaventura Mission). So many of these states evolved from a more recent history.

The Midwestern states were the bedrock of the rural Republican political base, starting with Lincoln and then running through a number of Republican presidents from the state of Ohio, culminating with Herbert Hoover, whose birthplace was Iowa. Also coming out of this Republican base was the Progressive movement, the most notable figure of the movement being Robert La Follette of Wisconsin. But the Midwest also had a strong rural populist base that supported Democrats of the likes of William Jennings Bryan of Nebraska who drew support from the upper plains states and other rural parts of the country. Also balancing the rural Republican bloc in later years was the growing Democratic urban bloc from the large cities on the Great Lakes such as Chicago, Detroit and Cleveland. So the net result is a politically dynamic region which although has been historically based in the Republican Party, has been an integral part of both Republican and Democratic strategy, and is the primary location of the battleground states in each election. In recent elections, Ohio, Michigan, and Missouri have been heavily contested and will be so in the future.

The Western States historically tend to be Republican for the simple reason that they were mostly admitted by Republican administrations. One of the key issues of the 1888 election was that Republicans under Harrison were ready to admit these states, while the Democrats under Cleveland were not. In the event, Harrison took New York and the electoral vote even though Cleveland won the popular vote (sound familiar?). With Harrison and the Republicans in control, the Dakotas, Montana, Idaho, Wyoming, and Washington were admitted to the Union in 1889–90, the first such states created since Colorado in 1876 and the biggest rush to statehood in the history of the country. While Cleveland would eventually admit Utah in 1896, the five remaining states after that were all admitted to the Union under Republicans. All except Hawaii and Washington are Red. So there is no surprise that there would be a strong Republican inclination from these states.

But the Western states have a far different political mixture than the other Red-state blocs. For starters, slavery was never a vital issue for them. They were legally defined as free or slave territories by a line drawn on a map, but the economy developed in its own ways. Their remoteness from the center of power gave them, then and now, a strong independence and libertarian streak. Nowhere is the myth of the American cowboy stronger than in these states. They were also the last portions of the frontier to be developed in the late nineteenth and early twentieth centuries. Indeed, a good case can be made that frontier life is still alive and well in Alaska. There was a strong Progressive streak in the West as well. The West was a major factor in the women's suffrage movement. Wyoming was the first state to grant women the right to vote and Montana was the first state to elect a woman, Jeanette Rankin, to Congress. Women's suffrage was a key plank for the Republican Party for decades and Rankin entered Congress as a Republican.

The West also has almost a schizophrenic nature between its urban and rural character. Although by area the Western states are largely rural, the population tends to be highly concentrated in cities and towns because it is extremely difficult to live in much of the arid regions of these states. As a result the Western states tend to have some of the highest percentage of their population living in urban areas. Thus we have the incongruity of a state like Arizona, which is synonymous with the desert and Wild West, having Phoenix as its state capital, one of the ten largest cities in the country. Similarly, one of the fastest growing large metropolises in the country is Las Vegas, a town that barely existed before 1930. Thus we have in the Red states, three areas of widely diverging backgrounds.

Finally, as can be seen in the population and electoral votes, the Northeastern states are the primary base for the Blue states, but this is not as monolithic a bloc as the Southern states are to the Red states, nor as cohesive. The Northeastern states started out as the base for the Federalist Party, centered in New York and New England. After the Federalist Party disappeared, the Northeastern States went through a transitional period, ending up in the Republican Party at the time of the Civil War. As the Northeastern cities grew in size and influence, the urban core tended to vote for the Democrats in the large states and the rural areas voted for the Republicans in those states. As such, states like New York and Pennsylvania became important swing states for both political parties. New York, in particular, was decisive in the 1884, 1888 and 1892 elections. The Republican Party remained strong in the Northeast, and in 1936, Maine and Vermont were the only states that Alf Landon won against Franklin Delano Roosevelt. Richard Nixon carried the

Northeast except for Massachusetts against George McGovern in 1972. It is only in recent times that the Northeastern states have become a Democratic bastion, with the entire region voting for John Kerry.

Although data was collected in a number of areas, for the purposes of the discussion in this chapter, the discussion will be confined to finance and income, and the data limited to Tables 3.1 and 3.2 [Tables A.1 and A.2 in the Appendix]. The entire collection is in the Appendix.

With two exceptions, the data presented in this book comes from the *US Statistical Abstract*. The exceptions are net federal revenue received [Tables 3.2a, 3.2b, and Appendix Tables A.1b, A.2b], which was taken from the Tax Foundation as net revenue received is a key concept in the Red state–Blue state discussion, and churches per 1,000 population [Appendix Tables E.1b, E.2b], as this statistic is not covered in the Abstract.

INCOME, FINANCE AND THE STATE ECONOMIES

The first data to look at is income. From the 2000 Census, the US Median Household Income for the calendar year 1999 was $41,994 [Table 3.1A and B, Column 3]. Not surprisingly, the median household income for the Red states was lower, at $37,934, as the Southern states continue to be the poorest region in the country. The median household income of the Southern states was at $36,360, well below the other two blocs of states in the Red category. The Red Midwestern states were better at $38,469 and the Red Western states were near the national average at $40,558. However, while these regions did substantially better than the Southern states, they were still substantially below the Blue states of the Midwest and West, both of which had median household incomes in excess of $45,000.

The average household income for the Blue states was $45,964 and the median income was $46,183, above the national average and well above the median household income of the Red states. Thus the median income of the Blue states was more than 20 percent higher than the Red states. This is not surprising since the Blue states contain most of the wealthiest states in the union. The Northeast states alone contain four of the five states with median household income over $50,000 (New Jersey, Connecticut, Maryland and Massachusetts; Alaska is the other).

The Median household income figures are mirrored in two other sets of income data. In looking at the 2002 median state personal income of the Red states we get a figure of $80.4 billion, just over half of the median Blue-state personal income of $150.3 billion [Table 3.1A and B, Column 4]. The Blue states are substantially more populous than the Red states, so one would expect their personal income on average to be larger. But when one looks at 2002 per capita income rankings of states, the Red states have an average ranking of 34 and a median ranking of 36 out of the 50 states. The Blue states have an average ranking of 13 and a median ranking of 12, about the figure one would expect to get since the two sets of rankings should total on or close to 50 [Table 3.1A and B, Column 5].

Since the per capita rankings eliminate the size of the state and focus strictly on income, the divergence between the Red and Blue numbers is quite substantial. Had they hovered inside the 30–20 range and were fairly close to a 25–25 split, the ranking differences would not seem so significant. But in fact, the ranking differences are closer to 40–10 than they are to 30–20, which is truly stunning. Once again, the primary weakness is in the Southern states that have a median per capita income ranking of 40, including Mississippi at 50, Arkansas at 49 and West Virginia at 48, the three lowest in the nation. In fact, the Red states have the 17 lowest per capita state income rankings in the nation. The median per capita state ranking of the Western Red states is 38 and the Midwestern Red states is 31. Only Colorado (ranked 9th) and Virginia (ranked 11th) are a major exception to the trend. The most populous Red states, Texas and Florida are ranked 34th and 27th, respectively. So even the largest Red states are not an exception to the rule when it comes to per capita income. In the Blue states, the Northeast has the states with the six highest per capita incomes in the country. Of the Blue states, fourteen of the nineteen were in the top 20 per capita income ranked states. Only Oregon at 29th and Maine at 33rd ranked in the lower half nationally. The above data shows that the Blue states are dramatically richer than the Red states.

In addition to the Blue and Red comparisons as a whole, comparisons between the Blue and Red states within the Midwest and Western regions are of interest because of differences in the region. In the Midwest, the Blue states have a median household income of $45,629 while the Red states have a median household income of $40,558. In the West, the Blue states have a median household income of $45,776 while the Red states have a median household income of $38,469. So not only does the rich Northeastern States have substantially higher income than the poor Southern states, but within the West and the Midwest, Blue states in each region are richer than Red states. In the case of the West, there are several Red states with income figures comparable to Western Blue states. But the Western Red states also have a chain of poorer states in the Northern Rockies (Idaho, Montana Wyoming) as well as New Mexico that bring the income figures down significantly. In the Midwest, all the Red Midwestern states have substantially poorer median household incomes than the Blue Midwestern states. Even in the case of the industrial Red states of Indiana ($41,567) and Ohio ($40,956), they are substantially below the neighboring states of Michigan ($44,667) and Illinois ($46,950). These intra-regional differences show that the above-income levels are not just the exclusive product of geographic differences (i.e. Northeast vs. South), but reflect certain political, economic and sociological differences within the Red and Blue states which have produced the income differences within regions.

TABLE 3.1A. RED-STATE POPULATION, INCOME, FINANCE (PART 1)

	Population (000)	Electoral Votes	Median Household Income	Personal Income $Billions	Per Capita Income Rank	Poverty % of Population
	2000	2004	1999($)	2002	2002	2003–04
UNITED STATES	281,422	538	41,994	8,033.1	(X)	12.6
South						
Alabama	4,447	9	34,135	101.5	43	16.0
Arkansas	2,673	6	32,182	57.4	49	16.4
Florida	15,982	27	38,819	445.3	23	12.2
Georgia	8,186	15	42,433	222.1	28	12.5
Kentucky	4,042	8	33,672	94.3	39	16.0
Louisiana	4,469	9	32,586	102.7	41	16.8
Mississippi	2,845	6	31,330	57.8	50	17.3
North Carolina	8,049	15	39,184	207.6	34	15.1
South Carolina	4,012	8	37,082	93.9	42	13.6
Tennessee	5,689	11	36,360	144.4	35	15.0
Texas	20,852	34	39,927	559.9	30	16.7
Virginia	7,079	13	46,677	216.2	11	9.7
West Virginia	1,808	5	29,696	38.4	48	15.8
Total South	90,133	166				

	Population (000)	Electoral Votes	Median Household Income	Personal Income $Billions	Per Capita Income Rank	Poverty % of Population
	2000	2004	1999($)	2002	2002	2003–04
Mean South	6,933		36,468	180.1	39	14.9
Median South	4,469		36,360	102.7	40	15.8
West						
Alaska	627	3	51,571	18.6	14	9.4
Arizona	5,131	10	40,558	128.6	38	13.9
Colorado	4,301	9	47,203	135.0	9	9.9
Idaho	1,294	4	37,572	30.3	44	10.0
Montana	902	3	33,024	20.5	45	14.6
Nevada	1,998	5	44,581	59.1	19	10.9
New Mexico	1,819	5	34,133	40.0	47	17.3
Utah	2,233	5	45,726	50.7	46	9.5
Wyoming	494	3	37,892	13.7	17	9.9
Total West	18,799	47				
Mean West	2,089		41,362	55.2	31	11.7
Median West	1,819		40,558	40.0	38	10.0
Midwest						
Indiana	6,080	11	41,567	156.6	32	10.8
Iowa	2,926	7	38,469	74.8	31	9.9
Kansas	2,688	6	40,624	71.3	26	11.1
Missouri	5,595	11	37,934	147.8	27	11.5
Nebraska	1,711	5	39,250	46.3	22	9.6
North Dakota	642	3	34,604	15.4	36	9.7
Ohio	11,353	20	40,956	302.4	25	11.3
Oklahoma	3,451	7	33,400	80.4	40	11.8
South Dakota	755	3	35,282	18.4	37	13.0
Total Midwest	35,201	73				
Mean Midwest	3,911		38,010	101.5	31	11.0
Median Midwest	2,926		38,469	74.8	31	11.1
Total Red	144,133	286				

	Population (000)	Electoral Votes	Median Household Income	Personal Income $Billions	Per Capita Income Rank	Poverty % of Population
	2000	2004	1999($)	2002	2002	2003–04
Mean Red	4,649		38,336	121.0	34	12.8
Median Red	3,451		37,934	80.4	36	12.2

Source: Statistical Abstract of the United States

TABLE 3.1B. BLUE-STATE POPULATION, INCOME, FINANCE (PART 1)

	Population (000)	Electoral Votes	Median Household Income	Personal Income $Billions	Per Capita Income Rank	Poverty % of Population
	2000	2004	1999($)	2002	2002	2003–04
UNITED STATES	281,422	538	41,994	8,033.1	(X)	12.6
Northeast						
Connecticut	3,406	7	53,935	133.1	1	9.1
Delaware	784	3	47,381	23.8	12	8.2
D.C.	572	3	40,127	21.6	(X)	16.7
Maine	1,275	4	37,240	32.3	33	11.6
Maryland	5,296	10	52,868	178.4	4	9.2
Massachusetts	6,349	12	50,502	227.1	3	9.7
New Hampshire	1,236	4	49,467	39.4	6	5.6
New Jersey	8,414	15	55,146	305.1	2	8.3
New York	18,976	31	43,393	621.7	5	14.6
Pennsylvania	12,281	21	40,106	352.3	15	10.9
Rhode Island	1,048	4	42,090	30.2	16	11.5
Vermont	609	3	40,856	16.4	24	8.2
Total Northeast	60,246	117				
Mean Northeast	5,021		46,093	165.1	11	10.3
Median Northeast	2,341		45,387	86.3	6	9.5
West						
California	33,872	55	47,493	1043.2	10	13.2
Hawaii	1,212	4	49,820	33.6	20	8.9
Oregon	3,421	7	40,916	91.1	29	12.1
Washington	5,894	11	45,776	178.6	13	12.0

	Population (000)	Electoral Votes	Median Household Income	Personal Income $Billions	Per Capita Income Rank	Poverty % of Population
	2000	2004	1999($)	2002	2002	2003–04
Total West	44,399	77				
Mean West	11,100		46,001	336.6	18	11.6
Median West	4,658		46,635	134.9	17	12.1
Midwest						
Illinois	12,419	21	46,590	379.0	8	12.4
Michigan	9,938	17	44,667	274.1	18	12.3
Minnesota	4,919	10	47,111	154.0	7	7.2
Wisconsin	5,364	10	43,791	146.6	21	11.0
Total Midwest	32,640	58				
Mean Midwest	8,160		45,540	238.4	14	10.7
Median Midwest	7,651		45,629	214.1	13	11.7
Total Blue	137,285	252				
Mean Blue	6,864		45,964	214.1	13	10.6
Median Blue	5,108		46,183	150.3	12	11.0

Source: Statistical Abstract of the United States

The income figures are also reflected in another related figure—poverty [Table 3.2A and B, Column 6]. The percentage of people in poverty in the US is 12.6 percent in 2003–04, up from the last years of the Clinton Administration. The Red states are just about the national average with an average of 12.8 percent and a median of 12.2 percent; the Blue states are 10.6 and 11.0.

Another statistic related to poverty is unemployment [Table 3.2 A and B, Column 1]. And in the case of the percentage of unemployed, there is very little difference between the overall Red-state and Blue-state number at 5.4–5.5 percent. In this instance, the Red Midwest at 4.5 percent was substantially below the South and West at about 5.7 percent. In the Blue states, the low unemployment area was the Northeast at 4.9 percent. At the other extreme were the Western Blue states at 7.0 percent, the highest of any regional group. Thus, income was not a determining factor on the unemployment data as it was for other data sets.

Another economic factor is the number of bankruptcies [Table 3.2 A and B, Column 2 and 3]. In this instance, we have comparative numbers for 1995 and 2002. Nationally, the number of bankruptcies increased from 858,000 in 1995 to 1,505,000 in 2002, a substantial increase which reflects the recession that occurred in 2001. Naturally, being smaller states on average, the Red states have fewer bankruptcies per state than the Blue states. But while bankruptcies nationally and in the Blue states increased approximately 50 percent from 1995 to 2002, bankruptcies in the Red states increased 100 percent, from a mean average of 14,000 to 28,000, and a median average 11,000 to 22,000. While all the regional blocs increased, the median number of bankruptcies in the South increased from 14 thousand to 35 thousand. In contrast, Northeastern states such as New York, New Jersey and Massachusetts saw their numbers increase by 50 percent or less, and some smaller states barely moved at all. The net result was that that median average number of bankruptcies per state in the Northeast rose from 6,000 in 1995 to only 8,000 in 2002, and as a result, kept the national Blue-state median average down as well. Likewise, California saw its number of bankruptcies move from 140,000 in 1995 to only 148,000 in 2002, this despite the dot.com bubble crisis in the middle of this period. At the same time, an industrialized Red state like Ohio saw its bankruptcies explode from 32,000 to 73,000. If there is any pattern to the results, it is that rural states and aging manufacturing economies like Ohio had greater difficulty during this period than a more high-tech economy like California or Massachusetts. Thus, when it came to bankruptcies, the 2002 data adversely affected the Red states in general and the Southern states in particular.

TABLE 3.2A. RED-STATE POPULATION, INCOME, FINANCE (PART 2)

	Unemployment % of Workers	Bankrupt (000)	Bankrupt (000)	Net Fed Revenue Received	State Revenue Per Capita Rank	Unions % of Workers
	2002(1)	1995(1)	2002(1)	2004(2)	2000(1)	2002(1)
UNITED STATES	5.8	858	1,505			13.3
South						
Alabama	5.9	24	40	$1.71	37	9.0
Arkansas	5.4	8	22	$1.47	25	6.0
Florida	5.5	43	88	$1.02	50	5.8
Georgia	5.1	42	73	$0.96	45	6.0
Kentucky	5.6	13	26	$1.45	21	10.0
Louisiana	6.1	13	27	$1.45	31	8.4

	Unemployment % of Workers	Bankrupt (000)	Bankrupt (000)	Net Fed Revenue Received	State Revenue Per Capita Rank	Unions % of Workers
	2002(1)	1995(1)	2002(1)	2004(2)	2000(1)	2002(1)
Mississippi	6.8	11	22	$1.77	28	6.7
North Carolina	6.7	14	35	$1.10	23	3.4
South Carolina	6.0	7	15	$1.38	32	5.0
Tennessee	5.1	36	62	$1.30	46	9.1
Texas	6.3	44	77	$0.94	49	5.2
Virginia	4.1	26	42	$1.66	34	6.0
West Virginia	6.1	4	10	$1.83	18	13.2
Total South						
Mean South	5.7	22	41	$1.39	34	7.2
Median South	5.9	14	35	$1.45	32	6.0
West						
Alaska	7.7	1	1	$1.87	1	24.4
Arizona	6.2	15	27	$1.30	47	5.6
Colorado	5.7	13	19	$0.79	43	7.8
Idaho	5.8	4	8	$1.28	33	7.1
Montana	4.6	2	4	$1.58	19	14.1
Nevada	5.5	7	19	$0.73	48	15.2
New Mexico	5.4	4	9	$2.00	9	6.9
Utah	6.1	7	21	$1.14	24	6.2
Wyoming	4.2	1	2	$1.11	16	7.7
Total West						
Mean West	5.7	6	12	$1.31	27	10.6
Median West	5.7	4	9	$1.28	24	7.7
Midwest						
Indiana	5.1	22	51	$0.97	41	13.3
Iowa	4.0	6	11	$1.11	29	11.0
Kansas	5.1	8	14	$1.12	36	8.2
Missouri	5.5	15	32	$1.29	44	13.2
Nebraska	3.6	3	7	$1.07	30	8.0

	Unemployment % of Workers	Bankrupt (000)	Bankrupt (000)	Net Fed Revenue Received	State Revenue Per Capita Rank	Unions % of Workers
	2002(1)	1995(1)	2002(1)	2004(2)	2000(1)	2002(1)
North Dakota	4.0	1	2	$1.73	8	8.1
Ohio	5.7	32	73	$1.01	35	16.8
Oklahoma	4.5	13	23	$1.48	39	8.9
South Dakota	3.1	1	3	$1.49	42	5.5
Total Midwest						
Mean Midwest	4.5	11	24	$1.25	34	10.3
Median Midwest	4.5	8	14	$1.12	36	8.9
Total Red						
Mean Red	5.4	14	28	$1.33	32	9.1
Median Red	5.5	11	22	$1.30	33	8.0

Source: (1) Statistical Abstract of the United States, (2) Tax Foundation. Used by permission.

TABLE 3.2B. BLUE-STATE POPULATION, INCOME, FINANCE (PART 2)

	Unemployment % of Workers	Bankrupt (000)	Bankrupt (000)	Net Fed Revenue Received	State Revenue Per Capita Rank	Unions % of Workers
	2002(1)	1995(1)	2002(1)	2004(2)	2000(1)	2002(1)
UNITED STATES	5.8	858	1,505			13.3
Northeast						
Connecticut	4.3	8	11	$0.66	5	16.9
Delaware	4.2	1	4	$0.79	2	11.2
D.C.	6.4	1	3			14.1
Maine	4.4	2	4	$1.40	12	13.0
Maryland	4.4	16	34	$1.44	27	14.5
Massachusetts	5.3	14	17	$0.77	10	14.4
New Hampshire	4.7	3	4	$0.67	38	9.8
New Jersey	5.8	26	40	$0.55	20	19.8

	Unemployment % of Workers	Bankrupt (000)	Bankrupt (000)	Net Fed Revenue Received	State Revenue Per Capita Rank	Unions % of Workers
	2002(1)	1995(1)	2002(1)	2004(2)	2000(1)	2002(1)
New York	6.1	49	68	$0.79	7	25.6
Pennsylvania	5.7	22	52	$1.06	26	15.7
Rhode Island	5.1	3	5	$1.02	17	17.4
Vermont	3.7	1	2	$1.12	3	9.5
Total Northeast						
Mean Northeast	5.0	12	20	$0.93	15	15.3
Median Northeast	4.9	6	8	$0.79	12	14.5
West						
California	6.7	140	148	$0.79	14	17.8
Hawaii	4.2	2	5	$1.60	6	24.4
Oregon	7.5	13	24	$0.97	13	15.7
Washington	7.3	19	37	$0.88	22	18.6
Total West						
Mean West	6.4	44	54	$1.06	14	19.1
Median West	7.0	16	31	$0.93	14	18.2
Midwest						
Illinois	6.5	39	77	$0.73	40	19.7
Michigan	6.2	23	50	$0.85	15	21.1
Minnesota	4.4	14	19	$0.69	11	17.5
Wisconsin	5.5	12	23	$0.82	16	15.6
Total Midwest						
Mean Midwest	5.7	22	42	$0.77	21	18.5
Median Midwest	5.9	19	37	$0.78	16	18.6
Total Blue						
Mean Blue	5.4	20	31	$0.93	16	16.7
Median Blue	5.4	14	21	$0.82	14	16.9

Source: (1) Statistical Abstract of the United States, (2) Tax Foundation. Used by permission

The last major set of statistics involving income and finance has to do with revenue flows between the states and the federal government, specifically how much does each state get for every dollar it gives to Washington [Table

3.2A and B, Column 4]. Obviously, the states that are net receivers from the feds get more than one dollar back, the states that are net providers get less than a dollar. As a group, the Red states, supposedly the bastion of conservative small government benefit handsomely from federal largess. In 2004, they received a mean average of $1.33 and a median average of $1.30 for every dollar they shelled out. The Blue states get back 93 cents for every federal dollar that they send to the federal government, so they subsidize everyone else to the tune of seven cents on the dollar. Needless to say, Washington has been a good investment for the Red states. In one sense, this should not be surprising. First, the Red states control the Congress as well as the White House so naturally they have been crafting expenditures to benefit themselves, as the majority always does. They are also poorer than the Blue states and so naturally do not provide the federal government with as much revenue. And like all poorer areas, they tend to receive more services than they are able to pay for. In addition to that, however, they have been the long-term beneficiaries of programs dating back to Franklin Delano Roosevelt's New Deal, when the Democrats controlled Congress. Of course that was a different Democratic coalition, and one of the key ingredients to that coalition was the Southern states. In both eras, then and now, the Southern states chaired key committees in Congress and benefited from federal appropriations in both eras.

Over the years the Red states have benefited from two key types of appropriations—agricultural subsidies and military expenditures. Agricultural subsidies dated back to the early days in the New Deal in the early 1930s with the Agricultural Adjustment Act. The law initiated several programs, the most famous of which was the policy of paying farmers for storing surplus or removing land from production. These programs were designed to help farmers who had been suffering from overproduction and depressed prices since the early 1920s. In particular it was focused on the farms that had gone into operation on the eve of World War I on the High Plains in the tier of states from Oklahoma to the Dakotas and parts of the adjacent states. Other rural regions in the South and the Midwest benefited as well. Military expenditures were another matter. Military spending skyrocketed after the attack on Pearl Harbor and tended to focus on the coastal states, so the South benefited more than the Midwest. In addition, Roosevelt saw that these expenditures were an opportunity to lift the South out of the poverty it had endured since the Civil War, and so military expenditures were emphasized there. Later on, Southern congressmen were able to secure NASA space exploration expenditures for Florida and Texas. Thus, both military and agricultural dollars have been the basis for the large cash flows that have gone to the Red states for the past seventy years.

With these numbers in mind, it should come as no surprise that the South got the most money, given the fact that it benefits from both sets of programs. The Southern states receive a mean average of $1.39 and a median average of $1.45 for each tax dollar it sends to the federal government. The Western states are next at $1.31 and $1.28, with the Midwestern Red states following up with a more modest $1.25 and $1.12. As for the regions of the Blue states, all are net providers to the federal government. The Northeast had median average net revenue received of 79 cents, the Midwest 82 cents, and the West 93 cents.

The individual states offer some interesting stories. While the Southern states get the most benefits, the undisputed title of money pit of the nation goes to two Western states—Alaska at $1.87 and the champion New Mexico at a whopping $2.00, a 100 percent return on their money. The biggest contributing Red state is surprisingly Nevada at $0.73, contributing 27 cents on every federal dollar. Nevada is proof that there is money in vice. Texas at $0.94 is also a net payer, while Florida is a marginal receiver at $1.02. Only five of the 31 Red states are net payers.

On the other side of the coin, most of the Blue states are net providers to the federal government, some substantially so. New Jersey is the most extreme example, getting back only 55 cents of every dollar it sends. Connecticut, the state with the highest per capita income, gets back only two-thirds (66 cents) of what it sends. New Hampshire is next at 67 cents. The big population Blue states of California and New York are both at 79 cents, giving more than a fifth of their large incomes in subsidies to Red states. There are exceptions to this picture, of course. Blue-state Hawaii (at $1.60 per dollar), like Red-state Alaska ($1.87) is heavily subsidized as an extra-continental state with a large military presence. Maine, probably the poorest Blue state, receives $1.40. And of course, Maryland ($1.44), like Virginia, is a beneficiary of the spillover of the federal government infrastructure into their state.

The question of why the Blues States tend to be net providers of funds to the federal government while the Red states tend to be net users is a fairly complex one, but there are some clear trends, many of which have been brought up in earlier discussions. First, the obvious reason is that the Blue states are richer—they simply have more funds available to the federal government. This not only happens between states and regions, but within them as well, as has been shown by the regional net revenue data. The state of New York has been a long-standing test case of this. Throughout most of the state's history, the New York state government has been a net receiver of funds from New York City (except in the period in the 1970s, when the city nearly went bankrupt) while it has made net expenditures upstate. So the revenue aspects of rich areas and poor areas are not that much of a surprise.

Another impact in the Red state–Blue revenue difference is federal programs. The major expenditures over the years have been defense related, which tended to go to the South or West, or agricultural subsidies, which tended to go to South and the states on the High Plains. So both agricultural and military expenditures have tended to go to Red states. Both the revenue and the program factors have influenced the net revenue data for decades.

One other factor has come into play more recently, however. Since the Republicans have controlled Congress for most of the period since 1994, appropriations have naturally favored the Red states (which tend to have more Republicans in Congress) over Blue states. While these decisions generally work on a Congressional District basis (former Rep. Bill Thomas of California was able to send substantial highway dollars to his constituents in Bakersfield, CA, even though Thomas came from a Blue state), the net result would tend favor Red states, with clusters of Republican members of Congress in their state. With the Democrats in control of the Congress, revenue patterns may shift to Blue-state urban areas.

In conjunction with net federal revenue is the data on per capita state revenue [Table 3.2 A and B, Column 5]. The ranking of the state based on per capita state revenue in 2000 is close to the data on individual per capita income discussed previously. The mean and median rank of state per capita revenue was at 32 and 33 respectively for the Red states while it was 16 and 14 for the Blue states.

Finally, related to income and employment is labor union membership [Table 3.2 A and B, Column 6]. The unions constituted 13.3 percent of the national labor force in 2002. For the Red states, the averages were about two thirds of that with the mean Red states average at 9.1 percent and the median average of 8.0 percent. The Blue states are roughly double that figure with median Blue-state union membership at 16.9 percent. In the South, the averages were a 7.2 percent mean and 6.0 percent median. In the libertarian West the averages were 10.6 percent for the mean and 7.7 percent for the median. And in the Red-state Midwest the figures were 10.3 percent and 8.9 percent. In a change of roles in the Blue-state regions, the Northeastern states trailed the West and Midwestern states in union membership. The Northeast has a median percentage of 14.5 percent, while the West had 18.2 percent and the Midwest had 18.6 percent. The lower union membership in the Red states parallels the lower income for those states. As non-union wages are being squeezed and real wages continue to stagnate for most people, the only area where wages are being maintained is where the unions are strong, although as GM and Delphi show, even they are not always successful. Still, union membership is strongest in wealthier states, which is an important statement in itself.

The above series of income finance and employment data provide some interesting conclusions. The most significant is one that has been drawn many times before—that is, that the majority created by the Republicans to control both the White House and the Congress was one made up of primarily poor, rural states. Considering the Republicans have historically been the party of business, this is a remarkable coalition. As Thomas Frank pointed out in *What's the Matter with Kansas*, the Republicans have done a remarkable job connecting with people who should be the Democratic Party's constituency. This has also been borne out by campaign contribution data going into the 2004 election where Democrats were only able to raise more money than the Republicans in the over–$1 million category and the Republicans dominate all the categories below $1 million.

Another factor is that the Red states are heavily dependent on the federal government. In the case of the Western Red states, some of them are practically owned by the federal government, given the high percentage of their states that are federal lands.

This fact also touches on the larger issue of sovereignty and self determination that goes along with their low income. For most of the Red states, it has long been an issue to what degree they control their own destiny. The Populist movement was strong in most of these states in the late nineteenth century because people were suspicious that that their livelihoods and property were being controlled by the Eastern Establishment. People in the South thought a local business and plantation elite were controlling their lives. The success of the Republicans is that they have been able to identify that elite with the Democratic Party; what the Republicans have not been able to do is alleviate the dependency on the outside financial support that imprisons Red-state economies and make them glorified colonies. And of course, the Republicans have no real interest in doing so since they are in fact the real elite that profits from the Red states' dependency. The problem for the Republicans is that a country and a party based on such an economy is building an economic path to nowhere, as the South has proved throughout its history. Ultimately, both the Republicans and the country need the economic strength of the Blue states to be the engine of economic growth to keep the country moving forward. The Red states face this essential contradiction when it comes to economic issues.

On the other hand the Blue states largely consist of a small number of heavily populated (or in the case of the New England, densely populated), wealthier states. While there are some rural states in the mix, such as Maine and Vermont, the Blue states have large urban and metropolitan areas such greater New York, Chicago and Los Angeles which are an important part of their makeup. The Blue states also sport a significant industrial and high-tech base with a significant union presence.

These are states that in a previous era would have been Republican or swing states. These former Republican and swing states have become Democratic states. Thus the wealth of the Blue states have been supporting the supposed party of working people—Democrats. It has been proposed on many occasions that catering to the large bank accounts of corporations and the well-off has alienated the Democratic Party from its working class base, and that is the reason that Democrats have been losing poorer states to the Republicans in recent elections. There is no doubt some truth to this. But is also true that newer high-tech industries have been attracted to the Blue states because they are more willing to meet the needs of such industries. The elitist label that Republicans in Red states have been able to tag them with in recent years has dogged the Democratic Blue states. But one man's elitism is another man's success story. If the Democrats were to convince the voters in the Red states that the Democratic model of the Blue states was a more successful for them than the Red-state model they have now, and the Democrats were able to lose the elitist image because of that success, then there is the potential for the Blue-state economic data to be a political advantage.

SUMMARY

As these statistics have shown, there are differences between the Red and Blue states that have economic, political, and social implications. Most important for this discussion, and the focus of this chapter, is the difference in economic characteristics. Blue states as a group are significantly wealthier than Red states. They have higher income and generate more revenue for the Treasury than they have received. They also generate more state revenues and the rankings of education expenditure mirror their per capita income rankings. And as the health data in Appendix Tables C.1 and C.2, Columns 3 and 4 shows, they tend to live longer and have lower infant mortality. In short, regardless of one's stand on other measures, Blue states tend to have better economic and health characteristics and many people would say that based on that, they are the more successful social model. This implies that a Blue-state dominated society has a much better chance of being successful than a Red-state dominated society. The issue for the Blue states and the current advocate for the Blue-state culture, the Democratic Party, is how to go about convincing the American people of the risk of a Red-state dominated society, which is the topic of the next chapter, and the need to shift to a Blue-state culture.

4. Implications of a Red-State Dominated America

In the fall of 2006 the World Economic Forum released its annual survey on global economic competitiveness. The survey is based on the opinions and interviews of thousands of business leaders around the globe. In the survey, the United States was knocked out of the number one position that it had previously held and fell all the way to sixth place. This was the result of the business communities' concern over the US budget deficit and a decline of respect for its institutions.[57] This came a week after the International Monetary Fund pointed out that an economic slowdown in the US, as the result of the bursting of the housing bubble, was the biggest threat to the world economy.[58] These economic forecasts by leading international organizations were no surprise; they are what one would expect of a Red-state dominated government and society that is prevalent in early twenty-first century America.

Historical Roots of Red-State America

The development of a Red-state dominated government was a long time in coming. At its core were the slave states of the Old South. The Civil War and Reconstruction formed what became known politically as the "Solid South," the bloc of states from the Old Confederacy and allied states that

---

57   World Economic Forum, *Global Competitiveness Report*, http://www.weforum.org/en/initia-tives/gcp/Global%20Competitveness%20Report/index.html.

58   International Monetary Fund, *World Economic Outlook*, September 2006, http://www.imf.org/external/pubs/ft/weo/2006/02/index.htm.

voted consistently for the Democratic Party from 1880 to 1944. The event that created this alliance was a political deal after the 1876 election in which three disputed Southern States (Florida, Louisiana and South Carolina) agreed to cast their electoral votes for Republican Rutherford B. Hayes in exchange for the pullout of federal troops in the South. This allowed local white Democratic officials to regain control of their states, institute Jim Crow laws, and systematically disenfranchise blacks, who had gained political influence in those states. More importantly, it created a bloc of states that promoted what could today be called formative stages of Red-state government and culture. Based on the exploitation of workers through slavery in the ante-bellum period, the post-war Southern states developed an elaborate economic and social structure to maintain the dominance of the Southern elite, first with the slave workforce converted into a tenant workforce, then an industrial workforce subject to state right-to-work legislation.. This forerunner of Red-state ideology was confined to the Southern states until after World War II, and as such, was a regional phenomenon.

The Southern bloc was in an odd political alliance with the Democratic Party in other states. Most of the time, it was an economic and populist alliance of the kind that William Jennings Bryan put together. This was put on the back burner with the onset of the Depression and the victories of the Roosevelt Administration. Labor issues were emphasized while issues involving civil rights and farm workers were downplayed. But with the ending of World War II and Republican control of the Congress after the 1946 election, the coalition began to unravel. With the pullout of the Southern Democrats and the establishment of the States Rights Party after the inclusion of the civil rights plank in the 1948 Democratic Party platform, the movement of the Southern States into the Republican column had begun. Eisenhower won some of them in 1952 and 1956, and by the 1964 election they became the base of Barry Goldwater's electoral vote. With Nixon's Southern Strategy, making the South part of the Republican Party's base and linking it with the conservative rural states of the Midwest and West, the Red states as we know them today were formed.

In the end, the movement of the Southern states to the Republican column was an odyssey where ideological compatibility overcame the divisiveness and legacy of the Civil War. The net result is that for the first time since the mid-nineteenth century, the political parties are separated along ideological lines without any historical baggage. Or, at least, that is the case with the Republicans. The Democrats today are functioning a lot like they did before Roosevelt, with either no message or conflicting messages. Thus early twenty-first century America has a Red-state dominated government and society.

ECONOMIC ROOTS AND CHARACTERISTICS OF RED-STATE AMERICA

As the beginning of this chapter has indicated, the coming of Red-state dominated policies on the nation has been a decisively negative issue for the country. The aforementioned competitiveness report by the World Economic Forum stressed that economic imbalances (such as income inequality, the draining of money from labor to capital, and the large public and private debt) were undermining America's overall competitiveness potential. The report's authors also noted that the nation's fiscal situation was compromised by open-ended debt obligations linked to the Defense and Homeland Security Departments. Further there was the low savings rate and the enormous trade deficits. There was a lack of transparency and efficiency in US public institutions. The health of the American economy ranked 69th out of 125 countries, astonishing for a nation that calls itself the world's sole superpower. The World Economic Forum report also ranked US health and primary education at 40th and the quality of its institutions at 27th. Business had soured on public spending and believed that such spending should be concentrated in the areas of education and infrastructure.[59]

Such a slide is what one would expect from a Red-state dominated economy. The ancestor of today's Red-state America in the ante-bellum South had most, if not all, of the distinctive traits that we see now: a sclerotic society, one that exploited rather than valued labor, one that avoided government investment in education and infrastructure, and a whole host of other similar attributes. The Old South was a society that disdained government economic development; it was also a society that discouraged innovation and adaptation to the economic, physical and social environment. As a result, it was a society that steadily lost ground to the North and continues to this day to be economically disadvantaged, only now it has joined forces with other Red states to affect the entire nation.

---

59   See note 56.

In the current World Economic Forum report, the US had been surpassed by Switzerland, Finland, Sweden, Denmark, and Singapore. Thus, countries like socialist Sweden and a highly centralized country like Singapore, both which show distinctly Blue-state attributes, were able to jump over the Red-state dominated US. What happened between regions of the US in the early nineteenth century is happening now on a global level with America playing the role of the Old South.

RED-STATE CULTURAL CHARACTERISTICS

1. Red-State Culture Exploitation Characteristics

Of all the characteristics that make up a Red-state culture, the key characteristic is that Red-state dominated economies have a class structure based on exploitation, and that it is exploitation based on people and natural resources. Whether it is the slavery of the nineteenth century or the union busting of the twenty-first, the goal is the same. Exploitation of natural resources are also a hallmark on Red-state activity, whether it was the depletion of the productivity of the cotton fields in the South, forcing the planters to travel west to new fertile soil, or the mining activity of the Mountain West. What we see in the Iraq War and Occupation is a combination of the factors of labor and environmental exploitation. The "slaves" in this case are US service men and women that have been shanghaied by the Bush Administration in order to occupy Iraq and take control of its oil fields and other assets. This has not only led to the deaths of thousands of American soldiers and Iraqi citizens, but it has spawned widespread environmental damage as the Iraqi insurgency sabotages the oil fields, the power grids and the water treatment facilities. As is the case of such exploitation practices, there is always the risk of a backlash. In the nineteenth century, it was the abolition movement and Civil War. Today, it is the Iraq insurgency and brewing civil war. In both cases, the supposed temporary short-term advantages were more than offset by the long-term costs. Even the more benign versions of this exploitation policy, such as the 1920s when business had the upper hand over labor, also inevitably led to the backlash of the Depression, the World War I Bonus Marchers and the labor battles in the auto plants.

In a macroeconomic sense Red-state dominated societies not only favor capital over labor, they support corporate America over small business. The example today that most people are familiar with is Wal-Mart. This is a com-

pany that simultaneously attacks labor and small business to attain its corporate agenda. It is anti-union and in many stores not only pay low wages but
attempt to put its employees on public assistance, using the local taxpayer as
its "benefits program." At the same time, it forces small businesses out of the
market, gutting the main streets of small towns. This in turn creates an environmental problem as shoppers commute longer distances to Wal-Mart's
regional outlets rather than purchase goods at the local merchants. The net
result is that communities pay an enormous subsidy for Wal-Mart's lower
prices, often in excess of the value of those lower prices. In California, Wal-
Mart helped fund a successful referendum to repeal legislation that required
large corporations to provide health insurance. The primary opponent to the
legislation was the California Chamber of Commerce, but the key member
funding the state chamber's campaign was Wal-Mart. Indeed, the California
Chamber of Commerce itself is primary funded by large corporations, whose
economic agenda is often at odds with the smaller businesses that tend to
be members of the local chambers. Nevertheless, local chambers tend to un-
critically endorse the state chamber positions on legislation and government
activity, often under the misguided impression that the state chamber has
"researched" certain bills without determining whether the interests of the
state chamber is the same as the local businessman.

Another classic case where the interests of the local business community
clash with large corporations was the California energy crisis of 2000–2002.
In 1996 California passed an electrical energy deregulation bill. The bill was
supported almost unanimously under the guise that bringing in competition
to the electrical energy market would lower prices. Under the old regulatory structure, the public utilities were allowed to charge a fixed rate which
would not only provide energy to the parts of the state that they served but
required a surplus of capacity to be maintained to ensure the delivery of
service. Thus the rate was set above the theoretical market rate. But it also
helped to maintain a delivery system, which while still inadequate because
California's tough environmental regulations made building new power
plants a long and difficult process, still provided some stability. With deregulation, the vertically integrated utilities were broken up and in many
cases, the power supplies were sold off to independent suppliers. This led to
the suppliers gaining control of the market, which led to a series of shortages
and price rises for natural gas, which was the raw material used to produce

electrical energy at the local power plants in California. The crisis occurred in San Diego in the summer of 2000, followed by a general crisis throughout the state in early 2001. The crisis showed an interesting pattern. Municipal utilities such as the Los Angeles Department of Water and Power and the Sacramento Municipal Utility District avoided the crisis because their government owned system retained control of their power supplies. It was the private investor utilities such as Pacific Gas and Electric that lost money paying the inflated price of natural gas to produce their electricity that triggered the crisis. Later on it was determined that there has been sufficient supply, but that power plants were being deliberately shut to create the crisis. In the end it was determined that California businesses as well as individuals had been scammed for several billion dollars by out-of-state power suppliers. While large businesses were affected, many of them had the alternative of going into the energy markets and purchase alternative sources. In fact, it was the pullout of the large business from the local market that had prompted the investor utilities to advocate for deregulated power in 1996. The small businesses that did not have that option were the primary victims of the crisis along with the individual ratepayer. As one conservative San Diego city council member was reported to have said, the events of the summer of 2000 in San Diego was enough to make him want to support socialism. The net result was that the Blue-state structured government utilities weathered the crisis better than the Red-state structured investor utilities.

2. Red-State Culture Social and Economic Imbalance Characteristics

This leads to the another result of the policy of Red-state exploitation, and that is the stratification of social classes, economic opportunity and development. In the Red-state South, small farmers found themselves at a major disadvantage to the large plantation owners, and other workers had very few options. In the Blue-state North, one could enter farming relatively easy. The technological innovations of the North allowed even small farmers to be efficient producers of their plot of land. And complementing the agricultural opportunities were an equal number of opportunities in manufacturing, although large-scale industrialization would pose labor-management problems in the late nineteenth century. As a foundation underlying all of this was a public and private educational system and an activist government that supported both. This created a much more fluid social structure with more opportunities for advancement than were made available to people living in the South.

In Red-state America today, studies show that an American's opportunity to climb the social ladder is much more difficult than it was a generation ago and that there are more opportunities for social advancement in other developed countries than there are in the United States. The plant closures in the auto industry and the number of companies filing bankruptcy and voiding their pension obligations have reinforced that fear. Wages and salaries are now the lowest percentage of gross domestic product since data collection of the subject was begun in 1947.[60] At the same time, the new plantation and factory owners of the twenty-first century, the corporate executives, continue to reap enormous benefits regardless of the performance of their respective companies. Many have had their bonuses untouched in bankruptcy proceedings while their employee's interests have been sacrificed. At the same their allies, the super-rich, have made unprecedented wealth. We now have extremes of wealth not seen since the late 1920s, or the Robber Barons of the late nineteenth century. In all cases, favorable tax and other regulatory legislation at the expense of workers enhanced this wealth.

David Cay Johnston has been writing about tax issues for the *New York Times* for a number of years. In his 2003 book *Perfectly Legal*, he has outlined the degree to which the rich have offloaded their tax burden on to everyone else. In the chapter on the growth rates of various levels of income, he pointed out work of French economists Thomas Piketty and Emmanuel Saez. They showed that the share of income going to the bottom 90 percent of the population had fallen from 67.1 percent to 52.0 percent from 1970 to 2000 while the share of income for the top .01 of 1 percent (13,360 households) grew from 1.0 percent of total income to 5.1 percent during the same period.[61] The period of course predates the George W. Bush Administration and covers both Republican and Democratic presidents from Nixon to Clinton. But it does cover a period when the Republican Party's Southern Strategy was put into place, when a more conservative political, social and economic philosophy was taking hold, and the current configuration of the Red states

---

60   Steven Greenhouse and David Leonhardt, "Real Wages Fail to Match a Rise in Productivity," *New York Times*, August 28, 2006.

61   Thomas Piketty and Emmanuel Saez, "Income Inequality in the United States 1913–1998," NBER *Working Paper no. 8467* (September 2001); cited in David Cay Johnston, *Perfectly Legal: The Covert Campaign to Rig Our Tax System to Benefit the Super Rich—and Cheat Everybody Else* (New York: Portfolio 2003), 33.

became a political majority in this country. Since then, the current Bush Administration has implemented tax policies that have only aggravated that trend. The one figure in this chapter of Johnston's book that does carry into the current administration is that the portion of federal revenues coming from corporations in 2002 was 10 percent, down from a third during the Eisenhower Administration in the 1950s.[62] And while the rich have been getting the lion's share of the tax breaks, everyone else has seen a large portion of their income increases eaten up by social security tax increases. As a result, during the same 1970–2000 period Piketty and Saez showed that average pre-tax income in 2000 dollars for the bottom 90 percent of Americans fell from $27,060 to $27,035 a drop of 0.1 percent, while those in 90 percent to 95 percent range rose 29.6 percent, those in the 95 percent to 99 percent range rose 54.2 percent, those in the 99 percent to 99.5 percent range rose 89.5 percent, those in the 99.5 to 99.9 percent range rose 144.8 percent, those in the 99.9 percent to 99.99 percent rose 322.0 percent, and finally those in the top .01 of 1 percent rose 558.3 percent, or from an average pretax income of $3,641,285 in 1970 to $23,969,767 in 2000.[63]

The above statistics were helped enormously in recent years by the numerous tax cuts enacted by the Bush Administration and a compliant Republican Congress. The proposals have been shamelessly put forward even as the massive expenditures brought on by the war in Iraq have been bleeding the treasury.

No other event could graphically highlight the manner in which the rich have been advanced at the expense of the poor than George W. Bush's 2005 inauguration after being re-elected in November 2004. The estimated cost of inaugural activities was $40 million.[64] Many of the events were for people who had raised a minimum of $100,000. What made the show doubly appalling was that while this extravagant display of wealth was being flaunted around the country, American servicemen and women were risking their lives in Iraq while being given inadequate armor and stale food. This gaudy display was brought into sharp relief when stories comparing the 2005 inauguration (ostensibly occurring during wartime), were compared to the subdued 1945 inauguration of Franklin Roosevelt. The last of the four Roosevelt

---

62   Ibid., 41.
63   Ibid., 38.
64   Spencer S. Hsu, "U.S. Tells D.C. to Pay Inaugural Expenses," *Washington Post*, January 11, 2005.

inaugurations, it was a deliberate low-key affair that reflected wartime atmosphere of sacrifice, privation and rationing. Not so the case in 2005, where one would have never known that there was a war going by judging by the events in Washington in January 2005, or by the fact that the well-to-do and corporate lobbyists had no problem groveling for tax cuts while Americans were getting blown to bits by roadside bombs in such garden spots as Baghdad and Fallujah.

Such imbalances between the rich and the poor ultimately lead to the same kind of imbalances for the economy with potentially devastating effects. These kinds of imbalances show up in market distortions such as the dot.com bubble, the current housing bubble and the manic speculation leading up to the stock market crash of 1929. They are the result of a wealthy elite that has so much money that they don't what to do with it all, so they end up speculating in the latest hot stock tip, the booming real estate market, and "investments" in antiques, modern art and other kinds of exotic assets. In the 1920s, corporation return on assets was so high that companies could fund their capital requirements internally without having to rely on external market sources such as new stock or bond issues.[65] Speculation not only occurred in the stock market, but also the famous Florida land crash of 1926.[66]

On the other end of the economic spectrum were large segments of the population that could barely get by, if that. In the late nineteenth century, it was the impoverished working class living in tenement slums in the cities. In the 1920s, it was the farmers on the High Plains who were in an economic recession/depression a good decade before everyone else. Even the manufacturing workers, who were making some gains, were still losing ground. Today most workers have not seen a real wage increase in decades; this is similar to what was going on with manufacturing workers from 1900 to the 1920s.[67]

---

65 Simon Kuznets, *National Income and its Composition 1919–1938* (New York: National Bureau of Economic Research, 1941), 316; cited in George Soule, *Prosperity Decade from War to Depression 1917–1929* (1947; reprint New York: Harper and Row, 1968), 122.

66 Kuznets, *National Income and its Composition*, 316; cited in Soule, *Prosperity Decade*, 319.

67 William Foster and Waddill Catchings, "Must We Reduce Our Standard of Living?," *Forum* 85 (February 1931): 75–77; cited in William E. Stoneman, *A History of Economic Analysis of the Great Depression in America* (New York: Garland, 1979), 37.

3. Red-State Culture Debt Characteristics

The major difference for workers (and corporations) between earlier periods and the twentieth century was another importance characteristic of Red-state behavior—the growing and increasingly reckless use of debt. Of course, borrowing has always been part of our economic system. As Benjamin Franklin famously noted, "If you want to know the value of money, go try to borrow some."[68] Borrowing for capital projects has always been a standard practice. Projects from the Erie Canal to the Golden Gate Bridge have been financed through bonds. The building of the railroads depended heavily on debt financing. In the early days of the republic, that money primarily came from England, and to a lesser degree, France and other European countries. Gradually, over time, foreign financing was replaced by domestic lending, but the United States was a net debtor until World War I. On my living room wall I have a beautifully engraved bond note issued in 1869 by the Blue Ridge Railroad Company shortly before it went under. The notes were defaulted on. Unlike today's practice of imprinting an ugly cancellation stamp on the document, the cancellation practice of the late nineteenth century was to cut an "x" through the signatures of the corporate officers. The result is that the document is almost pristine, and under glass in a frame the razor cuts are almost invisible. That is not what makes this bond so interesting. The real revelation of this document was that, when it was a viable company, the bond could be redeemed for either $1,000 US or £200 British pounds. Likewise, the interest coupons were also in dollars and pounds. This was standard practice for the era.

For individuals, borrowing was a different story. The only borrowing that the average person could do was for purchasing property. Even then, terms were very strict. Loans required large down payments and were for very short terms, such as three years, with balloon payments on the end. Not many people could qualify for such loans. There were also short-term working capital loans for businesses. The heavy indebtedness by the Southern plantations to the New York and London merchant bankers was part of this phenomenon.[69] But mostly, the old adage applied: you had to prove that you did not need a loan to get one.

---

68   Benjamin Franklin, *The Way to Wealth*, 1757. Included in the 1758 *Poor Richard's Almanac*.
69   Harvey C. Bunke, *A Primer on American Economic History* (New York: Random House, 1969), 38; Fred A. Shannon, *The Farmer's Last Frontier: Agriculture 1860–1897* (Armonk, NY: M.E. Sharpe, 1989), 99–100.

In the twentieth century, lending broadened enormously. Starting with Morris Plan in 1912, workers could get loans based on their monthly salaries. Innovative bankers such as A.P. Gianinni, the founder of Bank of America, began lending to groups of people who had been shut out of the lending process. (In Gianinni's case, it was the immigrant Italian community in his home town of San Francisco, and the original name of his bank was the Bank of Italy). So by the 1920s personal lending was on a vastly larger scale than it had been in the Robber Baron era. And in the gross economic imbalances that developed during the 1920s, workers turned to the new lending vehicles, primarily in the form of auto and appliance loans, to keep themselves afloat. As Henry C.K. Liu in an article from *Asia Times Online* has noted, the finances of the 1920s under the management of Treasury Secretary Andrew Mellon were very similar to what we got under the fiscal policies of the Bush Administration and the monetary policies of the Federal Reserve under its former Chairman, Alan Greenspan. Like his modern counterparts, Mellon advocated a policy of tax cuts and easy money. The four Mellon tax cuts were a major part of the financial structure of the 1920s. Unlike the modern era, the Federal Reserve was not the dominant player in the America economy that it is today. Most of that economic power still resided in the Treasury Department and Mellon was the key player during the eleven years he was Treasury Secretary. There, the debt expansion under Mellon was a key change from earlier eras.[70] Ultimately it was not auto or appliance loans that brought an end to the party. It was broker loans in the stock market which triggered the final massive speculation in 1928 (itself the result of the loosening of credit to avert a recession in 1927) that led to the crash in the autumn of 1929. Thus the economic imbalances caused by the pro-business anti-worker policies of the 1920s were violently thrown into reverse and brought into balance by the economic leveling effect of the Great Depression. The risk today is the same as it was then: the stifled income of the working class unable to purchase the surplus of goods from the speculative investments of an over-funded elite, resulting in economic collapse. Only this time, the potential collapse will be magnified several-fold because of the volume of debt fueling the speculation activity. Indeed, some financial writers are predicting that

---

70   Henry C. K. Liu, "America's Untested Management Team," *Asia Times Online*, June 17, 2006, http://www.atimes.com/atimes/Global_Economy/HF17Dj01.html.

the financial crisis emanating from the bursting of the housing bubble start-ing in 2007 will be of historic levels.

Looking from today's vantage point, the excesses and the imbalances of the 1920s seem trivial by comparison. The impact of debt has exploded all out of proportion. Liu estimated that at the time of the 1929 crash, private debt had reached $3 trillion in today's dollars.[71] Today, the level of debt that we can account for is more than double that. And because of the recently established derivative markets, there is a whole new segment of liabilities that even the bankers and the regulators admit that they have no idea how large it is in real terms, because, like the broker loans market in the 1920s, it is virtually out of control. Today's debt is the result of massive issues of paper at all segments of society. At the personal level, it is a flood of credit cards, equity loans, mortgages, much of which has gone to day-to-day living expenses. At the corporate levels, it has been equity for debt swaps, lever-aged buyouts, junk bonds and the now infamous sub-prime (i.e. junk) lend-ing on mortgages. And in the federal government, it has been massive budget deficits aggravated by reckless tax cuts.

The ultimate expression of fiscal recklessness is the current financial cri-sis fomented by the ongoing bursting of the housing bubble. Much of the commentary has revolved around the so-called "sub-prime" lending, and has centered on relief for the banks in the money markets or relief for the sub-prime borrowers. The media has simplified these extraordinarily complex financial transactions in order to make them digestible to the viewing public. But these stories encapsulate what are the most far-reaching set of financial transactions in economic history. And at the core of these transactions is classic Red-state economic behavior.

What we have today is mostly unregulated investment banks, the invest-ment banking arm of commercial banks (or their off-balance-sheet related companies) and mortgage brokers of various kinds (a financial elite, if you will) generating unprecedented quantities of loans and then lending to peo-ple who had no chance of paying them back either because the borrowers never had the ability to pay them back in the first place, or because they were engaging in the same kind of Ponzi schemes as the lenders. Then if that weren't enough, the financial companies would package these junk loans and either sell them to unsuspecting investors, or else sell them to their friends

---

71   Ibid.

in the business who would chop them in various maturities or tranches, and then resell them to the suckers on their customer list. As long as there were rich fools with too much money on their hands, or as long as housing prices continued to increase no one cared. And to compound this deviant behavior, large chunks of these garbage loans were used as collateral to borrow several times the nominal value of the collateral to make even more junk loans. It was, in effect, the financial equivalent of an epidemic of mad cow disease in which a sick cow was ground up and served as feed to a herd of healthy cows, with the resulting spread of the disease throughout the herds. All the while the financial elite are raking in fees and bonuses from these transactions while dodging the government and the tax man as investors and borrowers are taken to the cleaners. The ultimate price for such behavior will be a highly unstable financial situation followed by economic collapse and/or long-term stagnation.

In conjunction with these debt levels has been the dependence of Red-state dominated economies to fund themselves with outside financing. The dependency of the plantation owners on New York and London bankers has already been noted. Today that dependency has been transferred to the Asian central banks and now the sovereign wealth funds of Asia and the Middle East that are bailing out the US banking system. The current level of foreign financial dependency brought on by the Bush Administration is much closer to what eighteenth- and nineteenth-century America faced than any comparative twentieth century era.

4. Red-State Culture Dynamism Characteristics

The last major result of Red-state dominated society can be called a lack of economic and social dynamism. In societies that are heavily dependent on cheap labor and natural resources, the basic elements of an economy, there is less of an emphasis toward developing a more innovative kind of economic and social structure. In the Southern states of the nineteenth century, the emphasis was almost entirely on agriculture for most of the period. In fact, manufacturing and higher technology (which in the early nineteenth century meant extensive development of railroads) tended to be discouraged because it was perceived to be a threat to the social elite. Only technology such as the cotton gin that re-enforced the elite's political and economic dominance was accepted. Even when the textile industry came in the late nineteenth and early twentieth centuries, they tended to locate in places that would not compete with the agricultural establishment.[72] And what manufacturing that came to the South was basically industrial hand-me-down industries from the North. These were industries that were well into their product life cycles with businesses that were dependent on low cost labor. They were also industries that would eventually lose out to overseas competition. Likewise after the Civil War, not only was the infrastructure of Southern cotton industry in a shambles, but because of the Northern blockade of their goods to England and the rest of Europe, they lost markets. In this fashion, the Southern economy became the American equivalent of a third-world country. Its industries had all the characteristics of an underdeveloped country—they tended to be low value products that generated little real economic surplus to the region. And what economic surplus was created was done by denying it to the workers and the people living there. And like an underdeveloped country, their products had low barriers to market entry that meant that other places could produce those products cheaper.

Comparing the nineteenth century South with Red-state America today, you can see the same industrial characteristics. One of the most common complaints about the American economy today is that we don't make anything. That is not quite true. But a disturbing number of industries have moved outside the country, and whole chunks of the economy seemed to have disappeared. We are still making high-tech products, but we are seeing that these products are having a shorter and shorter life cycle in this country before the production of those products move elsewhere. And unlike Japan, we have not effectively kept other countries from acquiring our technology and developing competing products. What we call high tech jobs are being exported overseas. Even relatively sophisticated service jobs are disappearing.

On top of that, there has been an attitude that manufacturing jobs do not matter, that knowledge jobs in the service industry are the jobs of the future and that we can afford to abandon manufacturing jobs. The problem with this approach is two-fold. First, you have to have a product or a company

---

72   James C. Cobb, *Industrialization and Southern Society* (Lexington, Kentucky: The University Press of Kentucky, 1984), 16–18, 80–81, 24–25; William Falk and Thomas Lyson, *High Tech, Low Tech, No Tech: Recent Industrial and Occupational Change in the South* (Albany, New York: State University of New York Press, 1988), 5; Harold Hall McCarty, *The Geographic Basis of American Life* (Port Washington, New York: Kennikat Press, 1970), 376.

to service, and that is very difficult when products or companies disappear or move overseas. What service jobs there are tend not to produce the number of jobs or the economic value of manufacturing. Service jobs can also be moved around much more easily than plant and equipment.

Second, this attitude also tends to put Red-state dominated areas at an economic disadvantage when it comes to trying to adapt to new technologies and environments just as it did for the nineteenth century South. Societies that behave this way tend to pay a terrible price for this kind of behavior. One only has to look at China, which in the year 1500 was the greatest power on the globe, and which subsequently declined into subservience with the West when it attempted to cut itself off from the rest of the world. Likewise, Japan remained a feudal society until the Americans opened it up literally at gunpoint. It took the national humiliation of both countries to reconnect with the outside world and trigger the remarkable turnaround that both have experienced over the last 100 years. This is the risk that America is taking if it attempts to take the same path.

The ultimate outgrowth of such a stagnant and highly unequal society, which is governed by a financial and corporate elite with increasingly less social movement, is what could be called "government by a mediocrity of the rich," where those at the top benefit from their social and financial connections and are protected from their mistakes by the institutions controlled by their associates. There are numerous cases of this, the most glaring being the private college and universities in America. Of course, most people are aware that George W. Bush got through Yale with a "gentleman's C." This is what is known as "legacy" grants or admissions at private colleges where the large donors and alumni are allowed get their academically less than stellar children into these schools.[73] Since these schools and their social networking are the entryway into the corridors of power in both the public and the private sector, these policies pose the risk of allowing the idiot offspring of influential families to wreak havoc on the political and economic fabric of the nation. One of the justifications for the inheritance tax was to slow down the accumulation wealth that would create an aristocracy in America, something of an anathema to founding fathers like Thomas Jefferson, although many of them were quite wealthy.[74]

---

73 "Poison Ivy," *The Economist*, September 23, 2006, 38.
74 Thomas Jefferson to James Madison, October 28, 1785 in *The Writings of Thomas Jefferson*, eds. Andrew A. Lipscomb and Albert Ellery Bergh, 20 vols. (Washington, DC: The Thomas

Just as damaging, is the adverse impact of deregulation or the removal of checks and balances on the quality of decision-making in both the public and private sector. Laws and regulations not only set the rules by which various activities are conducted, they also are a form of artificial competition which sharpen the decision making instincts of managers. Those managers that can adapt to the rules and regulations and are still successful tend to be the better managers and improve the quality of managers for all organizations. Conversely, removing rules and regulations do not necessarily improve the business environment. They may make it easier to do business for companies and industries, but they may also allow for sloppy decision making and make businesses and organizations less competitive in more stringent markets. Many American businesses which have gotten away with loose environmental operations have found themselves shut off from markets, particularly in Europe, where there are more stringent environmental and procedural standards. Managers and businesses find themselves less competitive in such situations. This is particularly true in high-tech, high value markets where production and management standards are very high. The loss of market share by American automobile manufactures to foreign automakers is a classic example. The most glaring example was the collapse of the Savings and Loan industry after the removal of regulations in the 1980s. In such situations, the removal of regulations does not make companies more competitive, it makes them less competitive because it allows lousy managers to stay that way. And it is a well-known axiom that the primary cause of business failure is bad management, not government regulations (though bad regulations do not help things).

The most damaging is a society that is not only run by incompetent elites, but also one which either despises government or does not know to use it. This appalling combination was brought brilliantly into focus in the aftermath of Hurricane Katrina's devastation of New Orleans and the Gulf Coast. The Federal Emergency Management Agency (FEMA) under the Clinton Administration had been one of the most effective bureaucracies in the federal government. Under the Bush Administration, it was not only relegated to some dusty corner in the Homeland Security Department, the friends of cronies in the administration ran it. Even when those cronies made the effort to inform their higher-ups of the impending disaster that was approaching the Gulf Coast, they were ignored. In the months since Katrina made landfall, America has been inundated with story after story of incompetence, corruption, and neglect, before and after the event. FEMA and the events occurring before and after the assault by Hurricane Katrina would appear to be the quintessential example for screwing up a government operation.

The most celebrated act of incompetence by the George W. Bush Administration, however, is the Iraq War and Occupation. The Iraq War contains within it all of the corrupting aspects of a Red-state dominated society and culture. It was a war that was almost unilaterally prosecuted by the president and his administration. The decision to go to war was made just about from the time that the Bush Administration took office. Congressional approval was an afterthought, and in any event, the Congress was lied to anyway. The people deciding to initiate the war were part of the governing elite while the volunteer soldiers who assigned to do the fighting, killing and dying were, by and large, from the working class and the poor. Also, the people deciding the war were also the people who were financially benefiting from the war—the list of contractors with ties to key Bush Administration officials (such as Vice President Dick Cheney and his former employer Halliburton) is too long to mention and is well known to the public. We now know that from the earliest days of the Bush Administration that not only were plans made to invade Iraq, but that plans were also being drawn up to decided who got which oilfields. And the administration was not too subtle about this issue when it entered Baghdad as it deployed troops to protect the Oil Ministry building while the rest of the country was being looted. Then later when the Coalition Provisional Authority (CPA) was established, the administration attempted not only to privatize the oil fields but other state-owned businesses and anything else the CPA could get its hands on. The war was promoted using patriotic and nationalist symbols and the Administration attempted to brand people who opposed the war as unpatriotic. The administration not only ignored the Congress, it ignored its intelligence agencies and basically heard what it wanted to hear from pet sources such as Ahmed Chalabi, resulting in a series of arrogantly bad decisions that took a difficult situation and turned it into a catastrophe. The meltdown in Iraq is typical of the shoddy thinking that has characterized many of the Bush Administration's efforts, and it characterizes the risks inherent a Red-state dominated society.

In conjunction with the Iraq War and Occupation, the Red-state dominated tendency of being dependant on foreign financial interests impacts foreign policy in that America's ability to influence events is limited by its need to keep its creditors happy. As the old saying goes, debt restricts. And that is certainly the case with regard to US policy vis-à-vis China. Similarly, a foreign policy that sends billions of dollars down the rat hole in Iraq ties up what the country can do elsewhere. America literally has its hands tied in dealing with Iran because of its commitment in Iraq. Indeed, it has been reported that one of the parties that is most interested in seeing the US stay in Iraq is Iran, because as long as America is tied down in Iraq, the Iranians feel safe and can pursue their regional ambitions.

The Future of a Red-State Dominated America

The majority of the people live in Red states. The majority of the electoral votes are in Red states. The majority of the population growth in the near future will be in Red states. Red-state culture tends to be one of conservative values: God, mother and apple pie. But the history of conservative value societies is not a pretty one. Ask Imperial Spain. Ask the Russia of the Czars. Ask the rebel soldiers of Confederacy. Better yet, try asking the dinosaurs and the woolly mammoths what happens when an existing way of life disappears and you can't adapt to a new one.

In his book, *Collapse: How Societies Choose to Fail or Succeed*, author Jared Diamond discusses the stories of many societies past and present that had to make those choices. One of the more intriguing stories that take a large section of the book is his discussion of the rise and fall of the Greenland Norse who inhabited Greenland from AD 984 to sometime after 1410. In the end this community could not deal with the environmental changes, particularly the cooling of the region after a few hundred years of temporary warming that had occurred there. But it was also clear that the values that had allowed them to found and sustain the settlements were the ultimate source of their failure. Theirs was also a conservative society, and their existing ways of farming simply could not work in the long run in the fragile environment of Greenland. But they could have survived if they had adopted the ways of the Inuit tribes that also made Greenland their home. That meant above all putting a greater emphasis on fishing and adopting Inuit technology such as their harpoons and kayaks. But the Norse considered the Inuit an inferior pagan and could not bring themselves to adopt Inuit ways. In addition to an inability to adapt to their environment, Diamond points out that the Norse settlers were a top-down hierarchical and violent society where power was concentrated in the settlement chiefs and the clergy. Much of the activities, such as the importing of luxury goods that were of short-term benefit to the local elite deprived the colony of needed tools and resources that were ultimately damaging to the colony in the long run. Some of these decisions were made to advance the prestige of the leadership. Some decisions were made to ward off any potential threats to their position. In the end, however, the leadership found the settlement collapsing around them as those less well off fell by the wayside. As Diamond put it in the end of his chapter on the end of the Greenland Norse settlement, the last privilege that the Norse leadership was able to extract from the tenant farmers of their settlements was the privilege of being the last to starve. Not exactly the prerogative that most elites shoot for, but one where they often end up.[75]

The story of the decline and fall of the Norse settlements in Greenland offer a chilling story to those people that dominate Red-state America today. Like the Norse Greenlanders, Red-state America is a conservative society with conservative values. Like the Norse Greenlanders, Red-state America tends to be a top-down society run by corporate and social elites who treat the lowers classes as commodities to expand the elites' position in the world at the expense of everyone else. Like the Norse Greenlanders, Red-state America tends to treat its environment as an irrelevant factor to be ignored. Given those similarities the question that has to be asked is whether the inhabitants in Red-state America will also go the way of the Norse Greenlanders and have their society collapse around them? That is the question that the citizens in both Red and Blue states will have to address.

Already, much of Norse Greenland's sorry history is starting to show in Red-state dominated America. One can see the stagnant economies and the abandon jobs. One can see the mounting debts and the increasing reliance on foreign support. One can see the growing inequality where the leadership basks in their mushrooming wealth while those below are being brought to social and financial ruin. And one can see the increasing rot in the nation as billions are spent extravagant foreign adventures while the infrastructure

---

75 Jared Diamond, *Collapse: How Societies Choose to Fail or Succeed* (New York: Viking 2005), 248–276.

of the county keeps falling apart. Like the Greenland Norse, one can see the risks that these attitudes and events have in store for Red-state America. And in the end a society and culture that sustains itself by exploiting its people becomes itself exploited by societies that are more dynamic. This ultimately results in Warren Buffett's "Sharecropper Society."

The scale of the rot is immense at this point. We have a situation where the most powerful nation in the world is being fought to a standstill by a ragtag insurgency. Not only are we facing failure overseas, but with the advent of Hurricane Katrina, it is clear that the most powerful nation in the world couldn't even protect its own citizens on the Gulf Coast from a disaster that was known to be a serious danger several days in advance before Katrina made landfall. As newsman Keith Olbermann famously stated, the United States was defeated by that greatest of terrorist threats, "standing water."[76] And while we have been treated to wholesale ineptitude in Iraq and the Gulf Coast, behind the ineptitude lay corruption on a colossal scale—not only the Jack Abramoff lobbying scandal but the sheer scale of the looting in the no-bid Iraq reconstruction contracts given to Halliburton and other contractors, along with equally shady FEMA dealings from the aftermath of Katrina, with Halliburton back at the government trough again. This is on top of the multi-billion dollar disappearance of funds from the Iraq CPA, massive spending on unreliable defense weapons systems such as Star Wars anti-ballistic missile system to the serving of spoiled food and polluted water to our troops in Iraq. All the while, corporate America and the super rich, who have now treated us with the financial crisis par excellence in the current mortgage market scandal, keep pressing to get their taxes cut after being on the receiving end of several tax cuts already.

How much more of this looting of the nation can occur before the survival of the country is at stake is now an open question. First, the mountain of public and private debts continues to increase. While there are many out there (with a vested interest in maintaining the existing financial structure) who keep telling us that debt is not a problem and that any economic decline will be a relatively mild one with a "soft landing," economic experience tells us that the current debt situation is unsustainable and that the correction of the unprecedented current economic imbalances cannot be archived without some nasty consequences. A hard landing is virtually unavoidable, and

---

76   Keith Olbermann, "The 'City' of Louisiana," *MSNBC Countdown*, September 5, 2005.

the current financial crisis has all the characteristics of a major crash. Indeed, with newspaper articles about a possible collapse of the banking system or its bailout by foreign interests, the risks are very real.

Second, the increasing dependency on potentially hostile powers such as Russia and China should be a matter of concern to every American. The growing threat of China to our trading and financial system, of course, is well known. But in a recent development Russia, which has been literally re-energized because the demand for its enormous oil and gas reserves that has created a huge trade surplus, has decided to direct its giant Shtokman natural gas deposit to European customers rather than the United States. Even more disturbing is the fact that the project, which will be undertaken by Gazprom, Russia's state-owned gas company, was made as part of a tripartite agreement with the governments of France and Germany, signaling a new political entity in Europe which could have a potentially adverse affect on NATO and other European-American institutions.[77] The energy deal itself is the result of the simultaneous effects of an arrogant US foreign policy which drives away friends and increases the hostility level of enemies, combined with a blundering military campaign in the Middle East which emasculates any military response to just about any foreign threat at the current time. And of course, who could forget that the attacks on September 11 were accomplished by 19 people with box cutters— not exactly in the same firepower league as the Japanese Navy's attack on Pearl Harbor.

America not only faces military risks, but risks to its treasury, risks to its domestic economy, risks to its financial markets, and risks to its banking system. In spite of this, the governing elite continue to hollow out the country until just like the Norse chieftains, there will be no one else left to support the crumbling economic superstructure as the whole thing comes down in a hideous crash.

Those who say that such a scenario cannot happen here have forgotten the lessons of 1929 crash and the destabilized economy of that period. The same kind of imbalances favoring business over labor and the subsequent hollowing out of the economy created that crisis. A 1920s economy, where agriculture had been in a financial crisis for just about the whole decade, saw workers unable to sustain their segments of the economy at the end of the

---

77   F. William Engdahl, "Moscow Plays Its Cards Strategically," *Asia Times Online*, October 25, 2006, http://www.atimes.com/atimes/Central_Asia/HJ25Ag01.html.

decade, even after (what was for the period) heavy infusions of debt and easy money to prop things up. The combination of workers and farmers unable to carry the load, eventually lead to the collapse of the whole economy under the weight of debt, over-investment and under-consumption.

All of the ingredients that led to the Great Depression of the 1930s are in our economy today. The only difference being that the collapse in 1929 occurred when the US was the world's largest creditor nation. Today we risk the same scenario as 1929, but as the world's largest debtor nation. The risk to the nation in such a financial position makes the crisis of 1929–1933 puny by comparison. This is what makes the financial crisis of 2007–2008 particularly chilling.

But beyond the economic risks are the enormous political and social risks that a 1930s financial crisis could bring. Most of the history books talk about the stock market crash, the soup kitchens and the Dust Bowl. There is some discussion of the War Bonus Marchers on Washington and their violent removal by the US Army. But little is said about the food riots and the extremist organizations on both the left and the right that were spawned because of the crisis. Yet there were food riots, starting in England, Arkansas in 1931,[78] which spread sporadically to several cities across the country. Likewise there were marches organized by the Communist Party USA through their Unemployment Councils, the most significant being the coordinated national marches on March 6, 1930.[79] In the 1932 election William Foster received over one hundred thousand votes for the Communist party and Norman Thomas, in his second run on the Socialist Party ticket, saw his totals increase from two hundred sixty thousand to nearly nine hundred thousand. In California, socialist Upton Sinclair captured the Democratic nomination for governor in 1934, and just barely lost after the most intensive negative ad campaign of its time organized by the Republican Party and their big business allies. At the same time there were right-wing factions looking for a "strong man" to save the country in the manner of a Mussolini or Hitler. It found its voice in the American Liberty League, the German-American Bund, and the radio broadcast of Father Charles Coughlin. In addition, there were a host of demagogues such as Governor and then Senator Huey Long and the

---

78   Dale Ingram, "Drought-stricken Arkansas Farmers Only Wanted Food for their Families. They Stirred America," *Arkansas Times*, January 19, 2006, http://www.arktimes.com/Articles/ArticleViewer.aspx.

79   New York World, *World Almanac and Book of Facts for 1931*, 99.

Reverend Gerald L.K. Smith, who proposed their own radical agenda for the country.

These actions of political demagoguery and extremism in 1930s America were merely a local chapter of the political upheavals that were occurring elsewhere. Germany had been in turmoil for nearly a decade when Hitler came to power. Likewise, many authoritarian governments, a great many of them of them neo-fascists came to power in Europe as the American financial crisis spread overseas. Still other dictatorships blossomed in Latin America. And all of this political upheaval eventually set the stage for first the Spanish Civil War, and then World War II.

Of all the millions of words that have been written about Franklin Del-ano Roosevelt and the New Deal regarding whether it was a success or a failure, probably the greatest testament to the work of the people in that administration was that they were able to keep the country intact without having it fall into political chaos and revolution, as was happening elsewhere around the globe. World War II may have actually pulled the country out of the Great Depression, but without the New Deal, there may not have been a country, or at least the country as we know it today, that would have been worth preserving. There was no guarantee that 1930s America was not going to be taken over by communist or fascist extremists. It was a very close thing, and the Roosevelt Administration was always concerned about this group or that careening the country down the primrose path to chaos and revolu-tion. And this was only a few years after the unparalleled prosperity (at least outside the farms) of the 1920s.

The important point is that everything in the above scenarios that could still in America today. An economic crisis brought on by heavy debts and fiscal mismanagement could easily be used by fear mongers to stampede the populace into some extreme action. Indeed the Bush Administration has used heavy doses of fear to get support for their policies and more impor-tantly, to get themselves re-elected in 2004. They have used fear in order to obtain a concentration of power with an utter disregard for the protections detailed in the US Constitution, British Common Law, and International Law unimagined by the founding fathers or Bush's predecessors in the Oval Office. The stage has been set to use such tactics by any group who so desires to obtain such power. The potential political and social upheaval emanating from a financial and environmental crisis is a very real possibility if there are insufficient institutions to control it. Today's Red-state dominated America with its own brand of elitism, authoritarianism, and imperialist nationalism, has all the ingredients to make it so. That is the risk in continuing with the status quo, and why it is time to come up with an alternative vision for America.

PART II

Red States, Blue States
   and the
Democratic Party

5. The Democratic Party and the Advocacy of a Blue-State Culture

For the past several decades, certainly since the 1980 election, we have lived in a country with an increasingly Red-state dominated culture. The growing strength of business over labor, the growing exploitation of labor, and the denigration of government as an effective tool to improve the lives of Americans on the domestic front has been part of the Washington mantra for quite a long time now. So long, that most Americans have forgotten that this country used to do things a lot differently and was very successful at it. Under the Bush Administration, however, conservative principles have been combined with a fundamentalist Christian domestic policy, and a neo-conservative foreign policy hodge-podge. This has distorted the conservative model to the point where the huge financial and ideological contradictions (such as having very unconservative large government expenditures financed through huge infusion of debt) have brought a Red-state dominated America to a state of domestic policy exhaustion and foreign policy collapse. The flaws to the Red-state American model were extensively discussed in the previous chapter and do not need to be recapitulated here. The question is what do we do about it, and where do we go from here.

Red-State Model Alternatives

The response to the question brings up another question: can our Red-state dominated culture just be patched up, repackaged as new and improved, so that we can continue on our merry way as if nothing had happened before? There are certainly those who have benefited from the system who would like that to be the case. The problem, of course is that too few have benefited from the system, and those that have don't seem to particularly care about those that haven't. Politically that is always risky. And those followers of the Marie Antoinette School of Social Responsibility who engage in such activity risk losing their heads the way she did. In addition to the political problems are the economic problems, because a Red-state culture is a distinctly conservative culture that tends to advance the existing status quo. As such it is not a good vehicle for developing either reforms of the existing system, or developing new ideas for a restructuring or replacement of the existing system. This becomes a real handicap when it is clear the status quo needs to be changed. In the case of Jared Diamond's Greenland Norse, it was fatal.

So to answer the question of whether the current Red-state dominated culture can continue with adjustments, the answer would appear to be no. The economic distortions caused by reckless deficit spending, the foreign policy disaster that is Iraq, and domestic catastrophes such as Katrina all point to a system that is beyond a few superficial economic and political patches. Radical surgery is what now appears to be required.

BLUE-STATE MODEL

What kind of radical surgery needs to take place? Clearly, it means that the country needs a new model and that model needs to be based on a Blue-state cultural model. Why the Blue-state model? Because historically, the vehicle for changing the status quo has come from the culture developed by the Blue states. If the Red-state model has been based on the status quo and of a slave ethic, that exploits working people, then the Blue-state model has been one of rethinking or remodeling the status quo using a social ethic that involves various stakeholders in the process.

Some might infer that such a social ethic is a form of socialism, and to some degree, it is. It does not necessarily mean that the government owns or controls the means of production, although that is the case in some countries. But it does recognize that individuals cannot unilaterally make economic decisions that damage the long-term interests of society. In other words, the Marie Antoinettes of the world may as well not waste their time applying for a business license. This philosophy in its most significant form goes back to the founding of the original Bank of the United States by Secretary of the Treasury Alexander Hamilton, through the Interstate Commerce Act of 1887 and the Sherman Anti-Trust Act of 1890 to the development of the regulatory structure of twentieth century America. In general terms, it has meant that the means of production should be regulated, but not owned, by government.

It does mean an allowance for greater government activity. In the Blue-state cultural scheme of things this goes back to the Louisiana Purchase, then on through the road, canal and rail systems financed by nineteenth century state and federal governments on to the present day. It has meant active government funding of large infrastructure projects. Most importantly for Blue-state culture and government involvement has been public education. Even with the publicized failure and bankruptcy of some large metropolitan school districts, the debate about vouchers and charter schools as well as bilingual education, the role of the public education system is still as important as it has always been. As the recent fallout from the issue of legacy admissions at private universities indicates, private systems have their own bureaucratic pitfalls. Also recent studies on newly established private school systems or quasi-privatized public systems have shown that student performance is little changed from the public system. Performance is impacted more by the quality of the teaching and the quality of the program than whether they are funded publicly or privately.

Another important aspect of Blue-state culture is its ability to adapt to new issues. One of the issues that have become important in recent times is the environment. Of course, the issue of the environment in the form of conservation has been an issue since the late nineteenth century with forest and fisheries management, the national parks, and the protection of the bison and the bald eagle. Later, starting with Blue-state California's air pollution and auto fuel economy laws, chemical pollution became a new field of Blue-state activity. The recent push by several Blue states to enact new environmental legislation, including California's landmark greenhouse gas bill, as well as support of the Kyoto Protocol show how Blue-state culture evolves into new areas.[80] And the recent passage (but subsequently vetoed by the governor) of single payer health care legislation by the California leg-

---

[80]   Justin Blum, "'Blue' States Tackling Energy on Their Own," *Washington Post*, January 22, 2006.

islature offers an indication of one of the next issues that will be adapted and remolded in a Blue-state culture.

Most of the important political reforms have occurred in Blue states or in Blue-state dominated eras; same thing for most of the economic breakthroughs. America needs both political and economic change as we proceed after the 2006 elections. So if we are going to make the changes necessary to create a new national model it is only going to occur with a shift from a Red-state to a Blue-state dominated culture.

THE DEMOCRATIC PARTY ROLE IN A BLUE-STATE MODEL

How is such a cultural shift going to occur? Obviously, there has to be a political movement to create such a shift, and in today's America, that shift is going to have to come from the Democratic Party. Notice that I am talking in terms of today's America, because there is nothing sacrosanct about the Democratic Party being either the exclusive or historic carrier of political or economic reform in this country. Throughout much of the middle and late nineteenth century the principal reform party in this country was the Republicans. It was founded as a reform party in the mid-1850s from various other political factions and of course its initial lead reform issue was the abolition of slavery. But it also advanced a number of reform issues starting in the Civil War years when it had a stranglehold on Congress after the walkout of the Southern delegations. It was not until the 1920 election that a big business dominated Republican Party began moving inexorably into its current extreme Red-state shift. As late as 1924 the Democrats had to compete with Robert La Follette's Progressive Party for leadership in the reform element of American politics. And certainly, a Democratic Party that brought us the Jim Crow laws and the poll tax is an organization that has shown that it is as capable as any political organization of maintaining an anti-reform position.

But in today's political environment, the Democratic Party is the only realistic organizational vehicle for initiating the kind of changes that are necessary. This is for a number of reasons. The most important of those have already been mentioned, namely the most important reform movements are coming out of the Democratic Party organizations, or organizations related to the Democratic Party. The environmental and health legislation in California mentioned above, for example, came out the Democratic Party controlled legislature. Republican Governor Arnold Schwarzenegger signed Democratic Assembly Member Fran Pavley's landmark greenhouse-gas bill because he needed to co-opt Democratic Party environmental positions and act like a Democrat in his run for re-election for governor. Also as noted before, other Blue states are active in environmental issues. The movement to reform corporate governance after the abuses of Enron, World Com and the like came from people like New York Democrat Attorney General Eliot Spitzer and California Democratic Treasurer Phil Angelides. The clean money campaign movement has its first success in the Blue state of Maine. The Democratic Party has not been as proactive in the various reform movements as some people would like. This has always been true as early reform movements start outside party structures before being adopted by the major parties later on. Nevertheless, the current edition of the Democratic Party is active on a number of reform agendas.

Second, the Democratic Party is the only viable political organization at the current time that can effect such reform activities. Other organizations such as the Green Party may be more ideologically purer, but they have yet to show that they can impact a race beyond being a spoiler as they were in the 2000 race. Nor does any other organization have the scope to carry out a movement and elect people at the same time. There are national movements involving single issues, but they still are not political parties that can get people elected and enact those issues into law. The ultimate effectiveness of any political movement is to elect people, and the Democrats are the only organization that can elect people to reform programs on a large scale.

For argument sake, however, suppose it became clear that the Democratic Party was incapable of carrying out such an agenda and the Republicans made no changes either. What would have to occur to get a new national political party going and are any of the existing marginal parties capable of becoming that new party? The answer to that question is to be found in the founding of the Republican Party. First, the Republican Party was an entirely new party. It did not evolve out of any existing minor party of the day. The Republican Party's creation was from several sources including anti-slavery Democrats, but the most important sources was the anti-slavery faction of the defunct and dismembered Whig Party. Therefore the most likely manner in which a reform-minded political party would be formed would be if a large segment of the progressive wing of the Democratic Party broke off and the party was unable to reunite. With the increasing disenchantment of both major parties, the possibility of their fragmentation and a new political party emerging is increasing with each election. Registration figures in Ventura County in the 2006 election show that in the wake of the Iraq War and the sex scandals involving Congressional pages, Republican registration stopped dead in its tracks, while the increases in independent registration (known in California as "Decline to State") is outpacing the increase in Democratic registration. The trend toward independent party registration, unaligned with any major party, is showing up all over the country. But at the current time, we are probably still some ways away from either party breaking up. Therefore, as far as any political party being the focal point for a Blue-state agenda, it would have to be the Democrats.

Thirdly, and quite simply, the Democratic Party is in control or very strong in the existing Blue states, which would be the basis for any Blue-state national agenda. You have to start from somewhere, and the Blue states and the Democratic Party in those Blue states would be the logical place to start.

DEMOCRATS AND THE 2002/2004 ELECTIONS

So given that the Democratic Party is where one has to start a Blue-state national revival, the question that is begging to be asked is whether the Democratic Party can do the job? For some people, given the party's performance the last few years, particularly when it comes to the War in Iraq, the question of whether the Democratic Party can do the job is similar to asking how many angels can dance on the head of a pin. To these people, the party has been so "out of it" that the question is pointless. But to those of us, who are toiling in the fields of Democratic Party politics, this has become a critical issue.

The 2006 election in California is a case in point. Here in the year 2006 in what is supposed to be the bluest of the Blue states, one would think that there would have been all kinds of political energy pouring into the election. Not in California. How can that be? Quite simply, no one cared, or at least no one cared that much. Finding volunteers was an ordeal. One practically had to beat them over the head with a stick to get them into a campaign office. Some people in California have attributed it to burnout—with statewide special elections in 2003 and 2005 there really had not been a break in the election cycle. But Democratic campaign offices were overflowing with workers in 2004. Something happened in that election. I have attributed it to the dynamics of the presidential primary races in 2003 and 2004 and what subsequently happened that November.

The most important issue influencing the presidential race in 2004 was, of course, Iraq. After the vote in Congress on the Iraq War resolution, many Democratic activists were disaffected in seeing all, not just some, but all of the leading Democratic presidential contenders in Congress support the resolution. These activists have been summarily dismissed by the mainstream Washington media as being left wing, anti-war, cheese-eating surrender monkeys. The reporters did pick up that most of the opposition was coming from middle-aged, old-time antiwar activists rather than the current generation of college students, but beyond that, the Washington media was clueless.

Activists as a group, whether they be liberal or conservative, are generally more informed on political subjects than the average person, particularly on those issues that they have an interest. Obviously, that is why they are activists. And in the case of the second Iraq War, the Democratic Party had a core of activists who had gone through the Vietnam years and the first Iraq War, and had a good idea of not only the issues, but also how to track down information in a war. This was a group that had learned these skills in the Vietnam era, long before the advent of the Internet. What the Internet did was to make them that more efficient and effective in tracking down information through the propaganda fog surrounding Iraq. I, for one, was tracking the English-language edition of several foreign papers and relaying that information by email to Democratic activists in my part of the state. Other people were doing the same. So by the time that the Iraq resolution came to a vote, a large segment of the California Democratic Party had concluded that going into Iraq was crazy—it was an unwinnable situation. This decision was not made on the basis of some ideological conviction. It was made after looking at more dispassionate foreign and domestic sources.

Of course, the Bush Administration had scheduled this vote right before the 2002 election to put the Democrats on the spot and fully expected to turn their opposition into jelly. And of course the Administration was right. It was even more galling that one of the prospective presidential candidates, Congressman and Minority Leader Richard Gephardt of Missouri, actually cut a deal with the Bush Administration behind the backs of not only his own colleagues in the House (where he wasn't going to win a vote on the floor anyway), but undercut the Democrats in the Senate, where they were still the nominal majority. In the event, the vote was taken; the Democrats caved in on the resolution and then promptly got their tails kicked in the election, losing complete control of the Congress.

Needless to say, the Democratic activists and party leaders in California and elsewhere were doubly annoyed that a bad idea led to a bad vote and a subsequent failure at the polls. In their opinion, those Democratic members of Congress had shown poor judgment during the whole episode and all the presidential aspirants were suspect as presidential candidates. What made these candidates particularly weak on the Iraq issue was that, if the Democrats were going to win the presidential election (and the basic job of any official of any political party is to get their party members elected to office), just like any athletic coach, they had to put themselves in a position on the Iraq issue to win the election. With the Bush Administration in control of events on that issue, that was always going to be a long shot. There were four possible outcomes from the vote for a Democratic presidential candidate depending on whether he supported or opposed the war and whether the war was a success or failure. All the candidates and many of the Congressional leaders felt that the politically safe vote was to support the war. But a vote for the war by a Democratic presidential candidate was useless. If the war was a success for the Bush Administration, Bush would win the election regardless how the Democrats voted—incumbents with successful policies win elections. And voting for the war if the war was a failure does not make the Democratic candidate look any better. Ask John Kerry. The only vote that Democratic presidential candidates could have taken to position themselves in order to win the election was to vote against the war and hope the war would fail (even those of us pouring over all the information we could on Iraq did not know for sure what would happen). Cynical, but true.

The failure the Congressional Democratic presidential candidates to understand this basic piece of political logic underscored the Democratic catastrophes in 2002 and 2004. At the core of the Democrats problem was that they had no convictions behind the policies that they advocated: they couldn't tell the voters why they were running and why the voters should elect them. They knew they were against Bush and his policies, but they couldn't decide what they were for. Worse yet, in the case of Iraq, they were afraid to make a decision that might be unpopular. This vacuum of conviction on Iraq is what opened up the field for the Howard Dean campaign that understood the political dynamics of the moment and took advantage of it. Dean's campaign imploded for various reasons, and the electorate fell back to John Kerry, who was viewed as a safer, more "electable" candidate. But the fundamental problem for Kerry, which had begun by his vote for the Iraq war resolution, did not go away. The reservations that the Democratic activists (particularly the Dean activists) had about Kerry from the time of the Iraq vote continued through the campaign, but were suppressed because of their desire to get rid of Bush. But the Swiftboat fiasco and Kerry's statement that if he knew then what he knew later, he would still support the war, reconfirmed many of the activists' concerns. Kerry's loss merely affirmed the activists' original judgment about him and the other presidential candidates. After that campaign, the activists' general feeling was that they had supported Kerry to the maximum despite the reservations they had about him, but that they would never do that again for another mushy Democratic presidential candidate that did not stand for something.

The immediate reaction by these activists was to support Dean for chair of the DNC. But other supposed cave-ins, such as the bankruptcy bill, and especially the Alito Supreme Court nomination, has continued to alienate these people to the point that after a combination of burn-out and revulsion, they were conspicuous by their absence in the 2006 election in California.

DEMOCRATS AND THE CALIFORNIA 50ᵀᴴ CONGRESSIONAL DISTRICT ELECTION

The clearest example of the above trends in California occurred in the special election in the spring of 2006 in California's 50th Congressional District. The district is centered just above the city of San Diego in northern San Diego County and occurred when the former incumbent Representative Randy "Duke" Cunningham was convicted of bribery and other nefarious crimes that has put him in prison for roughly the next eight years. The special election was to fill the remainder his term which ended in January 2007. In the April special election primary Democrat Francine Busby, who was beaten by Cunningham soundly in 2004 and was running again when the Cunningham scandal exploded, entered the primary against another Democrat, an Independent, a Libertarian, and 14 Republican candidates, in this heavily Republican seat. The large Republican field was because the winner on the Republican side would be the odds-on favorite to win the June 6 run-off and be seated in Congress. But it also virtually guaranteed that no one would get 50 percent and trigger the June election.

In the April 11 primary, however, Busby registered just under 44 percent of the vote. This sent a mixed signal as far as the Democrats were concerned. The result was several points higher than the combined vote of Busby and the Green candidate in 2004. Yet despite the fact it was an open seat formerly held by a disgraced incumbent in the middle of a sea of Republican Congressional scandals, Busby was unable to get an outright 50 percent+1 win, let alone a landslide victory. In fact the combined Democratic vote was 45.06 percent compared to the combined Republican vote of 53.53 percent with the Libertarian candidate taking .60 percent and the Independent .81 percent. The turnout was a whopping 38.86 percent.

Less than two months later, on June 6, was the runoff with top candidates of the Democrat and Republican Parties (Busby and Brian Bilbray) facing off against the Libertarian and the Independent. This runoff coincided with the statewide California primary, and in fact, the voters in the 50th CD had to vote twice—once in the runoff and once in the primary. The results were disappointing for both major parties. The Republicans with Bilbray did hold onto the seat, but in the seven weeks between the primary and the runoff, the Republicans lost nearly 4 percent of the vote (actually 3.96 percent) falling from 53.53 percent to 49.57 percent, a shocking result by any measure. The problem for Francine Busby and the Democrats was that it didn't go to them. In fact the Democratic vote fell from 45.06 percent to 45.02 percent, totaling an even 4.0 percent loss for the major parties in 7 weeks. In the event, exactly 1.0 percent went to the Libertarian candidate and exactly 3.0 percent went to the Independent. Thus the long-term trend of California voters leaving the major parties to register "Decline to State" showed up to an unusual extent in the seven weeks of the special election.[81]

What caused these results in the 50th Congressional District? There were many theories. The election fraud conspiracy theorists were hard at work convincing anyone they could that the race was stolen from Busby. They not-

---

81   California Secretary of State, "Congressional District 50—Special Election," http://www. ss.ca.gov/elections/elections_cd50.htm.

ed that some precinct workers took the voting machines home them, which obviously was highly irregular. They were outraged when a court refused a re-count because the court bowed to House of Representative rules that give them the right to determine and seat their members once a member has taken the oath of office. In fact there were much more logical reasons for the results that were both good and bad for the Democrats. A lot of it showed up in the voting shifts that occurred between April and June. Clearly the Republican vote in Congressional races is soft. Party strategists can no longer take a high and/or solid Republican turnout for granted. This is also clearly showing in the flat-lining of Republican registration in Ventura County and the explosion of the "Decline to State" (DTS) registrations, which many of us believe is being augmented by the Jim Jeffords effect, where Republican registrations are shifting to Independent. That seems to have happened in the 50th CD vote, where the vote shifted to non-major candidates.

But there were other aspects to this race as well. The Courage Campaign, a progressive grassroots organization based in California and the progressive blog MyDD sponsored a poll on the 50th CD special election. The poll was conducted Wright Consulting Services who surveyed 691 people between July 6 and July 27, 2006. Five-hundred three of these people voted in the June 6 election, and 188 did not vote in the election, but had voted in recent prior elections. The poll had a margin of error of +/-3.8 percent for the whole sample and +/-4.5 percent for those who had voted. The poll showed that Democrats turned out better than Republicans, but Independents had a very low turnout. The failure to get a high turnout from Independents hurt Busby because she needed those voters. More importantly was the fact that she did not win a big enough share of the Independent vote. A surprisingly large 29 percent of DTS and third-party votes went to the Independent and Libertarian candidates, and as a result Busby only beat Bilbray by 40 percent to 34 percent from this set of voters. The polling indicated tremendous dissatisfaction with Bush, Cunningham and Bilbray as well as the direction of the country. But at the same time DTS/third-party voters didn't think Busby or the Democrats were capable of being effective and able to change the Bush policies. The polling on Busby's key issue, the "culture of corruption," fell flat on those voters since Bilbray was not personally part of the scandal. Also, a fuzzy, disunified Democratic position on Iraq allowed the Republican "stay the course" message to dominate in the heavily Republican district which was near major military installations. As a result, Independents turned to the two non-major party candidates or didn't vote at all. The poll concluded by issuing a hypothesis: swing voters want candidates who will stand up to the Bush Administration, stop his policies, and hold the administration accountable for its actions.[82]

DEMOCRATS AND THE LACK OF VISION AND MESSAGE

The California 50th Congressional District Special Election encapsulated all the grievances that the Democratic Party faithful have been conveying to the Democratic leadership in Washington since the 2002 election. They complain of a lack of vision. They complain of a lack of message or least a unified message. They complain of a lack of conviction in whatever message or messages are out there. They then infer that this lack of vision, message and conviction creates several problems in the political campaigns themselves. First, voters are confused; they don't know what the Democratic Party stands for. In addition, the party appears to them to be shiftless, groveling to the special interest of the day. The party tries to bend its message to appeal to the swing voter, and end up getting what happened in the California 50th where there were few of those voters, and those who went to the polls voted in non-traditional ways.

Second, the lack of conviction translates into a lack of integrity. This issue was highlighted in an article entitled "Remapping the Cultural Debate" in the February 2006 issue of *The American Prospect*. The American branch of Environics, a Canadian market research firm, based the article on extensive analysis of market research data on consumer behavior. The data was micro-sorted to what is called in the trade "neighborhood lifestyle segmentation." This analysis followed work done by Republicans who used consumer research data in the 2004 election to target potential voters based on lifestyle preferences, essentially a materialistic proxy for core value

The results of the American Environics micro-sort was that it led them to reject some of the more popular solutions to reviving the Democratic Party such as reframing the Democratic message in the manner of George Lakoff, or emphasizing a more populist image, which has also been fashionable. Instead, the study argued that the way to advance the progressive agenda of the Democratic Party was to selectively back off on policy in favor of val-

---

82 Todd Beeton, "Courage Campaign/MyDD Poll: Why Francine Busby Lost," *Courage Campaign*, August 2, 2006, http://couragecampaign.org/entries/poll-conclusions/#more.

ues. By emphasizing what the authors called "bridge values" Democrats can reach out to audiences who share their fundamental beliefs even if they don't agree with them on every issue. The authors of the study argue further that in the new atomized information economy, increasingly isolated voters first look at the character of the candidate (i.e., can they trust the person) before they assess the issues, and that even in places of the country that were under severe economic and social stress, questions of values trumped questions of social or economic policy. As the American Environics poll showed, voters first attempt to determine the character of the candidate before they focus on the issues. When there is a conflict, character trumps issues.[83]

Fuzziness on issues can imply a lack of character that puts the candidate at a severe handicap, for starters. Lack of conviction not only implies a lack of character, it in turn conveys weakness. In a nation traumatized by the events of September 11, 2001, security has become an overarching issue. Again, it is not only a question of which security and defense programs should be put in place. It is a question of which candidate has the character that makes the voters feel safe. The failure of the Democratic Party and the Democratic leaders to address this question in a meaningful way has cost them much grief at the polls. Democrats have been dealing with this problem through the 2002 election, through the Kerry campaign, and right up through the Courage Campaign/MyDD poll in the California 50th CD.

All of the above ultimately undermines the message. That is, assuming that there is a message; many Democratic activists are not sure that there is one. One of the favorite pastimes since the 2004 election has been the discussions on framing the message. These discussions have revolved around the work of George Lakoff. Lakoff analyzed how the Republicans have used words and how they have framed messages for years in order to get their message across. Lakoff's work has been to teach Democrats how to frame and project their own messages to compete with the Republicans in the national debate. This is all well and good and certainly useful information. The problem is that you have to have the message before you can frame it. You cannot frame empty space. In order for a message to be effective, it has to contain the aforementioned vision and conviction of the candidate, and it has to be done in a way that conveys the full scope of the campaign and the

---

83 Garance Franke-Ruta, "Re-mapping the Cultural Debate," *The American Prospect*, February 2006, 38–43.

candidate. And at its very base it has to show who the candidate is, why he or she is running for that particular office, and why people should vote for him or her. This in turn loops back to the issue of the character of the candidate and why it is more important than issues. The bottom line is that the message has to give the voter a reason to vote for the candidate and for this candidate on this issue. The voter can vote for other candidates on the same issue. It is the character of the candidate as embraced in his vision and conviction on the issues that ultimately allows the message to "make the sale."

It was precisely these concepts that were missing in the Kerry campaign in 2003–04. An April 21, 2004 Washington Post article highlighted the problem at the point in time when Kerry was consolidating the Democratic Party nomination. The article discussed how Kerry's campaign team tried to re-manufacture him as a modern centrist. As the article stated, the campaign's mission was to "position Kerry as a presidential candidate who is pro-national defense, pro-middle-class tax cuts, pro-balanced budgets—with the rhetorical dash and inspiration of John F. Kennedy."[84] It gave one the impression that staff was making a soufflé rather than a vision for the country. The whole process was to mould the message and the candidate into something he was not, and that the country was not. Based on the machinations going in April of 2004, one could easily see how something as blatantly fraudulent as the Swiftboat fiasco could succeed later that summer. In a world of make-believe, it is tough to sort out the genuine fraud from the merely manu-factured one. Arianna Huffington's articles about the Democratic campaign highlighted these deficiencies throughout the summer and fall. She called that campaign "timid, spineless...with no central theme or moral vision" that "played right into the hands of the Bush-Cheney team" and that the obsession with not alienating swing voters "turned a campaign that should have been about big ideas...into a narrow trench war fought over ludicrous non-issues" such as the Swiftboat debate.[85]

Likewise, the same thing appears to have happened in the Phil Angelides gubernatorial campaign in California. In a withering editorial the *San Francisco Chronicle* on October 18, 2006, the paper jumped all over Angelides' campaign and endorsed Governor Arnold Schwarzenegger. The paper wrote

84 Jim VandeHei, "Old-School Team to Sell Kerry as Modern Centrist," *Washington Post*, April 21, 2004.

85 Arianna Huffington, "Anatomy of a Crushing Political Defeat," *Arianna Online*, November 3, 2004, http://www.ariannaonline.com/columns/printer_friendly.php?id=742.

that Angelides "has not demonstrated the leadership traits required to build coalitions" and "has struggled to inspire Democrats in this election." They then noted that during their editorial board meeting with him, "many of his answers gave no indication that he either heard or cared about the question... [T]ime after time, he defaulted to his wind-up stump monologues about education or closing tax loopholes." Finally, in summing up their position on Angelides, the *Chronicle* said: "The lack of excitement about Angelides is not just about his deficiencies in campaign donations and charisma. He has yet to articulate a compelling case that his election would make a difference in California."[86] The *Chronicle* statements were not unique; such statements were heard from many sources during the campaign.

What was even more frustrating for Democratic activists was that while they realized that Angelides did not have the glamour of a movie actor like Schwarzenegger, they supported him precisely because he would be a credible alternative to the governor. Angelides won the Democratic primary over Steve Westly primarily on that belief. But in the general election race a different Phil Angelides emerged. The most startling event was Angelides' failure to support a bill passed by the legislature on single payer health insurance during the campaign. Schwarzenegger vetoed it, and with health care showing up as the number one or two issue in the campaign, it seemed like the perfect opportunity for Angelides to define himself and the campaign by supporting a bill that the Democrats had worked for years to pass through the legislature. It didn't happen. Like many things that occurred in the Angelides campaign after June, it did not have a message and it did not make a lot of sense.

When I brought up with a member of the California legislature the apparent disconnect between the Angelides of a year or two before and the one I saw just before the election, he had the same feeling. He had toured with Angelides during 2005 and said that the candidate was much more focused and defined himself much better then than he did in 2006. This legislator said it almost seemed as though a consultant had gotten hold of Angelides and put a fog over his campaign. We may understand better what happened to the Angelides campaign when all the post-election reports come in. But for many activists in California it had all the appearances of a West Coast

---

86   Editorial, "Gov. Schwarzenegger to Stay the Course," *San Francisco Chronicle*, October 18, 2006.

version of the Kerry campaign with its lack of focus and lack of message. It was a campaign from Mars—run by extraterrestrials for the benefit of extraterrestrials. It certainly had very little to say to the average Democratic activist, let alone the California voter.

The fuzziness of the Democratic message does not just come from campaigns, however. An article by Ari Berman in the October 16, 2006 issue of *The Nation* discussed the Democracy Alliance, a coalition of roughly 100 large donors who had banded together to support progressive projects. The group came together after the 2004 election and had been deeply frustrated by what had gone on in the Kerry campaign. In the nearly two years since, the Alliance has put over $50 million in center-left and progressive organizations and activists. But what has occurred is that many of the issues that have bedeviled the Democrats are now dogging this group. The most important of these problems are just who is the Democracy Alliance, what does it stand for, and what does it want to do. They have yet to decide whether they want to influence the party establishment or change it. The cautiousness that has been ascribed to the Kerry's and other Democratic campaigns seems to be active in the Alliance, and there has been difficulty in following a more adventuresome path.

As the article pointed out, the Alliance is making some of the same mistakes that certain camps have been making in the Democratic Party for years, and has been highlighted by the dispute between Democratic National Committee chair Howard Dean, and the chair of the Democratic Congressional Campaign Committee, Representative Rahm Emmanuel. Emmanuel wanted to spend money on races to take control of the House in 2006. Dean wanted a longer-term investment to build up party structure. But as the article on the Democracy Alliance pointed out, it takes more than throwing money at campaigns for a short-term victory to make a long-term strategic difference. You need conviction in what you are doing as well as the money to execute the plan and achieve victory. This was the lesson that the conservatives learned over a forty-year period in order to achieve power. James Piereson, who has been the long-time executive director of the John M. Olin Foundation, which has been one the leading funders on conservative issues, makes the point that you have to have a vision to execute your strategy. Piereson feels that conservatives have been successful not because they raised a lot of money and organized many foundations, but because of the ideas they were trying to sell.[87]

So just as is the case of a political party platform or the campaign speeches of candidates, the message coming out of the vision, and the convictions from that vision, determine the direction of the campaign. And the success of the candidate's message determines whether the campaign succeeds. Everything else flows from that. A successful message gets the volunteers and money for the campaign. It gives the donors and the volunteers a reason to work for the campaign. It gives the volunteers a reason to get people to the polls. Most important of all, a successful message gives the voters a reason to vote for the candidate and the campaign, which is the ultimate goal.

DEMOCRATS AND CLASS-BASED POLITICS

All of the above examples show various aspects of criticisms of the Democratic Party in terms of focus and message. But another part of the problem appears to be developing because of a strategic shift toward the voters that the Democratic Party started making in the early 1970s. This was an outgrowth of the reaction to the Vietnam Anti-War movement, the new rules that were promulgated for the 1972 convention, the nomination at that convention of George McGovern, and the subsequent crash and burn of the McGovern campaign and the Democrats in 1972. It was subsequently reinforced after the failed 1984 campaign of Walter Mondale. With those campaigns the so-called Democratic leadership came to the conclusion that the old Democratic strategy of liberalism and big government was dead as the dodo bird, as was playing to the various constituencies of the Democratic base. Furthermore, unions were dying and the party was being outspent big time by the big business fat cats that were bankrolling the Republicans. Simultaneously, the moderate Republicans were being edged out of their party by the new generation of social conservatives. So the Democrats answer was to cuddle up to Corporate America, abandon the Democratic base and their economic issues, and stump for a new set of social issues such as choice.

The result has been some of the things that Thomas Frank has described in his book, *What's the Matter with Kansas?* Frank shows how some of the poorest counties in Kansas (and throughout the United States) were voting in huge numbers for the Republicans and George Bush, while Bush and his

---

87   Ari Berman, "Big $$ for Progressive Politics," *The Nation*, October 16, 2006, 18–24.

friends were at best ignoring them and at worst ripping them off. Frank takes most of his book describing this Alice-in-Wonderland situation. He points out the cleverness with which Republicans developed their message. But he also shows in a couple of instances where he believes the Democrats helped them along the way. He points out the political activities of Republican activist Mark Gietzen who works in the Wichita area, a formerly Democratic stronghold in what had been a typically mainstream Republican state. As Gietzen stated, in earlier days, the Republican Party was the party of the rich and the Democrats were the party of the working poor. But the Democrats on their own discarded the idea that their party was the party of the poor. Now, a Democratic fundraising event was likely to cost as much as a Republican one. The result was that in 1994 long-time Democratic Congressman Dan Glickman lost his seat to a Republican. In the 1994 election, Glickman lost the precincts of his old Democratic base and the only precincts he carried were the affluent districts that were Republican.[88]

Frank's thesis is that the Democrats did themselves in by taking the corporate line and in the process taking economic issues off the table. This made the made the Democrats look like a slightly to the left version of the Republicans on economic issues and in the process neutralized those issues (the so-called Republican-lite approach). This also happened with environmental issues and some other categories and brings up Ralph Nader's old criticism that there isn't a dime's worth of difference between the Republicans and Democrats. The net result was two things. First, such strategies discouraged the liberal activists, who along with the labor unions, do the lion's share of the work in the Democratic Party. This is a problem that has been building up for a long time, and has now reached the point where it was very difficult in this election cycle to find volunteers for the 2006 election. Second, once the economic issues are neutralized, that leaves only the social issues such as abortion and gun control on the table. These social issues have been effective wedge tools for the Republicans to use to split off Democratic votes, which they have.

Many Democrats who have been courting the center and the corporate donations have done so in the belief that the working class voters and the poor have no other place to go. As the Republicans have shown, the Repub-

---

88   Thomas Frank, *What's the Matter with Kansas?: How Conservatives Won the Heart of America* (New York: Metropolitan Books 2004), 174–178.

lican's social issues can woo many of the working poor. Just as easily, these voters can stay home and say why make the effort to vote when there is no real difference, à la Ralph Nader.

Also Democrats for some reason do not identify culturally with the working class any more. Some Democrats may think it is irrelevant in a globalized world where unions are losing ground anyway. Some may think that labor issues are culturally passé in an economy that is increasingly dependent on the service sector. And some are indeed the elitists the Republicans say they are and think that the concerns of working people are beneath them. It is rare to find a Democrat speaking on class based issues these days. The only prominent Democratic politician basing his campaigns on the issue of poverty these days has been former Vice Presidential and Presidential candidate John Edwards. And when any other Democrat even approaches the issue of income inequality these days, he or she generally runs for cover when someone accuses him of fomenting class warfare. For whatever reason, it seems essential for "respectable people" not to mention the fact that we have economic classes in this country, a country where the gap between the rich and the poor has reached historic proportions.

While some may be embarrassed at admitting that Americans brought with them to the New World the old European classed-based baggage they thought that they had abandoned in the old country, others have always realized that such social behavior is universal in nature and cannot be ignored. It certainly has been a part of the American political landscape from the beginning and has been the basis of many of the great political movements of this country, including the Jefferson Republicans, Jacksonian Democracy, the Populist movement and the New Deal. Men like Jefferson, Jackson, William Jennings Bryan and Franklin Delano Roosevelt, among others, certainly had no problem addressing class-based issues. Indeed, it is a testament to the editorial, oratorical, and intellectual bankruptcy of the Democratic Party today that there appears to be few, if any, Democrats of note that can deal with this kind of material in any fashion. For a supposed "party of the people" this is a politically operational handicap of monumental proportions.

CAN THE DEMOCRATS LEAD?

Just as disturbing has been the party's inability to deal with Iraq, both as a policy question and the war itself. Of course policy questions involving war and peace are in the end infinitely more complex than any economic or class-based issue, if for no other reason that some of the key people in the policy about a war, namely the enemy, can never really be brought into the discussion while the war or foreign policy crisis rages on. But as Iraq disintegrates into chaos, once again we are brought face to face with the consequences of not having such a debate. What makes the present situation so appalling is how the country could so blindly stumble into such a mess while virtually no one in Washington objected. The Republicans have tried to cop their way out of this issue by saying that it was not their business to oppose the policies of a president of their own party. Of course, members of the same party of previous presidents managed to do that when necessary in their era. But the Democrats in opposition have no such excuse, which is doubly depressing. Those of us who remember the domestic battles going on during the Vietnam War wonder where the Eugene McCarthys, the Wayne Morses, the George McGoverns and their colleagues are in this Congress. The congenital gutlessness that envelope these people makes one wonder what they would do with power if they had it. The public, of course, has also asked the same question and has shown their response in the last several elections before 2006. Today's Senate reminds one more of the Roman Senate under the Caesars (with Karl Rove commanding the Praetorian Guard) than it does of anything the founding fathers had in mind. The question today is, how will the new Democratic Congress change things?

Can the Democrats pull it off and forge a new chapter in the history of their party? Are they capable of creating a new Blue-state model of government? Or will they wallow in the indecision and mediocrity that has been their lot for some time? We do know that parties coming into power tend to have fragmented agendas, and that things will consolidate. With the cross-currents surrounding the issues of the Iraq War, the economy, social issues such as abortion, the role of religion in state and society, the chasm of income inequality, the geographic differences and similar issues, one is right to ask whether the Democratic Party can find a solution to the political puzzle which makes it possible to fit these disparate pieces into an interlocking whole that advocates a Blue-state culture. To begin to answer that question we must first go back to the issues the Democratic Party faced the last time it was in the political wilderness without the control of the White House or the Congress—the period of the 1920s.

6. DEMOCRATS IN THE 1920s

When political experts discuss how a party out of power or a core of ideas such as liberalism can gain a national audience again, they invariably talk about the conservative ascendancy over the last forty years and all of the institutions and the structures that they put in place to advance their ideas. Certainly as a strategy it is worthy of discussion. There is much useful information from the conservative experience that has the potential to re-energize the Democratic Party. But while the events of what happened to conservatives and the Republican Party are interesting comparisons, the real comparisons for the Democrats is what happened to them the last time the Republicans seized long-term control of both the White House and the Congress. That period turned out to be 1921 to 1931, and the parallels of the two Democratic minority eras are striking.

The 1920s for the Democrats was actually the end of a long period of long-term Democratic minority status punctuated by shorter periods of Democratic victories. The recently organized Republican Party in the 1860 election had eclipsed the Democrats and the Civil War made the Republicans the dominant political party. With the exception of the Cleveland and Wilson Administrations, the Republicans maintained this majority until 1932.

The election of 1920 was a watershed in American politics. The changes brought about by World War I had completely transformed the country so that it was barely recognizable to the America of the 1912 election. Demo-graphically, the 1920 census had shown the change. For the first time in the history of the country, the population of the urban areas exceeded that of the rural areas. Cities like Detroit and Los Angeles had become major urban ar-eas almost overnight, and would rank with New York, Chicago and Philadel-phia as the dominant cities in the country for most of the twentieth century. Politically, the cities would be a growing force in the Democratic Party in future years, but at this point had not replaced the old Bryan coalition of ru-ral Southern and Western states. The overriding issue for most people was a negative reaction to the effects of the war and a desire to return to "the good old days," the pre-war society or something close to it. Warren Harding in his 1920 campaign called to "a return to normalcy," and such a sentiment had a profound impact on the electorate that year.

With the combination of a reaction against the war and the League of Nations, a desire to return to the status quo, the prohibition debate, con-cerns over immigration, and an organizational and the leadership vacuum brought on by Wilson's illness, the Democrats limped into their conven-tion in 1920. The convention itself would deal more lumps. The convention fought over prohibition and rejected Bryan's "dry" plank, created a platform that defended the League but was otherwise unremarkable, and then took forty-four ballots to name its nominee, James M. Cox, the governor of Ohio. Cox, like his platform, wasn't all that much different from his Republican opponent, Warren Harding. Both men were from Ohio and both men had been in the newspaper business. Harding and the Republicans supported Prohibition in public, if not in practice, while Cox was a "wet" who opposed Prohibition. That would go against Cox, as would the Democrats' support of the League and the general rejection of Wilson and his policies.[89]

The 1920 campaign itself was unexciting because there was not much to choose from. In the end, the people voted for normalcy and the Democrats were routed. Harding received 16 million votes to Cox's 9 million (impris-oned Socialist Eugene Debs received nearly a million, showing the alienation of a large number of people, particularly naturalized immigrants). Harding won the electoral votes by 404 to 127. The Congress was also a Republican rout with 301 Republicans to 131 Democrats in the House and 51 Republicans

---

89   David Burner, *The Politics of Provincialism: The Democratic Party in Transition 1918–1932* (1967; re-print Cambridge MA.: Harvard 1986), 62–64; Robert K. Murray, *The 103rd Ballot: Democrats and the Disaster in Madison Square Garden* (New York: Harper & Row 1976), 20–21.

to 43 Democrats in the Senate. The Republicans were in complete control of both branches of the government.[90]

From a party organizational standpoint, the rejection of the Wilson agenda in the election left the Democrats without one. One of the issues for the party out of power is to find a new message or refurbish the existing one when the old one has been rejected. Compounding the loss of message was the new social issues of prohibition and immigration, which would be the forerunner of a host of items that would start tearing the party apart. Gaining a consensus in the new polarized environment was going to be much more difficult. These social issues would in turn trigger a backlash that created new constituencies, fragmenting the electorate even more.

It does not take a psychic to see that many of the issues and strategies that the party struggled with in the early 1920s were similar to the problems that it would suffer with after 2000, and especially after 2004. Then as now there was a lack of recognized leadership, and what leadership there was tended to play it safe with ill-defined positions, not offering a real alternative to the Republicans—"me too" candidates. "Electability" becomes an important adjective in minority parties. But playing it safe and trying to be electable only makes things worse. As is usually the case, such safe politics fails to give the voters a reason for electing a minority party's candidates. Thus what happened to the Democrats after the 1920 election is important because it gives us some clues as to how the Democrats should respond in the early years of the twenty-first century, particularly after the 2006 election. It does not give us all the answers, but it does give us a basis for finding those answers.

In the 1920s, like today, the Democrats faced a number of issues that severely divided the party. One of the key issues throughout the period was Prohibition. The opposition to alcoholic beverages was fueled by a belief that alcohol was damaging to the social structure of the country, destroying lives and families, and that these destructive effects were a contributing cause of poverty and anti-social behavior in the country. Later on, support for prohibition would become a focal point and code words for another set of more unsavory issues with nativist and racist overtones. The people who supported prohibition tended to come to come from the evangelical Protestant Churches and tended to be anti-alien and anti-Catholic. They also tended to

---

90   *The American Heritage Book of Presidents and Famous Americans* (New York: American Heritage 1967) vol. 9, 787. Many other sources for this data.

be from the rural areas of the country and were hostile to the cities, which they saw as hotbeds of corruption, where they believed most of the drinking was being done. Thus, prohibition was the lead issue in a host of other issues that included immigration, the cultural split between the cities and the rural areas, and opposition to the Roman Catholic Church. The evangelical Protestant churches and the state legislatures, who were still dominated by rural districts, propelled the movement. Complementing these forces were the issues of drinking and corruption, and employer concerns about worker safety and worker productivity. The chief organizing force for prohibition was the Anti-Saloon League, which was founded in 1893. Originally founded for combating saloons and the deleterious effect it had on communities, it logically went on to fight the culture associated with saloons, namely alcohol itself.[91]

Beyond the reform nature of its message, prohibition also linked up with the other key domestic issue of the 1920 election—immigration. The immigration issue had multiple layers, all in some form tracing back their origins back to the Know-Nothing movement of the 1840s. Then, it was the case of the country being overrun by Irish immigrants seeking to escape the Potato Famine in their homeland. Some 4 million left Ireland in the late 1840s to avoid starvation, most of them coming to America. But at least the Irish represented mostly English speakers from a similar ethnic stock. By the end of the nineteenth and the beginning of the twentieth century, Southern and Eastern Europeans, primarily from Italy, the Balkans, and Russia, who represented a completely different ethnic group, replaced the Irish. For longer-established Americans, this was a far more serious problem than the Irish had posed, with the result that after the war there was much more active political work to limit immigration from these areas. In addition, China and Japan had always suffered from immigration restrictions to the West Coast.[92]

The combined prohibition and immigration issues masked two other issues that were important in the 1920s—nativism and religious fundamentalism. Nativism was obviously allied with the immigrant issue in that it was an attempt not only to limit further immigration, but it was an attempt to protect to White Anglo-Saxon Protestant American values from corrupting foreign influences. Its most virulent form came with the revival of the Ku Klux Klan. The Klan, a modern version of the old post-Civil War terrorist

---

91   Burner, *Politics of Provincialism*, 92–99; *Encyclopaedia Britanmnica* 15th ed., s.v. "prohibition."
92   Burner, *Politics of Provincialism*, 15–17; Dan Rather ed., Mark Sullivan *Our Times* (New York: Scribner 1996; abridged reprint of six volumes 1926–1935), 67–69.

organization, was a fraternal organization of primarily of lower class White Anglo-Saxon Protestants focused on stopping immigration from Russia and Eastern Europe, and as such, was anti-Catholic and anti-Jew, as opposed to the anti-black agenda of the historic Klan. The modern Klan was also linked to prohibition, and because of its tendency to use violence, it became the "enforcement" agent to keep various communities and organizations on the "dry" path. The Klan appealed to those people who supported small town traditional values and who considered the inhabitants of the cities as a threat to their way of life. But the thing that made the Klan such a force in the early 1920s was not the intimidation of targeted groups, although there was plenty of that. It was its political activity. With thousands of members the Klan became a force in several states. Like the Anti-Saloon League it was nonpartisan in the sense that it pressed its nativist issues to both parties and focused on the dominate party in each state whether that state was Democrat or Republican. For the Democrats, that meant the states of the South and West that formed the old Bryan coalition. The Klan was seen as representing the pro-farmer, pro-debtor, anti-tariff, Anglo-Saxon progressivism of Bryan and standing against foreign values and the influence of the Eastern cities, particularly New York and Wall Street.

Likewise, religious fundamentalism, which was again on the rise, was an important aspect in the support of Prohibition, principally because of the support given to it by the Protestant churches. Religious fundamentalism was the response of those people who felt threatened by the new age of science and the modernism of the post-World War I era which had been transformed by the conflict. Fundamentalism tended to be rural in character, was anti-intellectual and pro-traditional. In the North it tended to be anti-Catholic. In the South it was anti-evolution. The chief proponent of the link between religious fundamentalism and Prohibition was, of course, William Jennings Bryan. After World War I, Bryan focused on Prohibition, which would be his last great political cause and which he considered a moral good, and the sanctity of the Holy Scripture, most famously in the opposition to evolution. Naturally, he also supported "dry" candidates for public office, both on moral grounds and because he believed that a "dry" presidential candidate was necessary to carry the South and West in order for the Democrats to secure the presidency. With Bryan in the lead, other religious fundamentalist followed in his wake and supported "dry" issues and candidates.

Later as Prohibition lost support in the country, religious fundamentalism became its primary base. Needless to say, nativists and religious fundamentalist viewed the rise of cities political power within the Democratic Party with horror.[93]

With the approach of the 1924 election, the Democratic Party was divided into three segments. In the North and East where its city base had been expanding rapidly, it was primarily urban, ethnic with a large immigration base and "wet." In states such as New York, the 18th Amendment and the Volstead Act (the enforcing bill of the Prohibition amendment) may as well have not been enacted.[94] In the West, the party was primarily agricultural and "dry" with a progressive element to it from the Progressive, Populist and Grange movement of the late nineteenth and early twentieth centuries. The Farmer-Labor Party was a major force in Minnesota and the related states while the Progressive movement was still strong in Wisconsin, California and other states, although its elected officials tended to be Republican as was the case of Robert La Follette in Wisconsin and Hiram Johnson in California. This is why in Congress Democrats and Republicans from the West would join forces on key issues, particularly on farm bills.[95] Finally in the South, the party was also rural and "dry," but with the addition of religious fundamentalism and without the Progressive element that was in the West. In addition to the geographic breakouts of the party, there were the political pressure groups pressing on the party, which have been discussed and which were very powerful.[96]

Democrats in the Northeast cities did not act kindly to the combination of prohibitionist, fundamentalists, anti-immigration forces and the Ku Klux Klan that targeted them. They resented groups like the Klan that promoted white Anglo-Saxon Protestant Americanism to the exclusion of everyone else. They resented the prohibitionist and religious fundamentalists that told them how to live. Thus a backlash resulted in the Catholic and ethnic areas of the Northeast and Midwest against the old Bryan coalition elements.

That is where things stood on the eve of the campaign to select the nominee of the Democratic Party for president in 1924. For the Democrats, the 1924 election would be the most tumultuous election since 1860 when the

---

93   Murray, *103rd Ballot*, 10–20; Burner, *Politics of Provincialism*, 80–93.
94   Burner, *Politics of Provincialism*, 77.
95   Ibid., 73.
96   Ibid., 152.

party fragmented. The 1924 Democratic Convention in New York still has the distinction of being the longest and most bitterly fought-over convention in the history of national political conventions. It took 16 days and 103 ballots to nominate a presidential candidate, and when it was over, the party was in such a shambles that it was trounced in the November election.

As the convention approached, the political forces that had been described earlier went from a focus on the issues that were of interest to them to a presidential candidate that would embody those issues. For the delegates that represented the old Bryan coalition in the South and West, that meant a white Anglo-Saxon Protestant candidate that would be "dry," and protect the traditional small-town values of rural America. This in turn meant someone who not only supported prohibition and the Anti-Saloon League, but also had the support of the Protestant churches and the Ku Klux Klan. Just as important was the fact that he was not from an urban area, and, God forbid, was certainly not from Wall Street. For this group of delegates that person turned out to be William Gibbs McAdoo. Early on, McAdoo began to organize for a presidential nomination for 1924. At the time he looked like the consensus candidate. He was a "dry," anti-Tammany Hall (the New York City Democratic political organization), and anti-Wall Street, even thought he had lived in New York for some thirty years. Thus he was acceptable to the Bryan's South and West. But because of his service in the Wilson Administration, he had contacts with that segment of the party as well. While some of the Eastern establishment opposed him because of his regulatory activity involving the Federal Reserve and the Railroad administration, he had the support of labor because of his pro-labor railroad stance. He was able to put together a strong organization, raise a goodly amount of money, and was well positioned for the primary.

Then just when he had all the pieces together, disaster struck when he was linked to the Teapot Dome scandal involving the sale of naval oil reserves. This crippled McAdoo right up to the convention. He won some of the primaries, but was never in the commanding position that he had been before.[97]

Opposing McAdoo was the candidate of the East, Governor Alfred E. Smith of New York. Smith had been born on the lower East Side of Manhattan in 1873, gotten involved in New York City politics by 1902 and in 1918

---

97   Murray, 103rd Ballot, 39–50.

was first elected governor. After losing his re-election bid in 1920, he won re-election in 1922 and was now the most important Democratic politician in the Northeast. As much as he was supported in that part of the country, he was an anathema to the South and West. He was from the city, he was ethnic Irish, and German, he was a "wet," and just as repugnant, he was a Catholic. In addition, he was strongly opposed to the Klan because of their violent attacks on Catholics.[98] Thus in the candidacies of Smith and McAdoo, two candidates could not have been more diametrically opposed to each, and it showed in the political bloodbath that was to follow.

But before the ordeal of the balloting was to begin, the platform had to be resolved. The platform, like the nomination for president, was to reflect the deep divisions and bitter fighting that was characteristic of the convention. The real policy crisis for the convention was the Klan. The majority of delegates probably did not like the Klan and its activities, but the fact remained that it was too politically important to be publicly condemned. The compromise plank involving the Ku Klux Klan was actually a plank opposing the activity by any organization attempting to limit religious liberty or political freedom. This was as far as the committee wanted to go. But the opponents of the plank wanted the Klan to be specifically named. They were saying that the draft statement would not be acceptable to the Northeast. Supporters of the Klan said naming the Klan would be unacceptable to the South and Midwest. Given the situation regarding the Klan in the convention, there was bound to be a minority report to the full convention, and the minority report specifying the Klan made it to the floor with the support of the Smith delegates. The debate and vote on the minority plank went into the wee hours of the morning, involving fists fights, name calling, and all other kinds of sordid activity. Ultimately, with state delegations switching their votes and the entire voting procedure disintegrating into chaos, the anti-Klan minority report lost by one vote. The vote then created another disruption on the convention floor and the session was gaveled to a close. The division on the anti-Klan plank only gave a glimpse of what would happen on the presidential balloting.[99]

The process for the Democratic Party nomination for President would take a record 103 ballots over a period of ten days. Early on, it was clear that it

---

98 Ibid., 58–71.
99 Ibid., 144–161.

was deadlocked. McAdoo had the most votes and at times during the ten day stretch came close to having the majority. But the Smith forces had the votes to deny McAdoo the two thirds vote he needed for the nomination. Thus the ballots dragged on until by the 100th ballot nothing was going to change. On the 101st ballot, both Smith and McAdoo released their delegates. Eventually, with the help of James Cox, votes began to cluster around John W. Davis and he was eventually nominated on the 103rd on July 9.[100] But the Democrats were in a shambles and never had a viable campaign that year. Even more disruptive was that the more liberal voters along with the American Federation of Labor supported Senator Robert La Follette's third party Progressive ticket and were able to not only get Wisconsin's 13 electoral votes, but run a strong second in a number of states that siphoned of Democratic voters. In the end, Calvin Coolidge and the Republicans routed the divided Democrats. Coolidge got nearly twice as many votes as Davis and had 382 electoral votes to Davis' 136 and La Follette's 13.[101]

One of the outcomes of the wreckage of the 1924 election was that it pretty well dictated what was going to happen for president in 1928. While Davis, McAdoo and the rest self-immolated in the 1924 election, Al Smith won re-election as Governor of New York. He would then go on to win an unprecedented fourth term in 1926. By 1927, Smith was clearly the front runner for the 1928 nomination with no serious opposition. But just because Smith was going to be the nominee didn't mean that there wasn't going to be any problems. He was the reluctant choice of many delegates and all the issues that had kept Smith from the nomination in 1924 were still there in 1928. Large segments of the public were still opposed to the idea of a Catholic in the presidency. The Ku Klux Klan, which had been in membership freefall because the relatively good economic times of the mid-1920s, drained the source of dissatisfaction that a group like the Klan thrives on, suddenly was briefly re-energized because of the Smith candidacy. Likewise, the Anti-Saloon League, which was now on the defensive as support for prohibition was falling rapidly, also got a brief lease on life. Then there was Smith's continuing parochial behavior as a candidate who was unable to relate to people and issues outside his New York and Northeastern base. The Democratic platform that Smith ran on was barely distinguishable from the Republican platform,

---

100   Ibid., 205.
101   *American Heritage Book of Presidents*, vol. 9, 809. Many other sources for this data.

just as it was in 1924, with no ability to define itself from the other party. The "me too" politics of the Democrats would hurt them right up to the eve of the 1932 convention and election. Finally, the most important problem for the Democrats was Republican Party prosperity (although it was unraveling at the edges) and the popularity of their candidate, Herbert Hoover.

Even if no other problems for the Democrats had occurred in 1928, the economy and Hoover would have been enough for a Republican victory. But the other divisive elements within the Democratic Party led to the vicious "whispering campaign" which resulted in an even bigger loss at the top of the ticket. Hoover got 21 million votes to Smith's 15 million, and an overwhelming 444 electoral votes to 87. Smith's positions on prohibition, the Ku Klux Klan, as well as being a Catholic hurt him grievously in the South. For the Republicans, it was their biggest inroad into the South and was a rough draft of what they would do at the end of the century with the Red-state bloc. The Republicans picked up Florida, North Carolina, Tennessee, Texas, and Virginia.[102]

The issue that swept away all the others that the Democrats had been dealing with in 1928 was the stock market crash of October 1929 and the ensuing Great Depression. Hoover's and the Republican's inability to deal with the economic crisis made them as unpopular as they had been popular before. Moreover, the issues involving the economy dominated the political landscape to the exclusion of all others and gave the Democrats the means of becoming the majority party in the country. That process began with the congressional election of 1930. The Democrats took marginal control of the House of Representatives with 220 members to the Republicans 214, with one independent. It was a gain of 53 seats. In the Senate the Democrats gained 8 seats, with the result that the Republicans held the slimmest of majorities: 48 to the Democrats' 47 with Robert La Follette, Jr. holding a seat for the Wisconsin Progressive Party. The Democrats would take complete control in 1932, and in subsequent elections, the Democratic majority would reach levels unimaginable just a few years earlier.[103] The Democrats would be the majority party in this country until the 1994 Republican landslide.

But one would have never known that in 1931, the year they took control of the House. For the party had been so cowed into submission by then that

---

102   Robert Hunt Lyman ed., *The World Almanac and Book of Facts for 1931*(New York: The New York World 1931), 910–911. There are many other sources for this data.

103   *American Heritage Book of Presidents*, vol. 10, 835, 898–899. Many other sources for this data.

they were very hesitant to take action once they had control. After years of "me, too" politics, there were very little in the way of differences in the two parties. In the case of taxes the Democrats had gone from opposing the Mellon tax cuts in the early 1920s to adopting the Republicans positions. By the time of the Coolidge Administration, they were proposing tax cuts beyond what Coolidge had requested. And during the early years of the Hoover Administration, the Democrats tended to support the Hoover Administration policies. The Democrats went even so far as to say after the 1930 election that they would co-operate with Hoover and not propose any "dangerous" legislation.[104]

Thus, the Democratic drift of the previous ten years continued well after the 1930 election and into early 1932. The decisive break, and the beginning of the New Deal era Democratic Party, came with the revolt over the Hoover Administration's plans for a manufacturer's sales tax. Many Democrats in the House considered such a tax to be regressive and a tax on the poor. As a result, a bloc of Democrats broke away from the tax, rebelled against Speaker John Nance Garner, and killed the tax. This led to a series of votes which instituted an income tax surcharge similar to the one passed by Democrats in World War I. Speaker Garner then gave his support to an economic relief bill that had languished in Congress. These series of votes paved the way for the more radical solutions of the New Deal that would define the party for decades to come.[105]

The final chapter in the Democrats emergence from minority status came from the political strategy of Franklin Roosevelt. At the request of Al Smith, Roosevelt ran for governor of New York in 1928, and won the election by a mere 25,564 votes. To deal with the Depression after taking office, Roosevelt experimented with ideas such as supporting public power and borrowing to fund relief programs. Politically, he re-organized the Democratic Party in New York State. So, in an earlier version of Democratic National Chairman Howard Dean's 50-State Plan, Roosevelt set out to rebuild the upstate Democratic organization. He also at the same time developed programs for the upstate counties. When the results were in for the 1930 election, Roosevelt carried 41 of the 57 upstate counties and carried the state by over 700,000

---

104 Burner, *Politics of Provincialism*, 175.
105 Ibid., 177–178.

votes. Overnight the election made him the leading candidate for the Democratic nomination in 1932.

Roosevelt's next task was to unite the party nationally. He backed the growing city faction over the old rural coalition. Most importantly, he deemphasized the social issues of the previous two conventions, particularly prohibition, and emphasized the economic issues of the growing Depression. Finally, his last action to unify the party at the 1932 Convention was to get his leading opponent, Speaker John Nance Garner to join the ticket as Vice President, and then went on to win the 1932 election.[106]

Roosevelt's achievement from 1929 to 1933 was to create the foundation of the great mid-twentieth century Democratic Coalition that dominated the political landscape for the next sixty years. Roosevelt's advantage as a candidate was that he was not tied to any specific interest group and since 1924 had been talking to all of them. Another factor was that Roosevelt emphasized economic and class issues over the more divisive social ones. Most importantly, Roosevelt made the connection that Bryan, Smith, McAdoo, and everyone else had not made, and that was that both Smith and Bryan represented the working class of their respective constituents in the cities and the farms. It was Roosevelt that put the two groups together in a national working class coalition.[107] Finally, it Roosevelt's great assets as a candidate and his extraordinary ability to convey his message, particularly on radio, that solidified that coalition in the minds of the voters. It was the strategy and the message, plus the opportunity created by the Depression that ultimately made the Democrats the majority party.

What does this story of the Democratic Party of some ninety years ago mean for us today? Well, clearly there are a number of parallels. The most important of those parallels is that the Democrats were out of power. In both the 1920s and the recent era, the Republicans controlled both the Congress and the White House. This fragmented the policy message since the party was not in control of the legislative or executive branch of government in order to unify their message. The policy vacuum that was a result of being out of power created another similarity for Democrats of both eras: social issues created a lot of friction. Immigration was an issue that caused problems in both the 1920s and the 2000s, as it had in other eras as well. In 1924, it was

---

106   Ibid., 246–251.
107   Murray, *103rd Ballot*, 81, 285.

diffused by federal legislation, and in the current era it comes and it goes as a hot button issue, usually depending on the job situation. Immigration also has the capacity to impact other issues. Religious fundamentalism was also an issue for both eras. Like immigration, it was a flashpoint for other issues. It was also very polarizing. It strongly appealed to rural constituencies while urban areas were appalled by it. The Scopes trial ended it as a major issue after 1925, but like immigration, it has periodically surfaced. In both eras, though, religious fundamentalism fostered other key issues with strong religious overtones: in the 1920s it was prohibition and the Ku Klux Klan; today it is abortion and gay rights. Both eras not only saw religion energize other issues, but also brought about polarization between religious groups: in the 1920s, it was Protestants against Catholics and Jews; today, it is Christians and Jews against Muslims.

Because of the policy vacuum and because of these highly corrosive issues, the Democratic Party fragmented in both eras. This showed up in both the 1924 and 2004 campaigns. The differences in 1924 were quite stark and they were played out in the form of political theater in New York's old Madison Square Garden in 1924. The advent of the repeal of the two-thirds rule to obtain the nomination and the front loading of primaries helped insure that the 2004 convention would not have the histrionics of the one in 1924. But the divisions of the party, particularly with regard to social issues and the Iraq War were just as deep. And in both eras the party came out of the convention with a compromise or "electable" candidate that all factions could support, but not elect. In the case of John W. Davis and the Democrats in 1924, they never really had a chance, particularly since La Follette's Progressives fragmented what campaign their campaign could have been at the ballot box. John Kerry and the Democrats of 2004 did have a chance, but it was undercut by a lack of conviction and message as to what the Democrats stood for.

This leads to other similarities of both eras of Democrats: an inability to define their party, what it stood for, and why people should vote for it. Both eras suffered from a fear to be substantially different than the Republicans majority of the time. In both cases this led to the "me too" political phenomenon in which they mimicked the popular policies of the time and only tried to be marginally different. Even as late as 1932 and with the Great Depression having annihilated the Republican programs and agenda, the Democrats had only a marginally more progressive platform than the Republicans, some of which was finally the result of the progressive Democratic revolt in the House of Representatives in the spring of that year. Similarly, in 2000, Ralph Nader made his oft-repeated "dime" comment about George W. Bush and Al Gore. Then again, in 2004, with the Iraq War raging and popularity for it and for the Bush Administration plummeting, when Bush asked John Kerry whether he would have supported the Iraq Resolution if he knew then what he knew now, Kerry said "yes." In one word, the single most defining issue in the campaign disappeared.

Presidential campaigns are not the only place where defining issues and programs have been a problem for Democrats. Congress has been a major problem as well. Throughout the 1920s many issues regarding the economy, the tariff, farm relief, taxes and other such items came up for debate in the Congress. And as the decade proceeded, the Democrats drifted further away from their populist positions of the later nineteenth and early twentieth centuries, and aligned themselves more and more with the mainline business Republicans as opposed to the more progressive rural Republicans. By 1924, the merging of the two parties' positions was such that Robert La Follette in alliance with the American Federation of Labor and other agricultural groups created the Progressive Party with the idea of replacing the Democrats as the major political party in opposition. That did not occur and Democrats continued to be ideologically close to the Republicans right up to 1932. Even when it was clear that the economic crisis of the early 1930s would give them their opportunity to be the majority party again, many Democrats in Congress did not want to take a radically different approach to policy so as to not unduly alarm the business community and other conservative groups. The Democratic approach at that time was an anti-Republican/Hoover Administration approach which worked well in the 1930 election and was the logical strategy for 1932. But by mid-1932 the crisis was too great to be ignored any longer and the Democrats both in Congress and elsewhere began to develop the preliminary ideas that would later be the New Deal.

As was the case in the 1920s, the Democrats in Congress blended into the Republican landscape after 2002. They supported a number of conservative Republican initiatives such as tax cuts, a banker friendly bankruptcy bill, and controversial appointments of Chief Justice John Roberts and Justice Samuel Alito to the Supreme Court. In these and other domestic issues the Democrats in Congress found little real support in the country with the resultant losses in the 2002 and 2004 elections. But the defining issue of this era has been the war in Iraq, and on this issue the Democrats showed the same timidity that their counterparts showed with the Great Depression eighty years before. Even with the Iraq War having been demonstrated as a certified foreign policy catastrophe, the party as a whole was unable to challenge the Bush Administration in the 2006 election. Many in the party felt that their best position was to say and do little as the Republicans self-destructed. Much of the strategy for the Democratic Congressional Campaign Committee (DCCC) was to find Iraq War veterans (many who supported the war) as candidates. Outright opponents of the war were discouraged.

A case in point was California's 11th Congressional District, the district with the best opportunity in the state for the Democrats to gain a seat. The 2004 candidate was Jerry McNerney, a last minute anti-war candidate who was able to organize a successful write-in campaign in the March primary to get on the November ballot, where he eventually lost to the incumbent Republican Richard Pombo. Undeterred, McNerney began running again in 2006. But the DCCC felt that McNerney was not the right candidate for the district and so they encouraged Steve Filson, a veteran with less political experience and name recognition to run in the primary, backing him with a great deal of money. McNerney won the primary, and the DCCC abandoned the district. It was only late in the campaign when polls showed that McNerney could win that the DCCC gave him any support. McNerney went on to win his election. The DCCC ignored many anti-war candidates with opportunities to win and who won in 2006.[108]

But the signature event that showed Democratic timidity on the Iraq War issue was the treatment of Democratic Representative John Murtha of Pennsylvania. Murtha, an ex-marine and Vietnam veteran with thirty years in Congress and unparalleled access to the views of the opinions of the US military leadership advocated in 2005 the redeployment of US forces outside Iraq to staging areas in neighboring countries. Murtha also stated that the current policy was not only a failure but that it was destroying the military. Since Murtha was often known to state the views of the generals and admirals that these people could not publicly say themselves, Murtha's comments on Iraq were considered highly significant and his personal background was

108   John V. Walsh, "The War Loses, Voters Win, Rahm's Losers," *Counterpunch*, November 11, 2006, http://counterpunch.com/walsh11112006.html.

such that his patriotism and integrity on the subject could not be challenged. In other words, Murtha gave the perfect cover for his fellow Democrats in Congress to publicly attack the war. But aside from Minority Leader Nancy Pelosi and DNC Chairman Howard Dean, Democratic officials ran away from Murtha like scared rabbits. Just as was the case in 1932, Democrats in 2006 were waiting for political control to fall into their hands rather than seizing it.

The final piece of the analogy between the Democrats of the 1920s and the Democrats of today has yet to be written. That is, how do the Democrats achieve the majority party status in 2008 that they achieved in 1932? Some of the pieces are already there. The country was faced with an economic crisis in 1929–1932 that the Democrats took advantage of. Today, the Iraq War, and the devastating impact that it is having on the country, both domestically and overseas, provides a similar opportunity. Added to that is the potential economic crisis that could be triggered at any time by the mounting fiscal and trade deficits, the ongoing bursting of the housing bubble, and the potential for a majority shifting political alignment is very great. The question is how to put the pieces together. Roosevelt was able to put a coalition of Bryan's rural South and West with Smith's cities and the Northeast. He was able to do that because the economic crisis of the time allowed him to focus on class and economic issues and downplay the social issues that had ripped apart the party in the 1920s. Today, a Democratic leader will have to find a way to align all or part of the Red states with the Blue states to achieve that majority. In analyzing such a potential coalition, many political analysts have looked at the socially conservative Southern Red states and the libertarian conservative Western Red states and have tried to make a case to merge either group to the Blue states to form a majority. Some have pointedly said drop the South and align with the West where the party had some success at the state level in 2004 in places like Colorado and Montana. Others are saying that current polling offer opportunities in both parts of the country. Certainly Howard Dean believes that to be the case. Others debate which social issues will undermine any success in the Red states. But in looking at the historical political record, there is one man besides Roosevelt who was able present a progressive, even radical, message to the Red states and was able to retain their allegiance and support for election after election.

That was William Jennings Bryan, and it is to his speeches that we look to find some of the answers to appealing to Red states.

7. William Jennings Bryan and His Red-State Legacy

When the woes of the Democratic Party were discussed after 2004 election, one of the reasons that was given for the party's failure was its lack of substance or concern about "values." It was said that Democrats failed the "Budweiser test," that most Democrats were not the kind of people that you would want to sit down at a dinner or a picnic table and have a Budweiser with. Democrats are an elitist group that sent too much time groveling for corporate donations and really did not care about ordinary people or their values. This, of course, was much of the story line in Thomas Frank's *What's the Matter with Kansas?* Polling such as that done by American Environics has also shown that the character of a candidate is more important than his policies. Character acts as the gatekeeper in the voter's evaluation process. If the candidate fails the character test, the rest of his candidacy doesn't matter. But the character issue does not encompass all of the values-related issues of a campaign, and what issue constitutes a value is open to question. Finally, many analysts believe that the Democrats failed on the security issue rather than values issues. People, still shell-shocked by 9/11 were looking to presidential candidates that made them feel safe, and that John Kerry and an equivocating Democratic Party, failed the security test.

Regardless of what was the real reason for the Democratic defeat in 2004, many pundits, and politicians came out with their own reason of what happened and what was the miracle remedy or strategy to solve the problem. Some said that opposing the Iraq war cost the Democrats votes. Others said supporting the war was the problem. For some like Hillary Clinton it was a question of moving to the political "center," be less strident on abortion, gay rights, and other "values" issues. Above all, it meant being non-committal on Iraq beyond the fact that the Bush Administration had made a mess there. For someone like Russ Feingold, it meant doing what Karl Rove and the Republicans have done in all their elections—support the party's activist base.

One of the overarching themes has been that the next Democratic presidential candidate needs to show a greater display of his or her religious values in order to keep up with Republicans and their evangelical Christian base. As such, we have seen a great deal of political posturing bordering on the artificial on this subject. One Democrat who has made a better connection between political and the spiritual has been Illinois Senator Barack Obama. Obama has been praised for his ability to connect with churchgoers across the country. Beyond melding the sacred with profane, the overriding issue of all of this is how the Democratic Party can take back the Red states. Aside from Franklin Roosevelt and his coalition, only one Democratic leader has been able to blend a progressive agenda with the rural and Christian ethos of what are now the Red states. That person was William Jennings Bryan.

Bryan, if he is ever brought up at all, gets a rough going over by political analysts. For many people, their vision of Bryan is from the 1960 film *Inherit the Wind*, the movie based on the 1955 play about the Scopes "Monkey" trial in Dayton, Tennessee in 1925, which turned out to be Bryan's last moment on the public stage. The most famous scene from the trial and its stage and movie re-enactments is the cross-examination of Bryan, who was part of the prosecution team defending Tennessee's anti-evolution law, by famed defense attorney Clarence Darrow. In the proceedings, Darrow made Bryan out to be a bigoted fool as Bryan testified that certain stories in the Bible were actually true. Famed news writer H.L. Mencken, who attended the trail, shredded what was left of Bryan's reputation in a series of merciless columns run across the country. Five days after the conclusion of the trial, which was won by the prosecution, Bryan died in his sleep in Dayton at the age of sixty-five.

It was a sad end to a storied career, and for many people, it was a shame that Bryan had not pulled out of public life ten years earlier when he had resigned as Woodrow Wilson's Secretary of State, for his personal reputation would have been dramatically different. In that last ten years, Bryan's passion had turned away from the great progressive issues that he had advocated for decades and toward those issues of prohibition and anti-evolution which were close to his second love—the Christian church. But even in Bryan's pursuits at the end of his life, his actions were not those of a simple-minded religious fanatic, for they were based on his long-time support of progressive issues. Bryan saw the church as an agent of reform, not an authoritarian institution to be blindly obeyed. Prohibition was his response to the devastating toll that alcohol had on society, families, and its corresponding contribution to poverty. Anti-evolution was Bryan's and other Christians' response to the more sinister views of evolution made by the Social Darwinist. For Bryan, to support evolution was to support Herbert Spencer's cold blooded survival of the fittest doctrine, which not only was against most Christian beliefs, but was directly counter to what Bryan championed on behalf of the poor and politically powerless all his life. If his views on the Bible were overly simplistic, at least there was a human face on those views.

Today, looking back on those positions, most Americans have some ambivalent feelings about them. On an issue such as abortion, even supporters such as Bill Clinton have taken the contradictory position that they should be "safe, legal, and rare." More Americans probably support something like stem-cell research. But even the most ardently liberal persons have some second thoughts about genetically modified foods. And when one realizes that such "modern" people like Mencken were raving anti-Semites, and one looks at the dark corners where the Nazis took the issue of evolution and Social Darwinism, one can have a little more sympathy for the William Jennings Bryan that spoke on behalf of the state of Tennessee in Dayton during that hot July of 1925.

But it is the far greater legacy of the earlier Bryan before 1915 that is of importance to Democrats, for Bryan was one of the great Democratic leaders in the history of the party. For sixteen years, from his nomination for president in 1896 to his support for Woodrow Wilson in 1912, he was the undisputed leader of the party. No other politician, not even Franklin Roosevelt, led a major political party for so long. After Wilson's election 1912, he continued to be a major force in the party right up to the 1924 convention. What is even more remarkable is that throughout that period of twenty-eight years, he never held elective political office. In fact, in his entire political career, he held public office for only six years as a member of Congress from 1891 to 1895, and as Secretary of State from 1913 to 1915. During most of his political career he had to make his own living, mostly by giving speeches, and editing newspapers, such as the *Omaha World-Herald* and his famous newspaper, *The Commoner*. By today's standards, for someone to be a major national political figure from such a political base is extraordinary. Three times, he was an unsuccessful Democratic candidate for president, in the celebrated election of 1896, and then again in 1900 and 1908—the only failed candidate of a major political party to be nominated for a third time. Such was his influence during his political life that historians recognize that only Theodore Roosevelt and Woodrow Wilson were more important political figures during Bryan's thirty-five year political career.

More important from our standpoint was the fact that not only was Bryan a great Democratic Party leader, but that he was the champion of a number of progressive causes. In his day he was considered a radical who did not let facts get into the way of his opinions. The issues that he advocated read like a who's who of the Progressive Era: direct election of US Senators (eventually the 17th Amendment to the Constitution), a progressive income tax (which he ratified as the 16th Amendment as Secretary of State), prohibition (eventually the 18th Amendment), the establishment of the Department of Labor, and women suffrage (eventually the 19th Amendment), all enacted in his lifetime. In addition, he had come to national prominence for his stand on bimetallism, or the free coinage of silver in a ratio of 16 to 1 for gold. He was also the first major political candidate to address the issue of de facto American Imperialism in the election of 1900. Most striking was his advocacy of two issues that would not become realities until after his death. The first, the insurance of bank deposits, would not take effect until the establishment of the Federal Deposit Insurance Corporation in 1934. Most modern of all was his advocacy in the 1908 campaign of political campaign financial disclosure, an issue that would not become law until the 1970s. Bryan himself had been the victim of the first heavily-financed presidential campaign when William McKinley's campaign manager (and Bush political advisor Karl Rove's icon) Mark Hanna outspent Bryan and the Democrats by a factor of seven to one, with the support of large corporate campaign contributions.

So while Bryan's religious views may have seemed simplistic, his political views were well ahead of his time.

But it is not just Bryan's political views that should be important to us today; it is how he stated them and whom he stated them to that are important to modern-day Democrats. For Bryan was acknowledged as one the great orators in the history of this country. Even people who felt that Bryan's speeches relied more on emotion than on substance recognized that he was a spellbinding speaker. He is probably the only presidential candidate who won the nomination of a major political party based on a speech given at a political convention. Bryan began his career in the era before mature phonograph recording and before electronic voice amplification and the microphone. He had a resonant tenor voice that could carry large halls with thousands of listeners, essential for public speakers of his day. During most of his career, Bryan's gift as a speaker attracted large crowds, and he was able to obtain a substantial income from them to carry on his political work without being employed in other ventures. Long before Ronald Reagan was born, William Jennings Bryan was America's "Great Communicator."

In addition to being a great speaker, Bryan was an outstanding campaigner. He was just thirty-six when he received the Democratic nomination in 1896. Realizing that he was at a severe financial handicap against McKinley and Hanna, he set out to conduct what is considered operationally the first modern national political campaign. While McKinley was giving speeches from his front porch in Canton, Ohio, Bryan traveled by train across the country, the first campaign to go to the people on such a large scale. During the summer and fall of 1896, Bryan traveled over 18,000 miles in some twenty-seven states,[109] making hundreds of speeches and talking in person to tens of thousands Americans. By the late summer, he had made the seemingly invincible McKinley campaign look vulnerable. It was only with an unprecedented $3.5 million budget, over a thousand paid workers and a veritable blizzard of pamphlets extolling McKinley that Hanna was able to turn the tide and win the election.[110] Nevertheless, Bryan's campaign set new standards in creating the first truly national grassroots campaign and won him the devoted following of millions of Americans that would last through two more campaigns and throughout his lifetime.

---

109   *Encyclopaedia Britannica*, 15th ed., s.v. "Bryan, William Jennings."
110   *Encyclopaedia Britannica*, 15th ed., s.v. "Hanna, Mark."

Finally, even more important than his assets as a speaker and campaigner, the most important aspect of Bryan's career from the standpoint of modern Democrats was that he was able to accomplish all of this from a political base in what is now known as the Red states. A breakdown of the 1896 election shows that 171 of Bryan's 176 electoral votes came from Red states. He got one Blue-state vote from California (which split its nine votes) and Washington's four votes. The remainder came from his famous Southern and Western coalition, which included all the states of the old Confederacy in the South and much of the High Plains and Rocky Mountains. The notable exception was the Midwest that virtually all went for McKinley, including his home state of Ohio, as well as Indiana, and Iowa. Although Bryan lost some key Blue and Red states that Cleveland had won in 1892, such as New York, Illinois and Indiana (and which cost him the 1896 election), he was able to pick up traditional Republican states in the West. In any event, there is no question that Bryan had great appeal to much of what we now call the Red states.[111]

It is the totality of Bryan's appeal to voters that should interest Democrats today. As a private citizen most of his political life, he had no speechwriters or spin-doctors. He had no government public affairs office manufacturing his message. What came from Bryan, for better or worse (and to his opponents he was a wild-eyed radical demagogue), came from the man himself. In modern parlance, he was the real deal. While his message was not sufficient to win the presidency, it was loyally supported by millions of Americans, many of whom the Democratic Party is trying to re-establish contact with today. His ability to convey such a message and attract such voters is what makes him relevant today. The essence of Bryan's appeal is that he was able to take a progressive agenda and infuse it with religious symbolism that resonated with rural Middle America. The most famous example of this is in the closing of the "Cross of Gold" speech: "You shall not press down upon the brow of labor this crown of thorns" and "you shall not crucify mankind upon a cross of gold."[112] In these closing statements, Bryan has artfully combined the toil and the aspirations of working people with

---

111   *The 1929 World Almanac and Book of Facts* facsimile edition (Workman Publishing 1971), 908. Many other sources for this data.

112   William Jennings Bryan, *Speeches of William Jennings Bryan Revised and Arranged by Himself* (New York: Funk & Wagnalls 1909), vol. 1, 249. Subsequent notes from this source are in parenthesis in the text.

the Crucifixion. While this is his most famous example, it is typical of the kind of message he delivered throughout his career.

In order to appreciate Bryan's work, it is necessary to analyze the speeches he gave throughout his career, particularly the early years up to 1908 when he was a presidential candidate. And probably the best way to do that is to look at the collection of speeches that Bryan put together himself. While Bryan gave thousands of speeches in his lifetime, the best source is *Speeches of William Jennings Bryan Revised and Arranged by Himself*. This is a small, two-volume set of speeches edited by Bryan and published by the Funk & Wagnalls Company in November of 1909.

An excellent example of Bryan's handiwork on the stump is a very short speech by him entitled "Naboth's Vineyard," which is in Volume 2 of the Funk & Wagnalls speeches. It was delivered in the winter of 1898–1899 in Denver, Colorado and was one of the earliest speeches by anyone opposing the US colonization of the Philippines. This speech is transcribed in its entirety below:

> The Bible tells us that Ahab, the king, wanted the vineyard of Naboth and was sorely grieved because the owner thereof refused to part with the inheritance of his fathers. Then followed a plot, and false charges were preferred against Naboth to furnish an excuse for getting rid of him.
>
> "Thou shalt not covet!" "Thou shalt not bear false witness!" "Thou shalt not kill"—three commandments broken, and still a fourth, "Thou shalt not steal," to be broken in order to get a little piece of ground! And what was the result? When the king went forth to take possession, Elijah, that brave old prophet of the early days, met him and pronounced against him the sentence of the Almighty. "In the place where the dogs licked the blood of Naboth shall the dogs lick thy blood, even thine."
>
> Neither his own exalted position nor the lowly station of his victim could save him from the vengeful hand of outraged justice. His case was tried in a court where neither wealth, nor rank, nor power, could shield the transgressor.
>
> Wars of conquest have their origin in covetousness, and the history of the human race has been written in characters of blood because rulers have looked with longing eyes upon the lands of others.
>
> Covetousness is prone to seek the aid of false pretense to carry out its plans, but what it cannot secure by persuasion it takes by the sword.
>
> Senator Teller's amendment to the intervention resolution saved the Cubans from the covetousness of those who are so anxious to secure possession of the island, that they are willing to deny the truth of the declaration

of our own Congress, that "the people of Cuba are, and of right ought to be, free."

Imperialism might expand the nation's territory, but it would contract the nation's purpose. It is not a step forward toward a broader destiny; it is a step backward, toward the narrow views of kings and emperors.

Dr. Taylor has aptly exprest [sic] it in his "Creed of the Flag," when he asks: "Shall we turn to the old world again/ With the penitent prodigal's cry?"

I answer, never. This republic is not a prodigal son; it has not spent its substance in riotous living. It is not ready to retrace its steps and, with shamed face and trembling voice, solicit an [sic] humble place among the servants of royalty. It has not sinned against heaven, and God grant that the crowned heads of Europe may never have occasion to kill the fatted calf to commemorate its return from reliance upon the will of the people to dependence upon the authority which flows from regal birth or superior force.

We cannot afford to enter on a colonial policy. The theory upon which a government is built is a matter of vital importance. The national idea has a controlling influence upon the thought and the character of the people. Our national idea is self-government, and unless we are ready to abandon that idea forever we cannot ignore it in dealing with the Filipinos.

That idea is entwined with our traditions; it permeates our history; it is part of our literature.

That idea has given eloquence to the orator and inspiration to the poet. Take from our national hymns the three words, free, freedom and liberty, and they would be as meaningless as would be our flag if robbed of its red, white, and blue.

Other nations may dream of wars of conquest and of distant dependencies governed by external force; not so with the United States.

The fruits of imperialism, be they bitter or sweet, must be left to the subjects of monarchy. This is the one tree of which the citizens of a republic may not partake. It is the voice of the serpent, not the voice of God, that bids us eat (vol.2, 6–8).

The subject of "Naboth's Vineyard" was imperialism. The issues that Bryan is referring to are the outgrowths of the Spanish-American War of 1898. While Bryan supported the war and the liberation of the Cuban people from Spain, he had much different views of what was going on the Philippines, which was also acquired from Spain, but instead of being set up as an independent nation, became an American colony. In the Philippines, the reaction to the US was the resistance movement (shall we say insurgency) led by Emilio Aguinaldo who ran a guerilla war until he was captured and the resistance crushed in 1901. In the United States, Bryan and several prominent

Americans, including Mark Twain organized opposition to the new colonial-ist policies. Imperialism and the guerilla war in the Philippines would stand alongside the free-coinage of silver as the major planks in Bryan second pres-idential campaign against McKinley in 1900 and it would also be an issue in his 1908 campaign against William Howard Taft.

The above speech encapsulated much of Bryan's artistry. Like most of Bryan's speeches and written text, Naboth's Vineyard's is imbued with his-torical literary text, most significantly Biblical text. The title of the speech and the opening text refers to the story in 1 Kings 21 of the Old Testament. Likewise, the recitation of four of the Ten Commandments from Exodus, the use of the parable of the Prodigal Son from Luke, and the inferences to the Tree of Knowledge and the Serpent from the Garden of Eden in Genesis also adds powerful Biblical references. Bryan speaks of imperialism in the con-text of these references and directly links them in his statement that "wars of conquest have their origin in covetousness." A modern politician would probably use the word "greed" in place of the Biblical term, but to Bryan the great political questions of his time were moral questions, and Biblical references in his speeches were a logical outgrowth of this viewpoint. While the prose is of the late nineteenth century, the fundamental issues are not. When Bryan says that "covetousness is prone to seek the aid of false pretense to carry out its plans," one cannot help but think of the many fabrications that the Bush Administration used to get us into Iraq. Bryan also brought up another point that has been stated by many Democrats in the 2006 election, namely, our position in the world. He stated that "our national idea is self government, and unless we are ready to abandon that idea forever we cannot ignore it in dealing with the Filipinos." Invading another nation that did not attack us for the sake of regime change as was done in the case of Iraq puts us in the position of sacrificing our values, as Bryan said, and eroding our standing in the world.

"Naboth's Vineyard" is a succinct example of how Bryan combined moral imagery of the Bible with critical issues of the day. While Bryan most often used stories from the Holy Scripture, classic stories such as those by Homer were also employed. These sources would have been widely known to rural audiences who did not have the access to vast libraries of information, as was the case with Americans living in the cities. It allowed him to connect with these audiences in a way that speakers that are more sophisticated could not, and it was a natural part of his oratory and writings based on his educational and religious upbringing that gave his speeches an authenticity to rural voters that could not be fabricated or questioned.

A further clue into Bryan's approach to his speeches and writings come from a remarkable speech he gave on "Lincoln as an Orator" in Springfield, Illinois on February 12, 1909 on Abraham Lincoln's one hundredth birthday. This speech is also in Volume 2 of the Funk & Wagnalls speeches (vol. 2, 419–425). The speech is of note for two reasons. First, it is an analysis of one the greatest American public speakers by another. Second, it is an analysis of a famous Republican leader by a famous Democratic leader. It goes without saying that, although he never heard Lincoln give a speech and could only have read them, Lincoln's speeches were an inspiration to Bryan.

Bryan points out that Lincoln's political influence and presidential nomination was based on his speeches. He was little known outside of Illinois and it was his debates with Stephen Douglas that brought him to prominence. The very thing could be said of Bryan up to the "Cross of Gold" speech. Of the Gettysburg Address Bryan said it was "not surpassed, if equaled, in beauty, simplicity, force, and appropriateness by any speech of the same length in any language. It is the world's model in eloquence, elegance, and condensation." Like Bryan, Lincoln frequently used Bible language and illustrations. The famous "House Divided" speech from the Lincoln–Douglas debates had as its inspiration Mark 3:25. It is said that Lincoln spent several hours trying to develop the language to illustrate his point that the republic could not survive half slave and half free before he settled on the passage from Mark. Needless to say, much about what Bryan said about Lincoln equally applied to Bryan himself, and they were the guidelines that Bryan used in his own speeches.

But Bryan's speeches were more than about effect. True, he made his living primarily as a speaker, speaking on many topics. But the speeches would be forgotten today if it were not for the issues behind the speeches that he advocated. Bryan was not just a Bible-spouting evangelist, although he used the evangelist's tools. He was the greatest advocate of the working class (both in the field and in the factory) of his day. He was clearly the foe of the industrialist and Wall Street, and one of the reasons that he failed to win in 1896, in addition to being massively outspent, was the fear and intimidation that employers put on their workers not to vote for Bryan saying that a Bryan victory would cost the workers their jobs.

At the core of Bryan's politics was his belief that the capitalists were exploiting the common man. But like Lincoln on the slavery issue, Bryan was able to convey the economic issue on behalf of the working man better than any politician of his day. It is doubtful that Theodore Roosevelt or Woodrow Wilson would have been able to enact their progressive reforms without the foundation that Bryan laid. It is not surprising that Bryan was known as "The Great Commoner" throughout his political career and that his death in 1925 was cause for national mourning.

Bryan's most celebrated effort on behalf of working people is his famous "Cross of Gold" speech, given on July 8, 1896 at the Democratic National Convention in Chicago. It is arguably the most famous speech ever given at a national political convention and is the only one that got its presenter nominated for President. The speech as given at the convention was the closing speech of the debate of the free-silver plank of the 1896 Democratic platform. While the closing lines are well known, other parts of the speech are worthy of note. Probably the next most famous lines from the speech are the following: "Burn down your cities and leave our farms, and your cities will spring up again as if by magic; but destroy our farms and the grass will grow in the streets of every city in this country" (vol. 1, 248). But just as important, if not more important, are the two sentences just before: "You [the gold Democrats] come to us and tell us that the great cities are in favor of the gold standard; we reply that the great cities rest upon our broad and fertile prairies" (vol. 1, 248). One of the great themes throughout the speech is that the wealth of the country is based on its agricultural production and that is graphically represented in the "Burn down your cities" quote.

The "Cross of Gold" speech is littered with important themes and illustrations, many of which are still important to Democrats today, but were given their first real hearing through the leadership of Bryan. Most of these themes have to do with wealth, power, and the fight of the people against the entrenched power of the wealthy elite. At the beginning of the speech after recounting how the silver Democrats had organized, and then became the majority delegate bloc in the convention and on the platform committee, Bryan defines whom the silver Democrats represent at the convention in the following segment:

...but we stand here representing the people who are the equals, before the law, of the greatest citizens in the state of Massachusetts. When you come before us and tell us that we are about to disturb your business interests, we reply that you have disturbed our business interests by your course.

We say to you that you have made the definition of a business man too limited in its application. The man who is employed for wages is as much a business man as his employer; the attorney in a country town is as much a business man as the corporation counsel in a great metropolis; the merchant at the crossroads store is as much a business man as the merchant of New York; the farmer who goes forth in the morning and toils all day— who begins in the spring and toils all summer— and who by the application of brain and muscle to the natural resources of the country creates wealth, is as much a business man as the man who goes upon the board of trade and bets on the price of grain; the miners who go a thousand feet into the earth, or climb two thousand feet upon the cliffs, and bring forth from their hiding places the precious metals to be poured in the channels of trade are as much business men as the few financial magnates who, in a backroom, corner the money of the world. We come to speak for this broader class of business men.

Ah, my friends, we say not one word against those who live upon the Atlantic coast, but the hardy pioneers who have braved all the dangers of the wilderness, who have made the desert to blossom as the rose—those pioneers way out there, who rear their children near to Nature's heart, where they can mingle their voices with the voices of the birds—out there where they erected schoolhouses for the education of their young, churches where they praise their Creator, and the cemeteries where sleep the ashes of their dead—these people, we say, are as deserving of the consideration of this party as any people of this country. It is for these that we speak. We do not come as aggressors. Our war is not a war of conquest; we are fighting in the defense of our homes, our families, and posterity [vol. 1, 240–241].

This segment from the "Cross of Gold" speech highlights the central theme of Bryan's political career. Another rather lengthy version of the same topic, this time couched in terms of what direction the Democratic Party should take on economic issues, was delivered by Bryan at the end of the speech, as follows:

Mr. Carlisle said in 1878 that this was a struggle between the "idle holders of idle capital" and "the struggling masses who produce the wealth and pay the taxes of the country"; and my friends, the question we are to decide is this: Upon which side will the Democratic Party fight; upon the side of "the idle holders of idle capital," or upon the side of "the struggling masses"? That is the question that the party must answer first; and then it must be answered by each individual hereafter. The sympathies of the Democratic Party, as described by the platform, are on the side of the struggling masses, who have ever been the foundation of the Democratic Party [vol. 1, 247–248].

Bryan then follows up that segment with the one below:

> There are two ideas of government. There are those that believe that, if you will only legislate to make the well-to-do prosperous, their prosperity will leak through on those below. The Democratic idea, however, has been that if you legislate to make the masses prosperous, their prosperity will find its way up through every class which rests upon them [vol. 1, 248].

In still another version of this topic came from the middle of the speech:

> The gentleman from Wisconsin has said he fears a Robespierre [referring to the silver Democrats]. My friends, in this land of the free you need not fear that a tyrant will spring up from among the people. What we need is an Andrew Jackson to stand, as Jackson stood, against the encroachment of organized wealth [vol. 1, 241–242].

These excerpts given in 1896 pretty well defined the core values of the Democratic Party since that point in time. Indeed, much of the discussion in the Democratic Party since the 2004 election is that it has abandoned these core principles for the sake of moving politically into the center and also to obtain corporate donations to finance campaigns. Bryan's "leak through" prosperity is today's "trickle down" economics Much of what Bryan had to say over a hundred years ago is still being used in modern-day form.

A variation of this theme in the speech was Bryan's advocacy of a progressive income tax. In the "Cross of Gold" speech, he discussed it as follows:

> The income tax is just. It simply intends to put the burdens of government justly on the backs of the people. I am in favor of an income tax. When I find a man who is not willing to pay his share of the burdens of government which protects him, I find a man who is unworthy to enjoy the blessings of a government like ours [vol. 1, 242].

The tax issue was a relatively minor point in the "Cross of Gold" speech and was used to rebut the statement of earlier speakers during the silver debate. But Bryan had discussed the tax issue in more detail in his address to Congress on the subject on January 30, 1894 when he was a member of the House of Representatives from Nebraska. His speech was on behalf of an income tax as opposed to the regressive consumption taxes through tariffs that were used at the time. In that speech he noted that "everybody knows that a tax upon consumption is an unequal tax, and that the poor man by means of it pays far out of proportion to the income he enjoys" (vol. 1, 165). He pointed out that the 1890 Census showed that 91 percent of the people had 29 percent of the wealth while 9 percent has 71 percent (vol. 1, 174). In a speech on the tariff delivered in Des Moines Iowa on August 21, 1908 during the presidential campaign of that year, Bryan delivered an even more explicit attack on tariffs and the consumption tax.

> A tax upon consumption, even when laid with absolute impartiality, bears heaviest upon the poor, because our necessities are much more uniform than our possessions. People do not eat in proportion to their income; they do not wear clothing in proportion to their income; they do not use taxed goods in proportion to their income. As all taxes must come out of ones income, no matter through what system levied or collected, they are, in effect, income taxes, and taxes on consumption are really graduated income taxes, the largest per cent. being collected from those with the smallest income and the smallest per cent. from those with the largest income. It is only fair, therefore, that in an attempt to relieve the people from the iniquities of a high tariff, the poor, who are overburdened, should be given first consideration [vol. 1, 311].

Bryan's advocacy of the progressive income tax, his pointing out of the massive income inequity of the Gilded Age, and what he considered the unjust burden on the financing of the government by the working poor are all issues that had a prominent place in the 2006 election. The numerous minimum wage initiatives on the ballot and the number of candidates running on economic populism in spite of the commanding issue of the Iraq war is a testament to the power of these ideas.

Linked up to the tax issue was also the issue of the tariff, and here again, Bryan pointed out to the unfairness of the tariff on the poor. In a speech delivered in Congress on March 16, 1892, which was his first major speech in Congress, Bryan presented the House Ways and Means Committee bill on eliminating the tariff on wool and reducing the duties on woolen goods. About halfway into the speech Bryan attacked the concept of tariffs on so-called "infant industries" and the adverse affects on consumers:

> The reason our friends justify the principle [the protective tariff] is that they see the infant industry rise, but they forget the men on whom they are placing the burden. And the trouble with this country is that all over the land are the homes of forgotten men—men whose rights have been violated and whose interests have been disregarded in order that somebody else may be enriched. It is the principle involved in this little binding-twine bill. You see the industry that gets the $20,000, but you never think of the farmers that go down in their pockets and pay the little sums that make up the great amount [vol. 1, 43].

Tariff reduction has had many advocates over the years. In the nineteenth century the exporters of cotton supported low tariffs. Today it is a global issue where the benefits to consumers are the justification, but the primary beneficiary has been for multinational corporations to exploit foreign markets and flood the US with foreign goods. Neither approach showed any real sympathy for the working man. How Bryan would deal with the current situation would be problematical, but one aspect of the trade issue, contract labor and the treatment of labor, his view was very clear. In the very same tariff speech, he said the following:

> Why do we need a contract-labor law? It is to prevent the protected industries of this country from sending abroad to get cheap labor to take the place of American labor...We were told of the number of laborers to be employed because of the McKinley [tariff] bill; yet scarcely had the bill passed when there appeared in New York an advertisement for laborers to make tin plate; and the point of it was the statement that they would be paid higher prices than laborers were paid in Wales. Why was that stated in New York, except with a view to having that paper sent to Wales and importing here the labor to make these goods?...No, my friends, the manufacturer has not dealt fairly and honestly with the employee. What has been the result? Who has been getting the benefit? Is it the great mass of our people? Are they the ones that have profited by this transaction?... [vol. 1, 59].

From the above excerpt, it clear, though, that Bryan would have been a staunch opponent of the outsourcing of labor.

Along with the issue of the free coinage of silver is the parallel issue of the money supply. While the discussion on the money supply is an esoteric one, with the money issue is the larger issue of the privatization of what is considered by many a public function. It also brings up the greater issue of what activity should be private and what should be public. This was part of the national bank currency segment of the "Cross of Gold" speech, in which Bryan said:

> We say in our platform that we believe that the right to coin money and issue money is a function of government. We believe it. We believe that it is a part of sovereignty, and can no more with safety be delegated to private individuals than we could afford to delegate to private individuals the power to make penal statutes or levy taxes. Mr. Jefferson, who was once regarded as a good Democratic authority, seems to have differed in opinion from the gentleman who has addrest [sic] us on the part of minority. Those who are opposed to this proposition tell us that the issue of paper money is a function of the bank and that the Government ought to go out of the banking business. I stand with Jefferson rather than with them, and tell them, as he did, that the issue of money is the function of the government and that the banks ought to go out of the governing business [vol. 1, 243].

In a prepared statement that was entered in to the Congressional Record on June 5, 1894, two years before the above excerpt was given in Chicago, Bryan initially stated his point succinctly by saying: "No person or corporation has a natural right to issue money. It is 'an attribute of sovereignty' and the banks can no more demand as a right the power to supply a currency for a people than they can demand the right to enact laws for the general government of the people" (vol. 1, 216).

While this discussion may appear arcane, another aspect of this issue is very much with us—the private financing of elections and how to deal with them. Bryan was the first victim of massive campaign expenditures by the opposition in the campaign of 1896. By his third run for the presidency in 1908, Bryan had made it a key issue. The first written words that we have from Bryan in his speeches from the Funk & Wagnalls collection are found in his address to the 1904 Democratic convention in St. Louis.

> We have had the debauchment of elections. It was stated the other day that into the little State of Delaware, two hundred and fifty-six thousand dollars were sent at one time just before the election of 1896. Some say that our party must have a great campaign fund to bid against the Republicans. Let me warn you that if the Democratic Party is to save this nation, it must save it, not by purchase, but by principle. That is the only way to save it. Every time we resort to purchase, we encourage the spirit of barter. Under such a system the price will constantly increase, and the elections will go to the highest bidder [vol. 2, 60].

By the time of the 1908 election, the Democratic Party was advocating the disclosure of large campaign contributions. Bryan summed up the party's feelings on the subject in a speech that he gave in his hometown of Lincoln, Nebraska nine days before the De Moines speech on August 12, 1908. In the middle of the speech, he declared that an election is a "public affair," an activity of the government that should not be influenced by private considerations:

> An election is a public affair. The people, exercising the right to select their officials and to decide upon the policies to be pursued, proceed to their several polling places on election day and register their will. What excuse can be given for secrecy as to the influences at work? If a man, pecuniarily interested in "concentrating the control of the railroads in one management," subscribes a large sum to aid in carrying the election, why should his part in the campaign be concealed until he has put the officials under obligation to him? If a trust magnate contributed $100,000 to elect political friends to office with a view to presenting hostile legislation, why should that fact be concealed until his friends are securely seated in their official positions [vol. 2, 109]?

With the passage of the Bipartisan Campaign Finance Reform Act, also known more familiarly as McCain-Feingold, and various clean money campaigns around the nation, not to mention the numerous government investigations occurring at the federal and state level, campaign finance continues to be as sensitive an issue today as it was in Bryan's time.

On general principles as well as specific issues Bryan had much to say for the Democratic Party. While he did advocate government ownership of railroads because of their vital relationship to the economy, Bryan was opposed to socialism because he considered socialism to be government-sponsored monopoly and just another version of the corporate trust. Bryan's vision of the economy was one of many businesses competing in an industry rather than dominating large trusts. Bryan summed it up in his 1906 New York speech:

> The Democratic party is not the enemy of property or property rights; it is, on the contrary, the best defender of both, because it defends human rights and human rights are the only foundation upon which property and property rights can rest securely. The Democratic Party does not menace a single dollar legitimately accumulated; on the contrary, it insists upon the protection of the rich and poor alike in the enjoyment of that that they have honestly earned. The Democratic party does not discourage thrift, but, on the contrary, stimulates each individual to the highest endeavor by assuring him that he will not be deprived of the fruits of his toil. If we can but repeal the laws which enable men to reap what they have not sown—laws which enable them to garner into their overflowing barns the harvests that belong to others—no one will be able to accumulate enough to make his fortune dangerous to the country. Special privileges and the use of taxing power for private gain—these are the twin pillars upon which plutocracy rests. To take away these supports and to elevate the beneficiaries of special legislation to the plane of honest effort ought to be the purpose of our party [vol. 2, 89–90].

It is interesting to contrast Bryan's view of property and human rights with that of Ronald Reagan. For Bryan, human rights were the basis property rights; for Reagan, it was just the reverse. The current Republican administration that invaded a country that had not attacked it (Iraq) and stood by protecting the Oil Ministry building while the rest of the country was looted and thousands were being killed, is a graphic illustration of where Reagan's vision leads. America would have had a far better outcome in Iraq if it had followed the vision of Bryan.

Likewise, Bryan's treatise on the Republican Party of his day gives pause for thought. In accepting his second presidential nomination in Indianapolis on August 8, 1900 Bryan waxed forth on one of his major campaign themes— imperialism. In discussing imperialism, the national debt and the Republican Party he had several things to say:

> ...I do assert that on the important issues of the date the Republican party is dominated by those influences which constantly tend to substitute the worship of mammon for the protection of the rights of man.

In 1859 Lincoln said that the Republican party believed in the man and the dollar, but that in case of conflict it believed in the man before the dollar. This is the proper relation which should exist between the two. Man, the handiwork of God, comes first; money, the handiwork of man, is of inferior importance. Man is the master, money the servant, but upon all important questions to day Republican legislation tends to make money the master and man the servant.

The maxim of Jefferson, "Equal rights to all and special privileges to none," and the doctrine of Lincoln, that this should be a government "of the people, by the people and for the people," are being disregarded and the instrumentalities of government are being used to advance the interests of those who are in a position to secure favors from the Government....

Against us are arrayed a comparatively small but politically and financially powerful number who really profit by Republican policies; but with them are associated a large number who, because of their attachment to their party name, are giving their support to doctrines antagonistic to the former teaching of their own party.

...Republicans who used to boast that the Republican party was paying off the national debt are now looking for reasons to support a perpetual and increasing debt; Republicans who formerly abhorred a trust now beguile themselves with the delusion that there are good trusts and bad trusts, while in their minds, the line between the two is becoming more and more obscure; Republicans who, in times past, congratulated the country upon the small expense of our standing army, are now making light of the objections which are urged against a large increase in the permanent military establishment...[vol. 2, 17–19].

The references to the support of a "perpetual and increasing debt" and "a large increase in the permanent military establishment" are striking. The Democrats in the 2006 election could have just as easily made these statements. Also, the "permanent military establishment" has echoes of Dwight Eisenhower's "military industrial complex."

But of greater importance are the linkages of Bryan's statements on the concentration of wealth with the statements of Jefferson and Lincoln on the subject. In pointing out that Lincoln put "man before the dollar" and that Jefferson said "special privileges" to none, Bryan was one of the first Democratic leaders to attempt to appropriate the legacy of Lincoln for the Democratic Party. This was controversial because of the hostility to Lincoln in the Democratic South. But in his speech, Bryan attempted to do two things. The first was to show that Lincoln's principles were in the tradition of Jefferson and the Democratic Party. The second was that the modern Republican Party had abandoned its core values. Bryan constantly pointed out Jefferson's admonition that there were two natural political parties in any nation—a democratic [with a small "d"] party and an aristocratic party, and his criticism of the Republican Party as Jefferson's aristocratic party and its abandonment of Lincoln's principles was in keeping with the Jefferson theme.

The importance of the above segment is that the ideas in Bryan's speech were the beginning of the shift of the reform element of the Republican Party over to the Democratic Party. This shift was evident in the growing rifts in the Republican Party that Bryan spoke of. The progressive wing of the Republican Party with Theodore Roosevelt, Robert La Follette and Hiram Johnson was finding itself at odds with the McKinley wing of the party. A full-blown breech in the Republicans did not occur during Bryan's presidential runs, but by 1912, the rift in the Republican Party was so great that the party split, with the result that Democrat Woodrow Wilson won the presidency. The Wilson administration, in effect, would enact the Democratic Party vision of Bryan's speech (Wilson would make Bryan his Secretary of State) by appropriating the progressive program of Lincoln's twentieth century proxy Theodore Roosevelt and proceed to develop a progressive program of its own. Wilson would lay the foundation that Franklin Roosevelt's New Deal would complete, at which time the reform element of American political activity completed its shift over to the Democratic Party. Of all the various impacts that Bryan would have on the political structure of this country, this was probably the most important, for it defined the political landscape for the two major political parties right up to the present time. Name any issue that can be considered a core issue of the Democratic Party, or any statement of faith that represents the party, and in just about every case, at its foundation is the work of William Jennings Bryan.

With regard to core values and statements of faith of the Democratic Party, Bryan had much to say here as well. The closing arguments of his two Congressional speeches, the March 16, 1892 speech on the tariff and the August 16, 1893 speech on bimetallism, along with the Cross of Gold speech, say much about his political philosophy and the Democratic Party. The closing of the 1892 speech speaks of the people who supported him throughout the years:

> We cannot afford to destroy the peasantry of this country. We cannot afford to degrade the common people of this land, for they are the people who in time of prosperity and peace produce the wealth of the country, and they are also the people who in time of war bare their breasts to a hostile fire in defense of the flag. Go to Arlington or to any of the national cemeteries, see there the plain white monuments which mark the place "where rest the ashes of the nation's countless dead," those of whom the poet has so

beautifully written: "On Fame's eternal camping-ground/Their silent tents are spread."

Who were they? Were they the beneficiaries of special legislation? Were they the people who are ever clamoring for privileges? No, my friends; those who come here and obtain from Government its aid and help find in time of war too great a chance to increase their wealth to give much attention to military duties. A nation's extremity is their opportunity. They are the ones that make the contracts, carefully drawn, providing for the payment of their money in coin, while the Government goes out, if necessary, and drafts the people and makes them lay down upon the alter of their country all they have. No; the people who fight the battles are largely the poor, the common people of the country; those who have little to save but their honor, and little to lose but their lives. These are the ones, and I say to you, sir, that the country cannot afford to lose them...

We cannot put our safety in a great navy; we cannot put our safety in expensive fortifications along a seacoast thousands of miles in extent, nor can we put our safety in a great standing army that would absorb in idleness the toil of man it protects. A free government must find its safety in happy and contented citizens, who protected in their rights and free from unnecessary burdens, will be willing to die that the blessings which they enjoy may be transmitted to their posterity [vol. 1, 74–76].

With regard to the future of the Democratic Party, he had this to say in 1893:

To-day the Democratic party stands between two great forces, each inviting its support. On one side stand the corporate interests of the nation, its moneyed institutions, its aggregations of wealth and capital, imperious, arrogant, compassionless. They demand special legislation, favors, privileges, and immunities. They can subscribe magnificently to campaign funds; they can strike down opposition with their all-pervading influence and, to those who fawn and flatter, bring ease and plenty. They demand that the Democratic party shall become their agent to execute their merciless decrees.

On the other side stands that unnumbered throng which gave name to the Democratic party and for which it has assumed to speak. Work-worn and dust-begrimed, they make their sad appeal. They hear of average wealth increased on every side and feel the inequality of its distribution. They see an over-production of everything desired because of the underproduction of the ability to buy. They can not pay for loyalty except with their suffrages, and can only punish betrayal with their condemnation. Altho [sic] the ones who most deserve the fostering care of Government, their cries for help too often beat in vain against the outer wall, while others less deserving find ready access to legislative halls.

This army, vast and daily vaster growing, begs the party to be its champion in the present conflict. It cannot press its claims 'mid sounds of revelry. Its phalanxes do not form in grand parade, nor had it gaudy banners floating on the breeze. Its battle hymn is "Home Sweet Home," its war cry "equality before the law." To the Democratic party standing, between these two irreconcilable forces, uncertain to which side to turn , and conscious that upon its choice its fate depends, come the words of Israel's second lawgiver[Joshua 24:15]: "Choose you this day whom ye will serve." What will the answer be? Let me invoke the memory of him whose dust made sacred the soil of Monticello when he joined "The dead but sceptered sovereigns who still rule/Our spirits from their urns."

He was called a demagogue and his followers a mob, but the immortal Jefferson dared to follow the best promptings of his heart. He placed man above matter, humanity above property, and, spurning the bribes of wealth and power, pleaded the cause of the common people. It was his devotion to their interests which made his party invincible while he lived and will make his name revered while history endures. And what message comes from the Hermitage? When a crisis like the present arose and the national bank of his day sought to control the politics of the nation, God raised up an Andrew Jackson, who had the courage to grapple with that great enemy, and by overthrowing it, he made himself the idol of the people and reinstated the Democratic party in public confidence. What will the decision be to-day? ... [vol. 1, 143–144].

In the above 1893 speech on bimetallism Bryan was attempting to stop the repeal of the purchasing clause of the Sherman act which allowed for limited annual purchases of precious metals, particularly silver, by the government. The speech was given a few months after the Democratic victory in the 1892 election in which Grover Cleveland won his second non-consecutive term as president. The two sides of the Democratic Party that Bryan was talking about was Cleveland's conservative gold Democrats who had the backing of industry and Wall Street, and the silver Democrats of the agricultural South and West, of which Bryan was one of the key spokesmen, but not yet the leader of the movement. The choice that Bryan posed to the party in 1893 is roughly the same one that Democratic Party activists have been talking about for the past ten years. Of course the criticism leveled by activists today is that by selling out to corporate interests, focusing toward the political center and playing it safe, the party loses out anyway because if does not give voters a reason to vote, and thus the Democrats lose votes from both its base and from the political center. Whatever mistakes Bryan made during his presidential campaigns, being mushy on policies and ignoring his base was not one of them, as the above excerpts clearly show. Bryan promoted and projected his policies and issues with a passion and a zeal that is rarely heard today; playing it safe on the major issues of the time was simply not in his playbook.

Bryan's approach, nineteenth century flourishes and all, is in sharp relief from what we hear today. For a comparison, let's take a key issue and a prominent elected official of our time. Senator Barack Obama of Illinois is one of the current darlings of the media and the Democratic Party. There is no question that he is very charismatic and a fine speaker. He is one of the few Democrats today who have no problem injecting religious overtones in his speeches. A smattering of his speeches on his official Senate web site attests to his ability on topics involving labor, Africa, HIV-AIDs, various college commencement speeches, and a whole raft of other topics. Yet when it comes to the critical issue of the day—Iraq—a more cautious level appears to enter the language. Take for instance his November 22, 2005, speech on Iraq to the Council on Foreign Relations in Chicago. In the opening of the speech, he talks about the wounded servicemen and women that he encountered at Walter Reed Army Medical Center. In a very moving section, he describes what these people are going through. Then he gets to the following paragraph:

> And so the war rages on and the insurgency festers—as another father weeps over the flag-draped casket and another wife feeds her husband the dinner he can't fix for himself—it is our duty to ask ourselves hard questions. What do we want to accomplish now that we are in Iraq, and what is possible to accomplish? What kind of actions can we take to ensure not only a safe and stable Iraq, but that will also preserve our capacity to rebuild Afghanistan, isolate and apprehend terrorist cells, preserve our long-term military readiness, and devote the resources needed to shore up our homeland security? What are the costs and benefits of our actions moving forward? What urgency are we willing to show to bring our troops home safely? What kind of answers are we willing to demand from those in charge of the war?
>
> In other words—What kind of a debate are we willing to have?[113]

An interesting series of questions. The problem is why were these questions being asked in November of 2005? Why did not the Democrats in Congress (who controlled the Senate at the time) ask them in 2002? Why were not these questions asked in the 2004 election? Obama did not get to Congress until January 2005; he has some excuse. Where are everyone else's excuses, both Democrat and Republican? Also what kind of a debate have we had since this speech was given? Not much from Obama or anybody else. The debate, such as it was, occurred in the 2006 election, but nothing much beyond that. Again, when you look at the above statement, it has a kind of antiseptic quality about it, a laundry list of questions without any real passion to it. No such problem with Bryan's "Naboth's Vineyard" speech opposing imperialism at the beginning of the chapter. There was passion, hellfire, and brimstone to over flowing in that speech. The speech was given just months

---

113   Sen. Barack Obama, "Moving Forward in Iraq," *Chicago Tribune*, November 22, 2005.

after the end of the Spanish–American War, when the issue of what to do with the Philippines was just emerging, not three years later. The bloodless manner in which the Obama speech addressed Iraq is indicative of how the Democratic leadership has been unable to deal with the Iraq problem. And the inability to deal with Iraq and subjects like it illustrates the core of the Democrats' problem.

It is quite easy to dismiss someone like William Jennings Bryan as a religious crank, a demagogue, and a political loser. After all, he never won an election after 1892. Yet millions of Americans worshiped him. Furthermore, it can also rightfully be said that it is Bryan, and not Wilson or Franklin Roosevelt who is the father of the modern Democratic Party. While Bryan never won the presidency himself, his stature as the leader of the Democratic Party, and the issues that he promoted through his speeches and campaigns laid the groundwork for the reform agenda that was appropriated from the Lincoln mid-nineteenth century Republicans into the twentieth century Democrats. Many issues, such as the progressive income tax were important in Bryan's day and helped elect Wilson. Others would be important issues in New Deal legislation, and an issue such as campaign finance is still debated today. Of Bryan's competitors, Teddy Roosevelt's legacy is now a politically extinct branch of the Republican Party. And Woodrow Wilson, who at one time considered Bryan to be a political extremist, by 1912, recognized the importance of many of Bryan's issues. It was during Wilson's administration that many of Bryan's major platform points became reality. Franklin Roosevelt, who was also not a big fan of Bryan either, ultimately was the one that saw that Bryan's message to the rural disenfranchised could be combined with Al Smith's urban voters to form the great New Deal coalition beginning in 1932.

But it is also in the larger history and vision of the Democratic Party that Bryan has an important position, for he is the historical link between the early Democratic Party of Jefferson and Jackson and the twentieth century party of Roosevelt. Bryan lost the presidency primarily because he was leading a minority party during his period of leadership. But because he was the leader for so long (extraordinary for a political party out of power), he gave the party an aspect of continuity that it would not have otherwise had. In his day there were Bryan political clubs to deliver his message. No other Democratic politician was in a position to maintain such a network. Bryan himself referred to Jefferson and Jackson in many of his speeches.

Looking at Bryan today, it is safe to say that the kind of people that supported him would have supported Howard Dean, both during the presidential nominating process and for his run for Democratic National Committee chair. Bryan addressed what we would call today the democratic wing of the Democratic Party. Many of the progressive issues of today, such as supporting unions, raising the minimum wage, affordable health care would probably have been his issues as well. Taxes on the rich would be no different than the speeches he gave on the subject in the early 1890s. On foreign policy matters, his anti-imperialist position probably would indicate that he would have opposed invading Iraq. For someone with his fundamentalist religious background, abortion, gay marriage, and especially prayer in school would have been difficult for him. One of the issues that Bryan pushed at the end of his life was bringing the Bible into the classroom. But even here whatever moral reservations Bryan would have had about abortion would have come in conflict with concerns about the welfare of the poor providing for large families. As for civil rights and civil liberties, they were barely on his agenda. But in that regard, he was not much different than most Americans of his day. With regard to the leading racial and xenophobic issue of his later years, the Ku Klux Klan, Bryan was not a member or a supporter, and there are indications that he despised the Klan. But whatever reservations he had for the Klan, they were not such that he was ready to publicly denounce them, as many were ready to do at the 1924 Democratic convention. In this case politics (and Bryan could be a very political animal when it came to winning the presidency for the Democrats) trumped morality. Finally, while he didn't say a great deal about it, he did attend the 1908 White House conference on conserving natural resources called by President Theodore Roosevelt in which he gave a speech on the subject and showed support for Roosevelt's conservation efforts (vol. 2, 397–405). This would indicate that he would have supported many environmental initiatives that were enacted in the twentieth century, particularly soil conservation. As an agrarian reformer, it is difficult to see him support rampant development that would have destroyed valuable productive farmland, since he believed that the wealth of the nation was based on the crops produced from the land. As a general summary of Bryan, he would have been strong on economic issues, mixed or ambivalent on so-cial issues, and most likely a dove or isolationist on foreign policy issues.

In the end, what does Bryan's political experience mean for us today? As was stated at the beginning of this chapter, Bryan represents one of the mainstream branches on Democratic Party political thought. He represented the rural, populist element and his base of power was in the South and West, two areas where the party is sorely lacking. He created a religiously infused populist message focusing on economic issues. One would have to think that such a message would still be effective today in the areas that were his base, particularly one which promoted the Christian message of the Gospels as delivered in Matthew 25:40 ("as you did it to one of the least of my brethren, you did it to me"). These areas are still mostly as poor and as ignored as they were in Bryan's day. The main strategy for Democrats would be to use the economic message that Bryan used to offset the social message coming from these same parts of the country on such issues as abortion, gay rights, and the like. It will not always succeed, but it will provide a basis for developing a stronger Democratic message in these areas. It also provides the opening necessary to develop new themes in the Bryan tradition, such as health care, global warming and the environment, which were not important issues in Bryan's day, but which clearly can be adapted to Bryan's techniques in the advocacy of these issues.

In a society in which people find difficulty in making ends meet, in which the middle class is being squeezed into extinction, and in which workers feel that they are falling further and further behind, William Jennings Bryan has a lot to say to these people. And in a society where more people believe in angels than believe in evolution, Bryan has a lot to say as well. The work is in tailoring that message to a twenty-first century Red-state audience that is as meaningful to them today as Bryan's message was 100 years ago. As How-ard Dean said during his presidential campaign and then as he showed as DNC Chair, he would not write-off the South or any other part of Red-state America. It is necessary to reach out to the Red states, "that unnumbered throng which gave name to the Democratic party," as Bryan did, and bring them into the fold.

8. TOWARD A TWENTY-FIRST CENTURY NEW DEAL

Up to this point, this book has discussed the American economic, cultural, political, and geographic divide as it affects us today, and how this divide affects the Democratic Party. Much of the last two chapters have discussed how Democrats in earlier eras dealt with issues that affect Democrats and the rest of us today. In earlier eras it was the Democratic Party and their progressive Republican allies that revived this country from the political, economic and social wreckage that conservative Republicans had created during their tenure in office. Today we are faced with the same situation. The Democrats solution to the problems of earlier days was Woodrow Wilson's New Freedom program, and most importantly, Franklin Roosevelt's New Deal. The New Deal faced the most serious social and economic crisis that this country endured in the twentieth century. Therefore, when it comes to the Democratic Party answers to the current issues, the discussion must start with the New Deal.

While there is no golden age or ideal model from the past that can be lifted in its entirety and can be used in the modern age without adaptation, the New Deal has the aspects to it that makes it a good foundation for any progressive program. The New Deal was able to stop the Hoover Administration deflationary spiral, and it was able to lay an economic foundation for the country that lasted intact into the 1970s. Indeed, it can be said that had it remained mostly intact, the country would be in much better shape than it is now. Therefore, it is useful to look at how the original New Deal was formed in order to determine what kind of a program should be constructed by the Democrats to repair the damage of the Bush Administration.

The political aspects have already been discussed. In 1932, Franklin Delano Roosevelt and his brain trust put together a coalition consisting of the rural Bryan wing of the party from the South and the West, and the urban Smith wing of the Northeast and the urban centers of the Midwest and Far West. But the administrative aspects of governing the new coalition were a totally different matter. The vote in 1932 was basically an anti-Hoover vote. The voters wanted a change, and they had no real focus as to what kind of a change it should be. As for any clues as to where Roosevelt would head the new administration, the only indications were what he had done as governor of New York since the beginning of the crisis in 1929. The other problem was the sheer scale of the problem and the speed at which it was developing. Though the economy was in trouble, it had held reasonably well together until late 1930. Even the stock market had recovered about three-quarters of its value. Then the US banks started failing in earnest in late 1930 and with the collapse of the Credit Anstalt Bank in Austria in 1931 turning the recession into a global economic crisis, the economic collapse began its steep decline. The bottom occurred as Roosevelt took office in 1933 (in fact, the banking crisis peaked during the inauguration). No one could have dreamed of this crisis two years earlier after the prosperity of the 1920s. There simply were no policies to deal with such a disaster.

Roughly, the crisis was the result of several key factors. First, the unequal distribution of wealth and income, which Bryan and other Democrats had decried since the late nineteenth century, peaked in 1929. The wealth generated at the top of the economic ladder by tax cuts and other benefit simply was not enough to keep the economy afloat without strength down below. The actual peak occurred in 1926 and the economy started to gradually slide thereafter. With the country gradually sinking, the Federal Reserve increased the money supply one last time in 1927, creating the last manic boom of 1928–29, before the basic imbalances sunk things in the stock market. In conjunction with unequal individual wealth was the dominant position of business and corporations at the expense of labor. This led to an excess of production and investment (including the stock market) while there was a shortfall of consumption and distribution. Hugh Johnson, FDR's director of the National Recovery Administration (NRA) stated it eloquently in his 1935 book, *The Blue Eagle from Egg to Earth*, when he said: "If you want to know where the consuming power of America went, you need only look around you and see it congealed in icebergs of unnecessary building and un-needed plants—and in the dead leaves of the worthless securities which financed them, and our fatuous foreign loans." As Johnson indicated, there was also extensive rot in the banking system and highly irresponsible banking and financial practices, both large and small.[114] Finally there was an unstable international banking situation. All of these pieces conspired to aggravate the situation when the stock market crashed.

As Roosevelt began putting together his 1932 campaign, one of his key issues was getting people back to work, and the conservation program that he began in New York would be part of that. It would evolve into the famous Civilian Conservation Corps (CCC), variations of which are still active today at various government levels. The idea behind the state and later the federal program was to get idle young men off the streets. But it also established the principle that it was the duty of the government to find work for the unemployed. This was a radical departure from established government policy and would be a major feature of the New Deal in the various agencies that were set up.[115]

Other important early New Deal concepts were laid out in two speeches given by Roosevelt in April of 1932. As recounted by Samuel I. Rosenman in his 1952 book, *Working with Roosevelt*, the first of these was the "forgotten man" speech, which was a radio speech broadcast on April 7. This was the first significant campaign related radio speech that Roosevelt gave and it contained the initial ideas of several New Deal projects. The theme of Roosevelt's speech was that real prosperity depended upon supporting "the forgotten man" —the unorganized but essential economic units at the bottom of the economic ladder. Thus the economy should be built from the bottom up, not the top down. The concept of "the forgotten man" had first been used by Bryan his first speech in Congress on the tariff in 1892 in which he said "all over the land are the homes of forgotten men—men whose rights have been violated and whose interests have been disregarded in order that somebody

114   Hugh S. Johnson, *The Blue Eagle from Egg to Earth* (Garden City, NY: Doubleday, Doran 1935), 158–162; cited in Raymond Moley, *The First New Deal* (New York: Harcourt, Brace & World 1966), 226–227.

115   Samuel I. Rosenman, *Working with Roosevelt* (New York: Harper & Brothers 1952), 64.

else may be enriched." Roosevelt's image of "the forgotten man" would show up again memorably in FDRs Democratic Convention acceptance speech later in the year. The April 7 speech brought forth several proposals, including increasing purchasing power of farmers, which later became part of the Agricultural Adjustment Act, preventing foreclosures of home and farm mortgages, which led to a number of housing finance programs and the Farm Credit Administration, and assisting banks, which eventually became a role of the Reconstruction Finance Corporation (RFC) under the New Deal as it previously was under Herbert Hoover. Finally, the speech broached the subject of giving wartime emergency powers to combat the Depression.[116]

The second speech was given at Oglethorpe University in Atlanta on April 22. This speech also emphasized the purchasing power of consumers over capital investment, but this speech also pointed out that the country needed a more experimental approach to solving the economic problems. If one method fails, try another one, but try something. Unsuccessful action was preferable to inaction. This would be a hallmark of the New Deal and Roosevelt's managing style.[117]

The 1932 campaign starting with Roosevelt's acceptance speech at the Democratic Convention added further structure to the initial ideas. The acceptance speech outlined the overall philosophy of the campaign that was to come. In the final paragraphs of the speech Roosevelt first outlined his attack on the Republican Party. Conjuring images of Bryan's "Cross of Gold" speech, he said:

> Never before in modern history have the essential differences between the major American parties stood out in such striking contrasts as they do today. Republican leaders not only have failed in material things, they have failed in national vision, because in disaster they have held out no hope, they have pointed out no path for the people below to climb back to places of security and of safety in our American life.

This was not going to be a campaign fought over the political center. This was a campaign fought from the political left for the purposes of pulling the country to the left. Roosevelt then went on to speak about the "forgotten man" that had had first shown up in his radio speech and which Bryan in his advocacy of the "peasantry of this country" had so eloquently defended three decades before:

---

116 Ibid., 61–62.
117 Ibid., 65–66.

> Throughout the Nation, men and women, forgotten in the political philoso-phy of the Government of the last years look to us here for guidance and for more equitable opportunity to share in the distribution of national wealth.
>
> On the farms, in the large metropolitan areas, in the smaller cities and in the villages, millions of our citizens cherish the hope that their old stan-dards of living have not gone forever. Those millions can not and shall not hope in vain.

Any Democratic presidential candidate in the 2008 election could easily use both the attack on the Republicans in the first excerpt and the "forgot-ten man" excerpt with minor editing. Then Roosevelt opened the final para-graph of the speech with one of the two most famous lines he ever spoke, and then went on to rally the nation:

> I pledge you, I pledge myself, to a new deal for the American people. Let us here assembled constitute ourselves prophets of a new order of com-petence and courage. This is more than a political campaign; it is a call to arms. Give me your help, not to win votes alone, but to win in this crusade to restore America to its own people.[118]

While the "new deal" line is justly famous, the final line of the speech is equally important in our own time. Not only the usage of the religious im-age of the crusade, but the idea of restoring America back to its own people. This is reminiscent of Howard Dean's speeches in 2003 wanting his country back, and the "Take Back America" slogans plastered all over Democratic campaigns. Clearly, the theme of the final line of the speech has resonated with Democrats all over the country; it is the philosophical link between then and now.

Leaving Chicago, Roosevelt then laid out in a series of speeches that sum-mer and fall the issues that his administration would deal with. These in-cluded reciprocal trade agreements, agricultural relief, and the refinancing of residential and farm mortgages. Added to this list was just about all the programs that would eventually be enacted in the first term, such as bank-ing legislation, repeal of prohibition, regulation of public utilities, develop-ment of water power, public works, unemployment relief, and a whole host of other actions which are now part of the New Deal. The one issue that was mentioned that Roosevelt ultimately could not deliver on was balancing the budget.[119]

Although Roosevelt criticized Hoover for running deficits, and genuinely wanted to balance the budget in the early part of his first term, the economic

---

118 Ibid., 78.
119 Ibid., 85–86.

crisis simply did not make that possible. One of the biggest criticisms is that despite its deficits and its government expenditures, the New Deal did not get America out of the Depression, which is true. World War II got us out of the Depression. But when one looks at World War II, what was it in realistic financial terms? It was the New Deal on steroids. World War II represented government spending and fiscal deficits unprecedented in American history up to that time and on a scale beyond the comprehension of most economists, let alone the American people. Today we call such defense expenditures military Keynesianism, in reference to the deficit, economic pump priming theories of John Maynard Keynes, and consider such expenditures a structural part of the budget.

With the winning of the November 1932 election, the hard work of actually trying to set up an administration began. Up to this point, the New Deal was a theoretical construct; now it had to become a reality. In looking at their situation Roosevelt and his brain trust focused on some key points, some of which would be presented in the inaugural speech. The key point was that there had to be greater concentration of power in the federal government. There needed to be an impression of firmness with a heavy dose of leadership from the White House. The president needed to seize the initiative so that the Congress would not be able to broker and delay administration proposals. Also, because there was a lot of bureaucratic drag in the existing departments, the plan was to create new agencies to solve certain specific problems rather than try to cure them through the existing cabinet departments.[120] Although there was a wide range of administrative philosophies in the new Administration, decision making, particularly in the early days, was government by pragmatism rather than ideology. In addition to pragmatic thinking, the Roosevelt administration was willing to experiment in addressing certain problems and agencies. As was said earlier, if the experiments did not work it was on to the next experiment.

As for the people who drew up the plans, they were a varied group that came at the problems from many different approaches. Lead Brain Truster Raymond Moley in his 1966 book, *The First New Deal*, categorized these people into five groups. There were those who took a traditional approach such as balancing the budget and restoring the existing commercial and financial

---

120   Arthur M. Schlesinger, Jr., *The Coming of the New Deal* (Boston: Houghton Mifflin 1958), 534.

structures; there were those who wanted to put more money in the system by inflating the currency; there was the Progressive group that wanted to break up trusts and regulate business activity; there were those who favored economic planning; finally there were the socialists who wanted government ownership of key sectors of the economy.[121] Roosevelt chose from the first four groups, often combining ideas, and except for the Tennessee Valley Authority, avoided state ownership. Indeed, it can be said of the New Deal that it was a middle of the road approach that ended up being unsatisfactory to both Wall Street and the Socialists. But the net result was a shift to the political left and greater government control.

With regard to the New Deal programs themselves, they came from various sources, and were not conceived in a vacuum. Many, in fact, were the result of initial work that had been started by Congress and the Hoover Administration. The Hoover Administration had established the RFC to issue loans to key businesses in financial trouble. The most important industry that they targeted was the banks, which was only partly successful. By late 1932 the banking system was heading for collapse and it was Hoover's Treasury Department that did the legal research and the preliminary plan for freezing the transfer of gold and national banking holiday. In fact, the Hoover and Roosevelt Treasury staffs worked together through inauguration weekend (March 4, 1933 was a Saturday) to implement the system with the teams switching roles after the inauguration.[122] As for regulation of banks and securities, that work had gone on by Senator Carter Glass and Representative Henry Steagall during the just ended 72nd Congress. The bill was well on its way to passage before it became the famous Glass-Steagall Act in June 1933. There had also been various attempt to pass agricultural relief by the Congress in the 1920s, and Senator George Norris had long advocated public development of the Muscle Shoals project that later became the Tennessee Valley Authority.

But Roosevelt and his team had developed much on their own as well, and these ideas started appearing in Roosevelt's speeches starting in April 1932 right through to the election. The most complex, and ultimately the most controversial was the National Recovery Administration (NRA), the result of the National Industrial Recovery Act (NIRA), the last of the Hun-

---

121 Moley, *First New Deal*, 228.
122 Ibid., 151–164.

dred Days legislation passed on June 16, 1933 along with Glass-Steagall, the Farm Credit Act, and the Emergency Railroad Transportation Act. It was not seriously addressed until after the election by the Brain Trust.

As can be seen from the multiplicity of information input sources, there was no plan for the New Deal. There could not be. This was an economic crisis of unprecedented proportions and there was no book to follow. Much of what was done by the Roosevelt Administration was improvised, and that was the secret of its success as far as the voting public was concerned. It also reflected a lot of Roosevelt's management style, which could best described as organized chaos. [123]

Compare Roosevelt's working style with Hoover. For Hoover, there were nice clean lines of authority and everyone in his place. And if a problem or solution didn't fit his preconceived notion of how one should act or how the government should function, it wasn't tried no matter how extraordinary the emergency and no matter how extraordinary the need for innovative action. Nothing could have demonstrated his shortcomings more than the banking crisis of February-March 1933. His Treasury Secretary Ogden Mills and his staff had put together a bank relief plan, including a bank holiday that Hoover was unwilling to implement in the final days of his administration because he thought it was improper and he felt that he didn't have the authority, although his Treasury staff believed that he did. Roosevelt, concerned more about impending financial chaos than conflicting legal interpretations, implemented the banking holiday immediately on taking office. It is just about universally agreed that the bank holiday broke the downward spiral of the banking crisis and immediately raised public confidence in the banking system and the country.[124] The 1933 banking holiday story and Hoover's and Roosevelt's response it, illustrate the fundamental difference between a Red-state and a Blue-state culture in government. Hoover, in a Red-state tradition-bound conservative mode of government, was unable to act. Roosevelt, in a Blue-state adaptable liberal mode of government acted decisively and succeeded.

Two management issues characterized the New Deal. As previously noted, New Deal actions tended to be of a pragmatic nature; not much room for ideology. The other management issue that was important to the New Deal

---

123   Schlesinger, *Coming of the New Deal*, 526–529.
124   Moley, *First New Deal*, 212–213.

was the fact that there was very little corruption in the Roosevelt Administration. Interior Secretary Harold Ickes spent more than $5 billion on projects on such things as highways, buildings, and dams for the Public Works Administration with nary a whiff of scandal.[125]

When the 1934 elections were approaching, Roosevelt asked the voters if their lives had improved over the 18 months of his administration. The answer in the 1934 election was for resounding support for the New Deal and one of the rare instances where the party in power gained congressional seats. The 1934 election confirmed the Democratic Party as the majority party for years to come, but it was not evident to the Roosevelt strategists at the time. They felt that a new initiative, which resulted in the Second New Deal, would be necessary.

After the 1934 election FDR strategist Ed Flynn reviewed the national electoral situation with Roosevelt. The conclusion that they reached was that even up through the 1934 election the Democratic Party was still a minority party. So a new strategy got underway in 1935 by expanding the welfare state with general relief programs, as opposed to work relief programs such as the CCC. These programs were focused on the urban voters. In concert with the general relief programs was Social Security. Finally, the other key piece of legislation was the Wagner Act, directed at labor. These pieces of legislation formed the core of the Second New Deal, and laid the basis for the landslide of 1936, which would give Roosevelt and the Democrats their biggest margins in Congress.[126] After that came the "Court Packing" attempt in 1937 and the Congressional Purge of 1938, both of which were disastrous failures and dealt Roosevelt a major setback in the 1938 election. But Roosevelt's Democratic Coalition would remain intact until the 1960s. The initiatives of the Second New Deal did bring in the African American vote in 1936, which had gone to Hoover in 1932. It also brought in labor and other religious minorities. The break would begin with the South leaving for Strom Thurmond in 1948 and the Catholic vote splitting over social issues such as abortion. But the group held together for a long time.

The Second New Deal would also establish the formal cleavage with the business community, which had been supportive up to that point, and those supporters who supported "reasonable" reform, but opposed the expanding

125 Encyclopaedia Britannica 15th ed., s.v. "Ickes, Harold L."
126 Moley, First New Deal, 525–530.

welfare state. The assault on business and the upper class was much more strident (it is in the 1936 campaign that Roosevelt uses the term "economic royalists") with the Wagner Act, which was skewed heavily toward labor, and a proposed tax increase on wealthy incomes which was used to goad the wealthy into opposition and re-invigorate Roosevelt's base.

Since the end of World War II and right up to the present, the general trend has been to dismantle the New Deal. Leading this effort has been the business community and their Republican allies. Today most of the securities and bank regulation legislation is gone. The last of Glass-Steagall was repealed in the late 1990s. The Taft-Hartley Act and subsequent legislation diluted the Wagner Act. Many of the agencies are gone, although some of the programs, such as the agricultural subsidies, still exist in other forms. The most recent New Deal program under attack is Social Security, but its popularity with the public has kept it safe up to now. But the most successful program on which there is no ideological dispute is the one that Roosevelt personally didn't care for—the Federal Deposit Insurance Corporation. Thus, with a few exceptions, we have come almost full circle to where the New Deal began.

As for the overall success of the New Deal programs throughout the years, the verdict is decidedly mixed. The New Deal was a celebrated set of programs, and some of the most controversial government programs in US history. There is no end to the debate on it. The political lines are deeply drawn with liberals on one side supporting the New Deal and conservatives opposing on the other. The general tenor of the argument for the supporters is that the New Deal got the country out of the Depression and only the active drive of the New Deal would have been able to end economic stagnation and restore public confidence in the country and the capitalist system. The opponents say that the New Deal did not get out of the Depression; there were still over 10 million unemployed when World War II started. World War II got us out of the Depression. Furthermore the New Deal did a lot of harm to the economy, stifling investment, and that had the New Deal not intervened, the nation would have righted itself on its own. A final criticism is that other countries such as England recovered much more quickly with their policies than America did with the New Deal.

As is the case with such arguments, there is a little bit of truth on both sides. Clearly, the New Deal did not get us out of the Depression; World

War II did that. But the New Deal did stop the slide into economic chaos; basically standing idle from 1929 to 1933 and issuing pronouncements, as Hoover did, that the country was fundamentally economically sound wasn't going to do it. Raymond Moley in *The First New Deal* wrote extensively on the subject and was one of the participants in working on the February–March 1933 banking crisis. It was his opinion that the banks, which didn't want a bank holiday, simply had no idea of the gravity of the crisis; something had to be done, and they weren't the people who were going to do it.[127] It is true that some programs such as the initial securities legislation stifled investing until it was replaced by a more realistic piece of legislation the following year. But there was also actions like the bank holiday and legislation like the Federal Deposit Insurance Corporation that were ultimately viewed as essential to the recovery of the economy. As for other counties in the 1930s recovering before the United States did, that ignores the fact that the primary crash was in the United States, beginning in early 1929, and the downturn in other counties, though severe, was of a secondary impact, and more easy to recover from. The US part of the event involved a major credit bubble that destabilized the banking system, as was the case in Japan in the 1990s and the US today. The negative psychological impact of a lack of confidence in the financial system makes it much more difficult to conduct any transaction let alone stage an economic recovery.

Moley's writings are probably as close an informed source as there is on the early New Deal. Moley met Roosevelt in the late 1920s when FDR was governor of New York and Moley was a professor at Columbia University. Initially recruited into the Roosevelt presidential campaign to provide ideas and write speeches, Moley later recruited other Columbia professors such as Rexford G. Tugwell and Adolph Berle and formed what later became the Brain Trust, the group that fed ideas into the 1932 campaign. Moley worked on the banking crisis in early 1933 then became Assistant Secretary of State. He left the administration in the fall of 1933 and went on to become a journalist and writer. While he continued to advise and write speeches for Roosevelt until 1936, he gradually became estranged from the policies of the New Deal to the point of breaking with Roosevelt by supporting every Republican presidential candidate from 1940 right through to Barry Goldwater

---

127   Ibid., 149–150, 153.

in 1964. Thus, Moley presents the unusual opinions of an early insider who later broke with the New Deal.

Moley's point of departure came when the Second New Deal came on stream in 1935 and emphasized more in the way of relief and the welfare state than recovery, and more skewed toward labor and was too confrontational with business. The populist nature of the 1936 campaign was too much for him. But in the beginning he was a strong supporter of the original New Deal decisions. In writing about the period in his 1939 book, *After Seven Years*, Moley outlined what he considered to be the pluses and minuses of the program. On the positive side the New Deal outlawed many abuses and readjusted many skewed relationships such as those between consumption and investment. It also changed the philosophy of business enterprise and made improvements in social welfare activities. Many of the experimental project failures were valuable educational lessons. On the negative side, Moley noted that the economy did not revive, investment lay dormant for years, the agricultural problems were not solved, and many were alienated because the New Deal failed people's expectations.[128] For Moley, the fundamental problem with the Second New Deal was that it treated progress as a zero-sum game—that groups had to be restrained (i.e. business) so that other people could advance (workers). Moley was a Wilson Progressive who believed that progress depended on co-operation and regulation rather than conflict. As such, he favored the collaboration with business in the NRA, felt that codes of voluntary conduct would be sufficient to solve the problem, and that coercion would be counterproductive. In Moley's opinion, confidence rather than any specific program was the key to the early New Deal's effectiveness. Moley noted that the average person had no idea what the New Dealers were doing, but they were convinced that things were being done, and that was enough.[129] Arthur Schlesinger confirmed that Roosevelt's basic appeal was that he was a leader that was for action with a positive forward-looking vision, and that certainly added to public confidence.[130]

In addition to the opinions of others on the New Deal, we can look at subsequent economic events to gain a better perspective. The Great Depression and the New Deal occurred at a time when economic statistics were just coming into their own. Since then, economic events such as the bursting of

---

128   Raymond Moley, *After Seven Years*, (New York: Harper & Brothers 1939), 399–400.
129   Moley, *First New Deal*, xviii.
130   Schlesinger, *Coming of the New Deal*, 588.

the Japanese real estate bubble in the late 1980s and the resulting stagnation lasting more than a decade showed us how extraordinarily difficult it is to revive from a major economic crash even when it is localized to one country. In this country it took nearly four years to recover the jobs from the dot com bubble in the stock market and six years for Dow Jones Industrial Average to surpass its 2000 peak. The NASDAQ average is nowhere near its record peak of nearly 5,000 from that period. And despite tax cuts and giving business a virtual free hand in doing what they like, job growth since the dot com crash has been the lowest on record. So given these experiences, the economic results of the New Deal are not as disappointing as they may have looked in 1940. Furthermore, the Bush Administration's difficulty in creating jobs even with tax cuts, massive deficits, heavy indebtedness, and huge doses of money from the Federal Reserve, clearly points out that the option of doing nothing and hoping that economy corrects on its own without domestic government programs is not a viable option either.

So with this history of the New Deal in mind, what does it tell us in constructing a New Deal for the twenty-first century? Well, the first point of reference is looking that the kind of issues Roosevelt's New Deal was faced with and how they compare to what we face today. The most obvious similarity is income inequality. As stated before, the various income inequality indexes, known as Gini co-efficients, are the highest since the stock market crash of 1929.[131] In both 1929 and today, these income distortions were brought about by decades of relative wage stagnation for the mass of workers while the people at the top of the income ladder received unfathomable riches. Both then and now saw this gravitation of money to the upper incomes assisted by tax cuts that benefited primarily the rich, with both tax cuts justified by saying that they would generate growth, income and jobs. Both periods not only generated a surge of wealth for upper income individuals, they also generated enormous corporate profits. In both cases, these skewed income trends were able to outlast their natural economic life by the expanded use of debt (much larger today than the 1920s), and the manipulation of economic data (in the 1920s, the lack of data; today deliberate massage such as the decision to take discouraged workers no longer looking for jobs out of the unemployment statistics under the assumption that they no longer want jobs). What the 1920s showed is that such subterfuge did not

---

131   *Left Business Observer no.114, 4.*

solve the problem; it only delayed and made it worse. In the 1920s, bankers prodded their depositors to put money in the stock market to make money on commissions, rather than have banks funds sit idle because the bank's corporate clients were so profitable that they did not need bank loans.[132] Today, one is bombarded in the media by stock brokers willing to let you in on the latest hot deal, the mortgage brokers wanting the refinance your house, the credit card companies with every kind of inducement imaginable, and finally the debt relief and bankruptcy specialists who are doing a land office business from those who were taken in by the brokers and debt peddlers. Ultimately in the 1920s, the hollowing out of the wageworker sector of the economy and the imbalance created by overinvestment and under consumption in real terms, led to a collapse on the scale that the traditional remedies of the marketplace no longer worked, or did not work fast enough.

How things end up this time around is yet to be seen. The numerous obituaries for this economy have all been premature, and the Cassandras have seemed more like Chicken Littles, and have looked pretty foolish in the process. And it is very true that no economic cycle repeats itself in any exact detail. But one thing has been telling throughout most of this cycle since income inequality bottomed out in the late 1960s: with few exceptions, individuals have been saving less and borrowing more. Even in a growth period such as the 1990s, much of it was based on speculative bubbles with no real wealth or value behind the numbers. Alan Greenspan and the money managers at the Federal Reserve and elsewhere have done a remarkable job in putting off a potential financial crisis, and they may be able to continue to put it off for some time to come. But it is also clear that they have been unable to correct the fundamental economic imbalances that generated the mountains of debt in the first place, and that their long-term policies are unsustainable. If the existing scenario continues, at some point the consumption will simply not be there to maintain the existing superstructure. When it does go, the impact on the economic life of this country would be chilling. The effect would be doubly devastating because, unlike the 1920s, we have tremendous indebtedness in the international market as opposed to being the world's biggest creditor nation. The recovery from such a double crash would likely be extremely long regardless of what policies are implemented. The state of

---

132   Simon Kuznets, *National Income and its Composition 1919–1938* (New York: National Bureau of Economic Research, 1941), 316; cited in George Soule, *Prosperity Decade from War to Depression 1917–1929* (1947; reprint New York: Harper and Row, 1968), 122.

the financial and real estate markets in 2007–2008 may indicate the beginning of the long-predicted crisis.

The second point of reference in looking at the old New Deal in order to construct a new one is quite simply that such an effort to dig out of a mess similar to the one that faced FDR will not occur by rugged individualists in the private sector. The business leaders found out to their horror that it is possible to wreck the economy to the point that confidence in the marketplace (and the people that "run" it) is completely destroyed and the private sector in incapable of fixing the problem on their own. Despite all the hostility that is put on government involvement today, the business community was actively involved in the early New Deal and the programs of the NRA before the more populist aspects of it alienated them. Even today, those that profess keeping the government out of the marketplace are usually the first ones running to the Treasury to bail out their industries. Just witness the current pleading from Wall Street to the Federal Reserve to shower the banks with money in order to relieve the financial crisis of 2007. No addressing of the distortions in our economy today will effectively occur without federal government involvement. The essence of Blue-state governing principles throughout the history of this country has been government involvement in the economy is necessary for sustained economic advancement, whether it be public education in the eighteenth and nineteenth centuries, the development of the transportation infrastructure in the middle nineteenth centuries, or the stabilization of the financial structure early twentieth century. Clearly any New Deal in our time is going to have to operate in the same Blue-state cultural basis. It is going to have to place more focus on community and society rather than the individual.

What specific approaches will a modern New Deal take? In the old New Deal, there were several schools of thought of how government should operate, some them more prominent than others. Based on the experience over the last seventy-five years, neither the planners nor the money managers would appear to be effective in the system today. Government planning is not flexible enough and requires a level of management skill that most government bureaucracies do not have. Also, the government's ability to pick winners has always been open to question, although in this regard it is no worse than the private sector. What money manipulation there is, is being done by the Federal Reserve (whose powers have been enhanced since the

New Deal), and there is no need at this time for competing organizations. Traditional approaches to economic problems such as tax cuts and concessions to Wall Street and industry are always popular with some element of the electorate and are particularly popular today. But the problem with traditional approaches is that they tend to bail out the wealthy and the powerful at the expense of everybody else and have not proven very effective. In recent times this strategy certainly hasn't produced the economic growth that the country needed. When the crunch comes, certain bailouts will be necessary. But there will also have to be methods that insure that those who created or ignored the mess don't get rewarded for it. Government ownership of segments of the economy has always been distasteful in this country, but the abuses by Enron and their fellow crooks have renewed interest in some forms of ownership. The fact that in California, the municipally owned utilities fared far better than the investor owned utilities in the energy crisis of 2001 vindicated that form of ownership in key infrastructure segments of the economy. One can debate which industries in which situations should be publicly owned, but it is definitely a useful option. Finally, the most likely form of activity in a modern New Deal would probably be the one that was the most actively used in the twentieth century: regulation and the breakup of segments through anti-trust legislation. Most of the problems that we face are the result of these kinds of issues.

Objectives of a Twenty-first Century New Deal

1. Need for Law and Order

With the above strategies in mind, what would be some of the major objectives of a modern New Deal? The first would be to bring a sense of law and order to the current environment. At the very core of the original New Deal was the need for a sense of order. The Roaring Twenties were not called that by accident. On the economic front the era very much adhered to the ideal that anything goes—as long you can get away with it. The chaos of the stock market crash and the resulting social and economic upheaval were the logical result of an economic system out of control. The Great Depression unleashed social forces across the political spectrum and there was no guarantee that democracy would survive the aftermath. Although many of the economic elite and upper middle class considered FDR a traitor to his class, the New Deal in fact saved the capitalist system, and many on the left considered it a sellout of the working class. It was the "Third Way" ideology of its day. It is remarkable that many of the critics of the New Deal who were denizens of Wall Street at the time forgot one of basic tenets of their profession—that the market dislikes uncertainty. Raymond Moley was right to point out that one of the most important results of the New Deal was to restore public confidence in the government and the economic system. The New Deal saved the banks and the brokerage houses and protected them from their own missteps. The New Deal then went on to curb potential abuses of the system by the rich and powerful that could destroy public confidence or markets in the future.

This is a lesson that has been forgotten by far too many people, on both the left and the right. The recent view has been that developments in financial theory and new models as well as the development of new financial instruments have made the New Deal regulations obsolete. But this view fails to take into account (and could not adequately measure) the psychological impacts on markets and market activity. For, while there have been great changes over the years as to how markets work, human reactions with regard to money and possessions haven't changed in centuries. In both the 1930s and the current era we have seen economic theories swept away by financial bubbles that grew large enough to undermine public confidence in the financial system. In such cases, it can take a very long time to restore confidence; it cannot be resolved in the short run by fiscal or monetary policy. Confidence in the political leadership must be restored before there is any advance on the financial front, and even then, recovery takes time. The social and psychological aspects of financial crises are what most free market advocates and critics of New and New Deal-type programs forget to put in their economic equations.

What government restraints that have been enforced in recent times have been misplaced. Since the Reagan Administration, too much of the government's effort has been directed to curbing the abuse of the system by the poor—the "welfare queens" and the like. But comparing the local welfare queen to the no-bid contracts for Halliburton in Iraq makes it painfully obvious where government resources should be directed to curb systemic abuse and corruption most effectively.

The first thing that any modern New Deal needs to do is to instill confidence in and support for the stability of the government and the economic system. That means reinstitution of some of the original New Deal legislation, particularly the key portions of the Glass-Steagall Act that were repealed in the 1990s and not covered by the Sarbanes-Oxley Act. For those who say that such legislation would be too restrictive, the answer is that this legislation was in place for decades without hurting America's competitive status. In fact, the American economy was at least as successful under those restrictions as it is now that the restrictions have been removed. The same is true of other New Deal legislation that needs to be restored, such as the re-regulation of public utilities. What the recent deregulated period has reaffirmed is that management decisions, rather than government regulation, are the key factors in the success of a business or the economy as a whole. Much of what the Bush Administration has done has fallen into the category where economic "value" is the result of government manipulation rather than genuine wealth. Regulations that stabilize and provide confidence and order in the market have a much better chance to create economic values than the anarchy of the so-called "free market."

Additional steps that need to be taken to create law and order in the economy are Congressional scrutiny of government ethics and financial transactions. One of the most important traits that helped promote FDR's New Deal was the integrity of its appointees. Given the radical nature of the programs, support would not have lasted as long as it did but for the fact that there was a minimum of scandal. That contrasts sharply with the massive corruption in Iraq and on the Gulf Coast after Hurricane Katrina. The Democratic Party needs to demand a corruption-free administration and Congress from its elected officials. The last on the law-and-order agenda of a modern New Deal is to bring some sense of stability to the federal budget. This in turn means a complete revision of the priorities of the federal government, which will be discussed later.

2. Need for Openness and Fairness

The second key objective to a twenty-first century New Deal is a need for openness and fairness. One of the themes of Roosevelt's 1932 campaign was "the forgotten man"—those people either left out or abandoned by the economic system. Many people have that feeling of being "forgotten" by the economy today. John Edwards in his 2004 Vice Presidential campaign spoke of the "Two Americas," one reaping the benefits of the current economy, the other left behind. A key plank in any modern New Deal is that the average American can feel that they have a piece of the action. Beyond that, however, is a new issue that was not present in 1932. And that is that there is a sense that information is being manufactured and restricted by consolidation of media into large corporate groups. This has bred a great deal of distrust of the media establishment and led to the outburst of alternative media, particularly on the Internet. It has also led to concerns originally stated by Thomas Jefferson that a democracy can only survive through an informed public.

With those ideas in mind some of the actions that need to be taken to sustain fairness and openness in a modern New Deal is the repeal of the Telecommunications Act of 1996, the reestablishment of the Fairness Doctrine in broadcasting, and efforts to insure that the Internet remains free and open to the public, with this principle enforced by legislation is necessary. In effect, these actions would, impose anti-trust legislation on the media, breaking the half dozen or media conglomerates that dominate information sources in this country and ensure that the Internet is not privatized into another media conglomerate. In conjunction with the Fairness Doctrine regarding opposing viewpoints, it is time to publicly fund all election campaigns, not just the presidential election, and it is also time to ensure that every vote get counted fairly and accurately and can be publicly audited. Elections are a public activity and should not be impacted by the whims of private enterprise. Another aspect of fairness and openness would be the strict enforcement of anti-trust laws to remove concentrations of corporate power that threaten our democracy. At the same time we need to strengthen labor laws and rejuvenate the National Labor Relations Board so that workers have a viable voice in our economy. Unions also need to encourage the organization of independent free-lance workers, not affiliated with any trade or craft, which form a growing part of the workforce. Labor's Working America is a step in that direction.

3. Need for the Primacy of Community Values while Respecting Individual Initiative

One of the most important characteristics of the original New Deal also came out of the "forgotten man" concept. That was that the New Deal was to be a collective effort involving all aspects of the community in which no one was to be left behind. In digging out of the Depression, they followed the concept represented by the acronym WITT—we're in this together. With the unfortunate exception of agricultural workers, the New Deal of the 1930s covered just about all aspects of society.

In contrast, today's America is more accurately characterized by the acronym YOYO—you're on your own. This idea was advanced with the idea of advancing individual freedom and the activities of the entrepreneur. But its result has had the tendency to stifle freedom under fear and uncertainty. It has also tended to subjugate the individual to concentrations of power in government and the private sector. A notable aspect of this was the response by the Bush Administration to the attack on September 11, 2001. Instead of rallying the country, the administration approached what was essentially an international criminal act with the nebulous "war of terror" couched in a "them versus us" and a "good versus evil" mentality, injecting heavy doses of fear into the process as well. Another aspect of the fear factor was to insist that two hundred years of carefully preserved civil liberties should be thrown way in the futile and paranoid pursuit of "terrorist suspects," while other countries managed to protect their citizen's rights as they were actually finding and arresting terrorists. The result in America has been the failed apprehension of any legitimate terrorists, while someone such as the Anthrax Killer remains at large even though only a couple of dozen people in the country would have fit the killer's profile. YOYO is high on the value of individual responsibility, but whatever merits individual responsibility has, in our time, it has been used as the all-purpose cop-out to avoid the needs of society. It fails to recognize that throughout history, the viability of human society has been based on preservation of the group, not the exploits of the individual. While individual initiative is an important aspect of rejuvenating the community, it cannot be used as a license to undermine public confidence.

In both the old and a modern New Deal, the primacy of community values means that there are certain activities beyond public safety (which is a given) that are the responsibility of everyone and cannot be palmed-off as personal responsibility. These activities include education, justice, health care, elections, transportation, infrastructure, and other national assets. You cannot privatize society. As for specific initiatives in a modern New Deal, they would include the previously mentioned public funding of elections, both the campaigns and the counting and audit of the votes. Private companies using unauditable proprietary software are unacceptable after the fallout from the 2000 and 2004 elections. It would also include public works projects for transportation and infrastructure. While we have been showering the various security departments with money, the roads, bridges, dams, rail lines and a whole host of other project are literally falling apart, and this was even before the devastation on the Gulf Coast. We cannot expect to keep the country safe if the basic building blocks for running the country are not there. Likewise we cannot develop the economy for the same reason. At the same time, these projects continue to fulfill their role as a means of activating the unemployed. Part of the infrastructure to be maintained is prisons. It has been very fashionable to allow the private sector to handle this activity in recent years, but the prisons are part of a public justice system that is a community responsibility that is ultimately accountable to and by the public that cannot be realistically handed to the private realm.

An area where the private/non-profit sector has been involved has been education. This has been true for centuries. But while there is more leeway here, education is still a community responsibility and must cover those educational tasks that the private sector is unable or unwilling to. Even more important, the public education system of this country has been a cornerstone of its economic development for over two centuries. One of the failings of early Red-state culture in the South was its reliance on a private educational system for the almost exclusive benefit of a cultural elite that retarded its economic development right to the present day. Now in many states, tuition costs are skyrocketing at public universities, creating the possibility of Red-state productivity and technology gaps that cripples those states in the world marketplace. A Blue-state such as California, which built a huge portion of its high-tech economy on the basis of its public educational system, particularly the University of California system, is now at risk of losing those gains to domestic and foreign economies that are increasing the funding and the quality of their educational systems. The educational system in the province of Ontario was one of two important factors that landed a highly coveted Toyota factory in Woodstock for the Ontario government because the skill of its workforce required less training costs for Toyota. And if it was true for Toyota then it is no doubt true for any high tech company looking for a place to set up shop. The higher the technology needs, the higher the education needs—public education is not just a question of the classroom, but also research and development.

The other key factor that landed the Toyota factory for Ontario was health care. With US health care costs double those of the developing world for a system that doesn't even adequately cover everyone, health care is now a serious economic liability for any current or future American business competing with other businesses in the developing world. It is clear that health care is not an insurable risk in the private sector. Therefore, one of the programs of a modern New Deal would be a government-financed universal single-payer health care system for all Americans, similar to Medicare. This is the only way that the US will be able to compete effectively with the systems in the industrialized world.

One of the major items Roosevelt's New Deal foreign relations was his "Good Neighbor Policy," and a series of reciprocal trade agreements. A version of that in a modern New Deal would be the development of a fair trade policy, which would take into account the interests of workers and the environment in all the affected countries, which is not the case in trade agreements like NAFTA where corporations have been allowed to exploit both. With regard to corporations, the abuses that have been allowed under the Bush Administration have prompted the need to rethink the whole issue of corporate governance. One of the planks of a modern New Deal would be to restore the principles on which corporations were originally chartered. This was that charters were granted for the purpose of providing a public good in exchange for limited liability. All too often in recent years, limited liability has been emphasized at the expense of a public good. A modern New Deal needs to review what kinds of public goods are worth chartering and what forms of limited liability should be advocated. Do mutual or co-operative corporations as opposed to private corporations carry greater public benefit and are entitled to special tax rates and other forms of limited liability? This is one of the questions that should be asked by chartering authorities.

Finally, one of the major objectives of the first New Deal was conservation. This was an issue that Franklin Roosevelt acquired from his cousin Theodore, and was part of his economic recovery plan as Governor of New York and later came to fruition in the New Deal as the Civilian Conservation Corps. Today, conservation has expanded to cover all the issues revolving around the environment, including global warming and alternative energy sources. A modern New Deal must address the problem directly and come up with national and international solutions to these problems, not sweep them under the rug to please a few corporate constituents.

These are some of the key activities of a twenty-first century New Deal. Unlike the original New Deal, they do not encompass the wide variety of activities that the Roosevelt Administration worked on in the 1930s. But they provide a broad foundation on which to build for a future Democratic administration.

4. Priorities in a Twenty-First Century New Deal

In addition to the programs, priorities must set amongst the programs. The most important decision that will have to be made for an incoming Democratic administration will be the necessity of making domestic needs a priority over foreign ones, and that the financial structure of the country must be addressed. This means that, first, America will have to shed its quasi-imperialist foreign policy and recognize the fact that not every foreign objective can be obtained by military force, and not only in the Middle East. Given the growing domestic needs that have been deferred and the huge budget deficits that have been run up, the current defense budget (which is double the level of 2001) is unsustainable. The next president is going to have to do what British Prime Minister Clement Atlee did after World War II, and shrink the American empire to a financially stable level. The over 700 military bases overseas need to be reduced substantially. The security of this country cannot be maintained with a demoralized and economically stressed populace in tandem with an empty treasury. We will be lucky if the Chinese continues to finance our economy. They certainly will not bankroll our military.

Second, dependence on foreign governments and their cash reserves in order to maintain our standard of living effectively makes America a vassal state. In addition to defense cuts, taxes will need to be raised on upper incomes to finance the deficit. The wealthy have benefited the most from the Bush Administration's fiscal policy since 2001. With hundreds of thousands of middle and lower income families having to make sacrifices because of family members serving in the Middle East, it is only fair that people in the highest tax brackets make the financial sacrifices to sustain the war without having that placed on lower income people as well.

Third, as Democrats we must assert that the republic created by the founding fathers takes precedence over the imperial desires and bank accounts of the military-industrial complex, and that liberty will not be sacrificed on the false idol of security. The so-called "war on terror" must not be used to terrorize the public and destroy the principles on which country was founded.

Finally, we must assert as William Jennings Bryan and Martin Luther King did that every great political and economic question is at its core a moral question, and that the personal values of our religious faith and the values of the democracy enshrined in the Constitution and the Bill of Rights supersedes the material values of our government and our society. We will not sacrifice our people and privatize humanity for the sake of spurious economic gain.

SUMMARY

This statement of a twenty-first century New Deal defines the nature of a Blue-state culture for our time. As in all Blue-state cultures, it provides a greater role for government, and it emphasizes the importance of community and society in implementing that culture. It puts the emphasis on "we" rather than "I" or "they." It recognizes a culture that is a democratically collective effort to attain our goals as a people. And above all, it is a pathway to hope, not fear. Since the events of September 11, 2001, we have been inundated with messages of fear: fear of other places, fear of other people; fear in our workplaces, our commercial areas, our modes of travel, and in our neighborhoods. The leaders in our country have been profiting from fear, both at the ballot box and in their bank accounts, leaving in their wake a near bankrupt, hollowed out country vulnerable to the economic and political agendas of foreign states. But as Franklin Delano Roosevelt, one of the Democratic Party's greatest advocates for Blue-state culture, said as he faced the Great Depression in his first inaugural speech in 1933, "the only thing we have to fear is fear itself." It is time to banish fear. It is time to look out with hope to the broad vistas of this country, as Roosevelt did, and restore to our nation the gift of the republic that the founding fathers and the soldiers of the Revolution gave us, so that it may be cherished by generations to come.

APPENDIX A.1A. RED-STATE POPULATION, INCOME, FINANCE (PART 1)

	Population (000)	Electoral Votes	Median Household Income	Personal Income $Billions	Per Capita Income Rank	Poverty % of Population
	2000	2004	1999($)	2002	2002	2003–04
UNITED STATES	281,422	538	41,994	8,033.1	(X)	12.6
South						
Alabama	4,447	9	34,135	101.5	43	16.0
Arkansas	2,673	6	32,182	57.4	49	16.4
Florida	15,982	27	38,819	445.3	23	12.2
Georgia	8,186	15	42,433	222.1	28	12.5
Kentucky	4,042	8	33,672	94.3	39	16.0
Louisiana	4,469	9	32,586	102.7	41	16.8
Mississippi	2,845	6	31,330	57.8	50	17.3
North Carolina	8,049	15	39,184	207.6	34	15.1
South Carolina	4,012	8	37,082	93.9	42	13.6
Tennessee	5,689	11	36,360	144.4	35	15.0
Texas	20,852	34	39,927	559.9	30	16.7
Virginia	7,079	13	46,677	216.2	`11	9.7

	Population (000)	Electoral Votes	Median Household Income	Personal Income $Billions	Per Capita Income Rank	Poverty % of Population
	2000	2004	1999($)	2002	2002	2003–04
West Virginia	1,808	5	29,696	38.4	48	15.8
Total South	90,133	166				
Mean South	6,933		36,468	180.1	39	14.9
Median South	4,469		36,360	102.7	40	15.8
West						
Alaska	627	3	51,571	18.6	14	9.4
Arizona	5,131	10	40,558	128.6	38	13.9
Colorado	4,301	9	47,203	135.0	9	9.9
Idaho	1,294	4	37,572	30.3	44	10.0
Montana	902	3	33,024	20.5	45	14.6
Nevada	1,998	5	44,581	59.1	19	10.9
New Mexico	1,819	5	34,133	40.0	47	17.3
Utah	2,233	5	45,726	50.7	46	9.5
Wyoming	494	3	37,892	13.7	17	9.9
Total West	18,799	47				
Mean West	2,089		41,362	55.2	31	11.7
Median West	1,819		40,558	40.0	38	10.0
Midwest						
Indiana	6,080	11	41,567	156.6	32	10.8
Iowa	2,926	7	38,469	74.8	31	9.9
Kansas	2,688	6	40,624	71.3	26	11.1
Missouri	5,595	11	37,934	147.8	27	11.5
Nebraska	1,711	5	39,250	46.3	22	9.6
North Dakota	642	3	34,604	15.4	36	9.7
Ohio	11,353	20	40,956	302.4	25	11.3
Oklahoma	3,451	7	33,400	80.4	40	11.8
South Dakota	755	3	35,282	18.4	37	13.0
Total Midwest	35,201	73				
Mean Midwest	3,911		38,010	101.5	31	11.0
Median Midwest	2,926		38,469	74.8	31	11.1

	Population (000)	Electoral Votes	Median Household Income	Personal Income $Billions	Per Capita Income Rank	Poverty % of Population
	2000	2004	1999($)	2002	2002	2003–04
Total Red	144,133	286				
Mean Red	4,649		38,336	121.0	34	12.8
Median Red	3,451		37,934	80.4	36	12.2

Appendix A.1b. Blue-State Population, Income, Finance (Part 1)

	Population (000)	Electoral Votes	Median Household Income	Personal Income $Billions	Per Capita Income Rank	Poverty % of Population
	2000	2004	1999($)	2002	2002	2003–04
UNITED STATES	281,422	538	41,994	8,033.1	(X)	12.6
Northeast						
Connecticut	3,406	7	53,935	133.1	1	9.1
Delaware	784	3	47,381	23.8	12	8.2
D.C.	572	3	40,127	21.6	(X)	16.7
Maine	1,275	4	37,240	32.3	33	11.6
Maryland	5,296	10	52,868	178.4	4	9.2
Massachusetts	6,349	12	50,502	227.1	3	9.7
New Hampshire	1,236	4	49,467	39.4	6	5.6
New Jersey	8,414	15	55,146	305.1	2	8.3
New York	18,976	31	43,393	621.7	5	14.6
Pennsylvania	12,281	21	40,106	352.3	15	10.9
Rhode Island	1,048	4	42,090	30.2	16	11.5
Vermont	609	3	40,856	16.4	24	8.2
Total Northeast	60,246	117				
Mean Northeast	5,021		46,093	165.1	11	10.3
Median Northeast	2,341		45,387	86.3	6	9.5
West						
California	33,872	55	47,493	1,043.2	10	13.2
Hawaii	1,212	4	49,820	33.6	20	8.9
Oregon	3,421	7	40,916	91.1	29	12.1
Washington	5,894	11	45,776	178.6	13	12.0
Total West	44,399	77				
Mean West	11,100		46,001	336.6	18	11.6
Median West	4,658		46,635	134.9	17	12.1
Midwest						
Illinois	12,419	21	46,590	379.0	8	12.4
Michigan	9,938	17	44,667	274.1	18	12.3
Minnesota	4,919	10	47,111	154.0	7	7.2
Wisconsin	5,364	10	43,791	146.6	21	11.0

	Population (000)	Electoral Votes	Median Household Income	Personal Income $Billions	Per Capita Income Rank	Poverty % of Population
	2000	2004	1999($)	2002	2002	2003–04
Total Midwest	32,640	58				
Mean Midwest	8,160		45,540	238.4	14	10.7
Median Midwest	7,651		45,629	214.1	13	11.7
Total Blue	137,285	252				
Mean Blue	6,864		45,964	214.1	13	10.6
Median Blue	5,108		46,183	150.3	12	11.0

Source: Statistical Abstract of the United States

APPENDIX A.2A. RED-STATE POPULATION, INCOME, FINANCE (PART 2)

	Unemployment % of Workers	Bankrupt (000)	Bankrupt (000)	Net Fed Revenue Received	State Rev. Per Capita Rank	Unions % of Workers
	2002(1)	1995(1)	2002(1)	2004(2)	2000(1)	2002(1)
UNITED STATES	5.8	858	1,505			13.3
South						
Alabama	5.9	24	40	$1.71	37	9.0
Arkansas	5.4	8	22	$1.47	25	6.0
Florida	5.5	43	88	$1.02	50	5.8
Georgia	5.1	42	73	$0.96	45	6.0
Kentucky	5.6	13	26	$1.45	21	10.0
Louisiana	6.1	13	27	$1.45	31	8.4
Mississippi	6.8	11	22	$1.77	28	6.7
North Carolina	6.7	14	35	$1.10	23	3.4
South Carolina	6.0	7	15	$1.38	32	5.0
Tennessee	5.1	36	62	$1.30	46	9.1
Texas	6.3	44	77	$0.94	49	5.2
Virginia	4.1	26	42	$1.66	34	6.0
West Virginia	6.1	4	10	$1.83	18	13.2
Total South						
Mean South	5.7	22	41	$1.39	34	7.2
Median South	5.9	14	35	$1.45	32	6.0
West						
Alaska	7.7	1	1	$1.87	1	24.4
Arizona	6.2	15	27	$1.30	47	5.6
Colorado	5.7	13	19	$0.79	43	7.8
Idaho	5.8	4	8	$1.28	33	7.1
Montana	4.6	2	4	$1.58	19	14.1
Nevada	5.5	7	19	$0.73	48	15.2
New Mexico	5.4	4	9	$2.00	9	6.9
Utah	6.1	7	21	$1.14	24	6.2
Wyoming	4.2	1	2	$1.11	16	7.7
Total West						

	Unemployment % of Workers	Bankrupt (000)	Bankrupt (000)	Net Fed Revenue Received	State Rev. Per Capita Rank	Unions % of Workers
	2002(1)	1995(1)	2002(1)	2004(2)	2000(1)	2002(1)
Mean West	5.7	6	12	$1.31	27	10.6
Median West	5.7	4	9	$1.28	24	7.7
Midwest						
Indiana	5.1	22	51	$0.97	41	13.3
Iowa	4.0	6	11	$1.11	29	11.0
Kansas	5.1	8	14	$1.12	36	8.2
Missouri	5.5	15	32	$1.29	44	13.2
Nebraska	3.6	3	7	$1.07	30	8.0
North Dakota	4.0	1	2	$1.73	8	8.1
Ohio	5.7	32	73	$1.01	35	16.8
Oklahoma	4.5	13	23	$1.48	39	8.9
South Dakota	3.1	1	3	$1.49	42	5.5
Total Midwest						
Mean Midwest	4.5	11	24	$1.25	34	10.3
Median Midwest	4.5	8	14	$1.12	36	8.9
Total Red						
Mean Red	5.4	14	28	$1.33	32	9.1
Median Red	5.5	11	22	$1.30	33	8.0

APPENDIX A.2B. BLUE-STATE POPULATION, INCOME, FINANCE (PART 2)

	Unemployment % of Workers	Bankrupt (000)	Bankrupt (000)	Net Fed Revenue Received	State Rev Per Capita Rank	Unions % of Workers
	2002(1)	1995(1)	2002(1)	2004(2)	2000(1)	2002(1)
UNITED STATES	5.8	858	1,505			13.3
Northeast						
Connecticut	4.3	8	11	$0.66	5	16.9
Delaware	4.2	1	4	$0.79	2	11.2
D.C.	6.4	1	3			˙14.1
Maine	4.4	2	4	$1.40	12	13.0
Maryland	4.4	16	34	$1.44	27	14.5
Massachusetts	5.3	14	17	$0.77	10	14.4
New Hampshire	4.7	3	4	$0.67	38	9.8
New Jersey	5.8	26	40	$0.55	20	19.8
New York	6.1	49	68	$0.79	7	25.6
Pennsylvania	5.7	22	52	$1.06	26	15.7
Rhode Island	5.1	3	5	$1.02	17	17.4
Vermont	3.7	1	2	$1.12	3	9.5
Total Northeast						
Mean Northeast	5.0	12	20	$0.93	15	15.3
Median Northeast	4.9	6	8	$0.79	12	14.5
West						
California	6.7	140	148	$0.79	14	17.8
Hawaii	4.2	2	5	$1.60	6	24.4
Oregon	7.5	13	24	$0.97	13	15.7
Washington	7.3	19	37	$0.88	22	18.6
Total West						
Mean West	6.4	44	54	$1.06	14	19.1
Median West	7.0	16	31	$0.93	14	18.2
Midwest						
Illinois	6.5	39	77	$0.73	40	19.7
Michigan	6.2	23	50	$0.85	15	21.1
Minnesota	4.4	14	19	$0.69	11	17.5

	Unemployment % of Workers	Bankrupt (000)	Bankrupt (000)	Net Fed Revenue Received	State Rev Per Capita Rank	Unions % of Workers
	2002(1)	1995(1)	2002(1)	2004(2)	2000(1)	2002(1)
Wisconsin	5.5	12	23	$0.82	16	15.6
Total Midwest						
Mean Midwest	5.7	22	42	$0.77	21	18.5
Median Midwest	5.9	19	37	$0.78	16	18.6
Total Blue						
Mean Blue	5.4	20	31	$0.93	16	16.7
Median Blue	5.4	14	21	$0.82	14	16.9

Source: (1) Statistical Abstract of the United States, (2) Tax Foundation. Used by Permission

APPENDIX B.1. RED-STATE TECHNOLOGY, INFRASTRUCTURE

	Highway Miles (000)	Education $ Per Capita Rank	Use of Computers %	Use of Internet %
	2001	2002	2001	2001
UNITED STATES	3,948		56.5	50.5
South				
Alabama	94	47	43.7	37.6
Arkansas	98	45	46.8	36.9
Florida	117	42	55.9	52.8
Georgia	116	19	52.4	46.7
Kentucky	79	26	49.8	44.2
Louisiana	61	36	45.7	40.2
Mississippi	74	46	41.9	36.1
North Carolina	101	37	50.1	44.5
South Carolina	66	31	52.2	45.0
Tennessee	88	44	51.3	44.8
Texas	301	32	53.7	47.7
Virginia	71	40	58.8	54.9
West Virginia	37	13	48.0	40.7
Total South				
Mean South	100	35	50.0	44.0
Median South	88	37	50.1	44.5
West				
Alaska	14	4	68.7	64.1
Arizona	55	48	59.4	51.9
Colorado	86	28	64.7	58.5
Idaho	46	39	62.8	52.7
Montana	70	24	56.0	47.5
Nevada	39	43	58.2	52.5
New Mexico	60	29	67.7	61.6
Utah	42	49	67.7	54.1
Wyoming	27	12	58.1	51.0
Total West				
Mean West	49	31	62.6	54.9
Median West	46	29	62.8	52.7
Midwest				
Indiana	94	17	53.2	47.3
Iowa	113	35	59.4	51.0

	Highway Miles (000)	Education $ Per Capita Rank	Use of Computers %	Use of Internet %
	2001	2002	2001	2001
Kansas	135	20	57.5	50.9
Missouri	124	30	55.3	49.9
Nebraska	93	33	55.6	45.5
North Dakota	87	50	53.0	46.5
Ohio	117	25	57.6	50.9
Oklahoma	113	41	49.9	43.8
South Dakota	84	38	55.3	47.6
Total Midwest				
Mean Midwest	107	32	55.2	48.2
Median Midwest	113	33	55.3	47.6
Total Red				
Mean Red	87	33	55.2	48.4
Median Red	86	35	55.3	47.6

APPENDIX B.2. BLUE-STATE TECHNOLOGY, INFRASTRUCTURE

	Highway Miles (000)	Education Exp Per Capita Rank	Computer Use % of Households	Internet Use % of Households
	2001	2002	2001	2001
UNITED STATES	3,948		56.5	50.5
Northeast				
Connecticut	21	3	58.7	55.0
Delaware	6	7	58.4	52.5
D.C.	2		49.3	41.4
Maine	23	11	62.8	53.3
Maryland	31	21	64.1	57.8
Massachusetts	35	5	59.1	54.7
New Hampshire	16	18	55.0	50.2
New Jersey	36	2	61.2	57.2
New York	113	1	50.6	43.1
Pennsylvania	120	16	53.5	48.7
Rhode Island	6	8	58.6	53.1
Vermont	14	6	60.4	53.4
Total Northeast				
Mean Northeast	35	9	57.6	51.7
Median Northeast	22	7	58.7	53.2
West				
California	169	34	61.5	55.3
Hawaii	4	23	63.1	55.2
Oregon	67	15	65.8	58.2
Washington	81	27	66.5	60.4
Total West				
Mean West	80	25	64.2	57.3
Median West	74	25	64.5	56.8
Midwest				
Illinois	139	9	53.0	46.9
Michigan	122	14	58.3	51.2
Minnesota	132	22	64.6	55.6
Wisconsin	113	10	56.4	50.2
Total Midwest				
Mean Midwest	127	14	58.1	51.0

	Highway Miles (000)	Education Exp Per Capita Rank	Computer Use % of Households	Internet Use % of Households
	2001	2002	2001	2001
Median Midwest	127	12	57.4	50.7
Total Blue				
Mean Blue	63	13	59.0	52.7
Median Blue	36	11	58.9	53.4

Source: Statistical Abstract of the United States

Appendix C.1. Red-State Health

	Doctors per 100K	Nurses per 100K	Infant Mortality per 1000	Life Expectancy Yrs
	1999	1999	1999	1991
UNITED STATES	254	833	7.2	75.8
South				
Alabama	200	771	10.2	73.6
Arkansas	192	780	8.9	74.3
Florida	243	872	7.2	75.8
Georgia	211	728	8.5	73.6
Kentucky	212	838	7.5	74.4
Louisiana	251	809	9.1	73.0
Mississippi	164	784	10.1	73.0
North Carolina	237	935	9.3	74.5
South Carolina	213	834	9.6	73.5
Tennessee	248	897	8.2	74.3
Texas	205	659	6.4	75.1
Virginia	243	837	7.7	75.2
West Virginia	219	893	8.0	74.3
Total South				
Mean South	218	818	8.5	74.2
Median South	213	834	8.5	74.3
West				
Alaska	170	1,186	5.9	
Arizona	203	767	7.5	76.1
Colorado	244	770	6.7	77.0
Idaho	155	601	7.2	76.9
Montana	191	889	7.4	76.2
Nevada	177	631	7.0	74.2
New Mexico	214	724	7.2	75.7
Utah	202	651	5.6	77.7
Wyoming	172	1,049	7.2	76.2
Total West				
Mean West	192	808	6.9	76.3
Median West	191	767	7.2	76.2
Midwest				
Indiana	198	831	7.6	75.4
Iowa	175	1,088	6.6	77.3

	Doctors per 100K	Nurses per 100K	Infant Mortality per 1000	Life Expectancy Yrs
	1999	1999	1999	1991
Kansas	204	891	7.0	76.8
Missouri	232	985	7.7	75.3
Nebraska	221	897	7.3	76.9
North Dakota	224	1,177	8.6	77.6
Ohio	237	924	8.0	75.3
Oklahoma	167	610	8.5	75.1
South Dakota	188	1,009	9.1	76.9
Total Midwest				
Mean Midwest	205	935	7.8	76.3
Median Midwest	204	924	7.7	76.8
Total Red				
Mean Red	207	849	7.8	75.4
Median Red	205	837	7.6	75.3

APPENDIX C.2. BLUE-STATE HEALTH

	Doctors per 100K	Nurses Per 100K	Infant Mortality per 1000	Life Expectancy Yrs
	1999	1999	1998	1991
UNITED STATES	254	833	7.2	75.8
Northeast				
Connecticut	361	995	7.0	76.9
Delaware	238	1,120	9.6	74.8
D.C.	245	833	12.5	68.0
Maine	232	1,085	6.3	73.1
Maryland	379	855	8.6	76.4
Massachusetts	422	1,180	5.1	74.8
New Hampshire	234	904	4.4	76.7
New Jersey	301	807	6.4	75.4
New York	395	939	6.3	74.7
Pennsylvania	293	1,137	7.1	75.4
Rhode Island	339	1,179	7.0	76.5
Vermont	313	869	7.0	76.5
Total Northeast				
Mean Northeast	313	992	7.3	74.9
Median Northeast	307	967	7.0	75.4
West				
California	248	532	5.8	75.9
Hawaii	269	805	6.9	78.2
Oregon	227	892	5.4	76.4
Washington	237	777	5.7	76.8
Total West				
Mean West	245	752	6.0	76.8
Median West	243	791	5.8	76.6
Midwest				
Illinois	263	909	8.4	74.9
Michigan	226	845	8.2	75.0
Minnesota	254	1,088	5.9	77.8
Wisconsin	232	905	7.2	76.9
Total Midwest				
Mean Midwest	244	937	7.4	76.2

	Doctors per 100K	Nurses Per 100K	Infant Mortality per 1000	Life Expectancy Yrs
	1999	1999	1998	1991
Median Midwest	243	907	7.7	76.0
Total Blue				
Mean Blue	285	933	7.0	75.6
Median Blue	259	905	7.0	76.2

Source: Statistical Abstract of the United States

APPENDIX D.1. RED-STATE ENVIRONMENT

	Per Capita Water Use Gallons	Per Capita Energy Use Mil. BTUs	Toxic Spills Mil. Lbs	Urbanization % of Population	Public Transportation % of Workers	Carpools % of Workers
	1995	1999	2001	2000	2000	2000
UNITED STATES	1,280	327	1,430.1	79.0	4.7	12.2
South						
Alabama	1,670	459	61.0	55.4	0.5	12.3
Arkansas	3,540	472	33.5	52.5	0.4	14.1
Florida	509	255	26.3	89.3	1.9	12.9
Georgia	799	359	35.3	71.6	2.3	14.5
Kentucky	1,150	462	28.6	55.8	1.2	12.6
Louisiana	2,270	827	70.3	72.6	2.4	13.6
Mississippi	1,140	437	36.3	48.8	0.6	15.2
North Carolina	1,070	320	35.8	60.2	0.9	14.0
South Carolina	1,690	384	52.0	60.5	0.8	14.0
Tennessee	1,920	378	62.8	63.6	0.8	12.5
Texas	1,300	574	130.2	82.5	1.9	14.5
Virginia	826	3,254	31.6	73.0	3.6	12.7
West Virginia	2,530	407	9.0	46.1	0.8	12.7
Total South						
Mean South	1,570	661	47.1	64.0	1.4	13.5
Median South	1,300	437	35.8	60.5	0.9	13.6
West						
Alaska	350	1,122	0.5	65.6	1.8	15.5
Arizona	1,620	255	52.7	88.2	1.9	15.4
Colorado	3,590	285	2.5	84.5	3.2	12.2
Idaho	13,000	414	8.6	66.4	1.1	12.3
Montana	10,200	467	18.2	54.1	0.7	11.9
Nevada	1,480	340	3.2	91.5	3.9	14.7
New Mexico	2,080	365	0.6	75.0	0.8	14.8
Utah	2,200	326	48.4	88.2	2.2	14.1
Wyoming	14,700	879	0.8	65.1	1.4	13.2
Total West						

	Per Capita Water Use Gallons	Per Capita Energy Use Mil. BTUs	Toxic Spills Mil. Lbs	Urbanization % of Population	Public Transportation % of Workers	Carpools % of Workers
	1995	1999	2001	2000	2000	2000
Mean West	5,469	495	15.1	75.4	1.9	13.8
Median West	2,200	365	3.2	75.0	1.8	14.1
Midwest						
Indiana	1,570	460	106.5	70.8	1.0	11.0
Iowa	1,070	391	19.2	61.1	1.0	10.8
Kansas	2,040	396	12.8	71.4	0.5	10.6
Missouri	1,320	323	43.0	69.4	1.5	11.6
Nebraska	6,440	361	12.2	69.8	0.7	10.5
North Dakota	1,750	577	0.9	55.9	0.4	10.0
Ohio	944	384	90.5	77.4	2.1	9.3
Oklahoma	543	410	12.3	65.3	0.5	13.2
South Dakota	631	326	1.1	51.9	0.5	10.4
Total Midwest						
Mean Midwest	1,812	403	33.2	65.9	0.9	10.8
Median Midwest	1,320	391	12.8	69.4	0.7	10.6
Total Red						
Mean Red	2,772	538	33.8	67.9	1.4	12.8
Median Red	1,620	396	28.6	66.4	1.0	12.7

APPENDIX D.2. BLUE-STATE ENVIRONMENT

	Per Capita Water Use Gallons	Per Capita Energy Use Mil. BTUS	Toxic Spills Mil. Lbs	Urbanization % of Population	Public Transportation % of Workers	Carpools % of Workers
	1995	1999	2001	2000	2000	2000
UNITED STATES	1,280	327	1,430.1	79.0	4.7	12.2
Northeast						
Connecticut	389	256	3.6	87.7	4.0	9.4
Delaware	1,050	370	5.2	80.1	2.8	11.5
D.C.	18	327	0.0	100.0	33.2	11.0
Maine	178	422	5.0	40.2	0.8	11.3
Maryland	289	267	7.7	86.1	7.2	12.4
Massachusetts	189	254	4.5	91.4	8.7	9.0
New Hampshire	388	279	1.2	59.3	0.7	9.8
New Jersey	269	318	26.8	94.4	9.6	10.6
New York	567	235	13.6	87.5	24.4	9.2
Pennsylvania	802	310	97.5	77.1	5.2	10.4
Rhode Island	138	264	0.9	90.9	2.5	10.4
Vermont	967	278	0.1	38.2	0.7	11.9
Total Northeast						
Mean Northeast	437	298	13.8	77.7	8.3	10.6
Median Northeast	339	279	4.8	86.8	4.6	10.5
West						
California	1,130	253	16.7	94.4	5.1	14.5
Hawaii	853	204	0.4	91.5	6.3	19.0
Oregon	2,520	335	21.9	78.7	4.2	12.2
Washington	1,620	389	11.7	82.0	4.9	12.8
Total West						
Mean West	1,531	295	12.7	86.7	5.1	14.6
Median West	1,375	294	14.2	86.8	5.0	13.7
Midwest						
Illinois	1,680	320	67.8	87.8	8.7	10.9
Michigan	1,260	328	59.9	74.7	1.3	9.7
Minnesota	736	351	13.5	70.9	3.2	10.4

	Per Capita Water Use Gallons	Per Capita Energy Use Mil. BTUS	Toxic Spills Mil. Lbs	Urbanization % of Population	Public Transportation % of Workers	Carpools % of Workers
	1995	1999	2001	2000	2000	2000
Wisconsin	1,420	345	25.5	68.3	2.0	9.9
Total Midwest						
Mean Midwest	1,274	336	41.7	75.4	3.8	10.2
Median Midwest	1,340	337	42.7	72.8	2.6	10.2
Total Blue						
Mean Blue	823	305	19.2	79.1	6.8	11.3
Median Blue	769	314	9.7	84.1	4.6	10.8

Source: Statistical Abstract of the United States

APPENDIX E.1A. RED-STATE CULTURE (PART 1)

	Abortions per 1000 Women	Marriages per 1000 People	Divorces per 1000 People	Divorces/ Marriages %
	2000(1)	2001(1)	2001(1)	2001(2)
UNITED STATES	21.3	8.4	4.0	47.6
South				
Alabama	14.3	9.6	5.3	55.2
Arkansas	9.8	14.8	6.6	44.6
Florida	31.9	9.7	5.4	55.7
Georgia	16.9	6.3	3.8	60.3
Kentucky	5.3	9.1	5.5	60.4
Louisiana	13.0	8.6		
Mississippi	5.9	6.7	5.4	80.6
North Carolina	21.0	7.8	4.5	57.7
South Carolina	9.3	9.3	3.5	37.6
Tennessee	15.2	13.9	5.2	37.4
Texas	18.8	9.4	4.1	43.6
Virginia	18.1	9.0	4.3	47.8
West Virginia	6.8	7.9	5.2	65.8
Total South				
Mean South	14.3	9.4	4.9	52.2
Median South	14.3	9.1	5.2	57.1
West				
Alaska	11.7	8.2	4.1	50.0
Arizona	16.5	8.0	4.2	52.5
Colorado	15.9	8.7		
Idaho	7.0	11.4	5.6	49.1
Montana	13.5	7.2	2.6	36.1
Nevada	32.2	75.0	6.8	9.1
New Mexico	14.9	7.9	5.1	64.6
Utah	6.6	10.6	4.4	41.5
Wyoming	0.9	10.3	6.1	59.2
Total West				
Mean West	13.2	16.4	4.9	29.7
Median West	13.5	8.7	4.8	54.6
Midwest				
Indiana	9.4	5.7		0.0
Iowa	9.8	7.2	3.2	44.4

	Abortions per 1000 Women	Marriages per 1000 People	Divorces per 1000 People	Divorces/ Marriages %
	2000(1)	2001(1)	2001(1)	2001(2)
Kansas	21.4	7.6	3.2	42.1
Missouri	6.6	7.6	4.3	56.6
Nebraska	11.6	8.1	3.7	45.7
North Dakota	9.9	6.6	2.7	40.9
Ohio	16.5	7.3	4.0	54.8
Oklahoma	10.1	4.9	3.4	69.4
South Dakota	5.5	9.1	3.4	37.4
Total Midwest				
Mean Midwest	11.2	7.1	3.5	49.0
Median Midwest	9.9	7.3	3.4	46.6
Total Red				
Mean Red	13.1	10.8	4.5	41.7
Median Red	11.7	8.2	4.3	52.4

Appendix E.1b. Blue-State Culture (Part I)

	Abortions per 1000 Women	Marriages per 1000 People	Divorces per 1000 People	Divorces / Marriages %
	2000(1)	2001(1)	2001(1)	2001(2)
UNITED STATES	21.3	8.4	4.0	47.6
Northeast				
Connecticut	21.1	5.6	2.9	51.8
Delaware	31.3	6.7	4.0	59.7
D.C.	68.1	6.8	2.3	33.8
Maine	9.9	9.0	3.9	43.3
Maryland	29.0	7.1	3.0	42.3
Massachusetts	21.4	6.4	2.4	37.5
New Hampshire	11.2	8.6	5.0	58.1
New Jersey	36.3	6.6	3.5	53.0
New York	39.1	7.9	3.0	38.0
Pennsylvania	14.3	6.0	3.2	53.3
Rhode Island	24.1	8.6	3.3	38.4
Vermont	12.7	9.9	4.0	40.4
Total Northeast				
Mean Northeast	26.5	7.4	3.4	45.4
Median Northeast	22.8	7.0	3.3	46.8
West				
California	37.2	6.6		
Hawaii	21.7	20.4	3.8	18.6
Oregon	23.5	7.7	4.9	63.6
Washington	20.3	7.2	4.5	62.5
Total West				
Mean West	25.7	10.5	4.4	42.0
Median West	22.6	7.5	4.5	60.4
Midwest				
Illinois	23.2	7.3	3.2	43.8
Michigan	21.6	6.7	3.9	58.2
Minnesota	13.5	6.8	3.3	48.5
Wisconsin	9.6	6.5	3.2	49.2
Total Midwest				
Mean Midwest	17.0	6.8	3.4	49.8

	Abortions per 1000 Women	Marriages per 1000 People	Divorces per 1000 People	Divorces / Marriages %
	2000(1)	2001(1)	2001(1)	2001(2)
Median Midwest	17.6	6.8	3.3	48.1
Total Blue				
Mean Blue	24.5	7.9	3.5	44.7
Median Blue	21.7	7.0	3.3	47.5

Source: (1) Statistical Abstract of the United States, (2) Stephen D. Cummings based on data from (1)

APPENDIX E.2A. RED-STATE CULTURE (PART 2)

	Drug Use % 12 yrs & over	Liquor % 12 yrs & over	Cigarettes % 12 yrs & over	Executions	Churches per 1000 Population
	2001(1)	2001(1)	2001(1)	1977–2002(1)	2005(2)
UNITED STATES	6.7	20.6	24.9	1069	
South					
Alabama	5.8	18.3	25.0	31	2.6
Arkansas	6.7	19.2	28.0	32	2.7
Florida	6.0	18.8	24.4	62	1.2
Georgia	6.1	19.8	24.7	35	1.9
Kentucky	6.7	18.3	32.5		1.8
Louisiana	6.7	22.3	29.7	29	2.1
Mississippi	5.7	18.3	26.5	6	2.9
North Carolina	7.9	17.0	27.6	31	2.4
South Carolina	5.7	19.7	26.2	33	2.4
Tennessee	6.2	16.0	28.4		2.1
Texas	5.3	21.5	23.7	381	1.5
Virginia	5.5	17.8	25.0	111	1.5
West Virginia	5.0	18.2	29.4		1.7
Total South					
Mean South	6.1	18.9	27.0	75	2.1
Median South	6.0	18.3	26.5	33	2.1
West					
Alaska	9.2	20.2	24.1		1.8
Arizona	6.7	21.5	23.1	32	0.8
Colorado	9.2	22.0	24.2		1.0
Idaho	5.4	19.6	23.0		1.5
Montana	6.3	23.2	23.0		1.8
Nevada	7.3	23.8	28.6	11	0.7
New Mexico	7.5	22.7	25.7		1.2
Utah	5.0	14.2	16.8		1.0
Wyoming	5.7	24.1	27.2		1.9
Total West					
Mean West	6.9	21.3	24.0	22	1.3

	Drug Use % 12 yrs & over	Liquor % 12 yrs & over	Cigarettes % 12 yrs & over	Executions	Churches per 1000 Population
	2001(1)	2001(1)	2001(1)	1977–2002(1)	2005(2)
Median West	6.7	22.0	24.1	22	1.2
Midwest					
Indiana	5.2	19.0	27.4	12	1.7
Iowa	4.5	21.9	24.8		1.9
Kansas	6.1	19.9	24.9		2.0
Missouri	5.7	20.0	27.7	80	1.9
Nebraska	4.6	22.8	24.4		1.8
North Dakota	4.1	29.0	25.5		2.2
Ohio	5.9	21.7	29.2		1.5
Oklahoma	5.4	18.3	26.9	90	2.1
South Dakota	4.5	24.5	26.4		2.1
Total Midwest					
Mean Midwest	5.1	21.9	26.4	61	1.9
Median Midwest	5.2	21.7	26.4	80	1.9
Total Red					
Mean Red	6.1	20.4	25.9	65	1.8
Median Red	5.8	19.9	25.7	32	1.8

APPENDIX E.2B. BLUE-STATE CULTURE (PART 2)

	Drug Use % 12 yrs & over	Liquor % 12 yrs & over	Cigarettes % 12 yrs & over	Executions	Churches per 1000 Population
	2001(1)	2001(1)	2001(1)	1977–2002(1)	2005(2)
UNITED STATES	6.7	20.6	24.9	1069	
Northeast					
Connecticut	7.5	22.3	25.1		1.0
Delaware	7.6	21.5	25.5	18	1.4
D.C.	8.1	22.0	25.2		1.7
Maine	8.4	22.7	26.2		1.3
Maryland	6.2	19.5	24.4		1.2
Massachusetts	10.7	25.9	23.0		0.7
New Hampshire	8.0	21.9	25.8		0.9
New Jersey	5.8	21.3	23.1		0.9
New York	6.8	19.7	23.2		0.9
Pennsylvania	5.9	22.3	26.3		1.4
Rhode Island	8.2	24.2	27.0		0.7
Vermont	10.5	23.2	24.6		1.2
Total Northeast					
Mean Northeast	7.8	22.2	25.0	18	1.1
Median Northeast	7.8	22.2	25.2	18	1.1
West					
California	8.2	19.1	21.3	13	0.8
Hawaii	7.5	18.7	20.7		1.0
Oregon	8.7	18.1	23.2		1.2
Washington	7.7	18.9	23.4		1.1
Total West					
Mean West	8.0	18.7	22.2	13	1.0
Median West	8.0	18.8	22.3	13	1.1
Midwest					
Illinois	7.2	24.1	26.7		1.3
Michigan	7.5	21.9	27.1		1.3
Minnesota	6.6	24.1	24.7		1.3
Wisconsin	6.3	28.3	24.2		1.3

	Drug Use % 12 yrs & over	Liquor % 12 yrs & over	Cigarettes % 12 yrs & over	Executions	Churches per 1000 Population
	2001(1)	2001(1)	2001(1)	1977–2002(1)	2005(2)
Total Midwest					
Mean Midwest	6.9	24.6	25.7		1.3
Median Midwest	6.9	24.1	25.7		1.3
Total Blue					
Mean Blue	7.7	22.0	24.5	16	1.1
Median Blue	7.6	22.0	24.7	16	1.2

Source: (1) Statistical Abstract of the United States, (2) Stephen D. Cummings based on data by (1) and American Church Lists.

Bibliography

Allen, Frederick Lewis. *Only Yesterday*. 1931. Reprint, New York: Bantam, 1959.

Associated Press, "Reid: 'Dangerously Incompetent.'" *CBS News*, March 23, 2006. http://www.cbsnews.com/stories/2006/03/23/politics/main1432159.shtml.

Associated Press. U.S. Savings Rate Hits Lowest Level Since 1933." January 30, 2006. http://www.msnbc.msn.com/id/11098797/.

Bawden, Tom. "Buffet Blasts System That Lets Him Pay Less Tax Than Secretary." *Times Online (London)*, June 28, 2007. http://business.timesonline.co.uk/toll/business/money/tax/article1996735.ece.

Beeton, Todd. "Courage Campaign/MyDD Poll: Why Francine Busby Lost." *Courage Campaign*, August 2, 2006. http://couragecampaign.org/entries/poll-conclusions/#more.

Berman, Ari. "Big $$ for Progressive Politics." *The Nation*, October 16, 2006.

Blum, Justin. " 'Blue' States Tackling Energy on Their Own." *Washington Post*, January 22, 2006.

Bowers, Simon. "Buffett Attacks American Spending Junkies." *Guardian(UK)*, March 7, 2005.

Bruchey, Stuart. *Growth of the American Economy*. New York: Dodd, Mead, 1975.

Bryan, William Jennings. *Speeches of William Jennings Bryan Revised and Arranged by Himself.* 2 vol. New York: Funk & Wagnalls, 1909.

Bunke, Harvey. *A Primer on American Economic History*. New York: Random House, 1969.

Bureau of Economic Analysis. *Current Dollar and Real Gross Domestic Product*. http://bea.gov/nation/xls/gdplev.xls

————. *Personal Income and Outlays, December 2006 Table 7.* http://www.bea.gov/bea/ newsrelarchive/2007/pil206.htm.

————. *U.S. International Transactions: Fourth Quarter and Year 2006.* http://www.bea.gov/ newsreleasesw/international/transnewsrelease.htm

Bureau of Labor Statistics. *Employment, Hours and Earnings from the Current Employment Statistics Survey (National).* http://data.bls.gov/cgi-bin/surveymost.

Burner, David. *The Politics of Provincialism: The Democratic Party in Transition 1918–1932.* 1967. Reprint, Cambridge, MA.: Harvard, 1986.

California Secretary of State. "Congressional District 50–Special Election." http:// www.ss.ca.gov/elections/elections_cd50.htm.

Chase, Stuart. *A New Deal.* New York, 1932.

CNN. "First Bush–Gore Debate Alternates Between Issues, Attacks." *CNN.com,* October 3, 2000. http://archives.cnn.com/2000/ALLPOLITICS/stories/10/03/ debate.wrap/.

Cobb, James C. *Industrialization and Southern Society.* Lexington: The University Press of Kentucky, 1984.

Corpus, Victor N. "If It Comes to a Shooting War." *Asia Times Online,* April 20, 2006. http://atimes01.atimes.com/atimes/China/HD20Ad03.html.

Crutsinger, Martin. "Family Income Falling." *Associated Press,* February 23, 2006. http://pqasb.pqarchiver.com/ap/access/9966778531.html.

Cummings, Stephen D. *The Dixification of America: The American Odyssey into the Conservative Economic Trap.* Westport, CT.: Praeger, 1998.

David, Paul. "The Growth of Real Product in the U.S. Before 1840: New Evidence, Controlled Conjectures." *Journal of Economic History* 27, no. 2 (June 1967).

Diamond, Jared. *Collapse: How Societies Choose to Fail or Succeed.* New York: Viking, 2005.

Economist. "In Comes the Waves." June 18, 2005.

————. "Poison Ivy." September 23, 2006.

———— "The South: Among Hills and Hollow." April 13, 1996.

————. "Still Waiting for the Big One." April 8, 2006.

————. Trade, Exchange, Budget Balance and Interest Rates. March 24, 2007.

————. "The Yen Also Rises." March 18, 2006.

Economist.com. "Ever Higher Society, Ever Harder to Ascend." December 29, 2004. http://www.economist.com/world/na/displayStory.cfm.

Falk, William, and Thomas A. Lyson. *High Tech, Low Tech, No Tech: Recent Industrial and Occupational Change in the South.* Albany: State University of New York Press, 1988.

Fisher, Irving. "Debt–Deflation Theory of Great Depressions." *Econometrica* 1 (October 1933).

Fogel, Robert and Stanley L. Engerman. "The Economics of Slavery." In *The Reinterpretation of American History*, eds. Fogel and Engerman.

———. "Explaining the Relative Efficiency of Slave Agriculture in the Antebellum South." *American Economic Review* 67, no. 3 (June 1977): 285 Table 7.

———. *The Reinterpretation of American History*. New York: Harper and Row, 1971.

Foster, William, and Waddill Catchings. *Business Without a Buyer*. Boston: Houghton Mifflin, 1927.

———. "Must We Reduce Our Standard of Living?" *Forum* 85 (February 1931): 75–77.

Frank, Robert, and Phillip J. Cook. *The Winner-Take-All Society*. New York: Free Press, 1995.

Frank, Thomas. *What's the Matter With Kansas?: How Conservatives Won the Heart of America*. New York: Metropolitan, 2004.

Franke-Ruta, Garrance. "Re-mapping the Cultural Debate." *The American Prospect*, February 2006.

Franklin, Benjamin. "The Way to Wealth." *Poor Richard's Almanac*, 1758.

Fukuyama, Francis. *The End of History and the Last Man*. New York: Free Press, 1992.

Galbraith, John Kenneth. *The Great Crash, 1929*. Boston: Houghton Mifflin, 1955.

Gallman, R.E. "GNP in the U.S., 1834–1909." In *Structures in Income and Wealth*, vol. 30, *Output, Employment and Productivity in the U.S. After 1800*. New York: Columbia University Press, 1966.

Greenhouse, Steven, and David Leonhardt. "Real Wages Fail to Match a Rise in Productivity." *New York Times*, August 28, 2006.

Habakuk, H.J. *American and British Technology in the 19th Century: The Search for Labor-Saving Inventions*. Cambridge, England: Cambridge University Press, 1962.

Hansen, Alvin. *Fiscal Policy and Business Cycles*. New York: Norton, 1941.

———. *Full Recovery or Stagnation*. New York, 1938.

Harris, Paul. "37 Million Poor Hidden in the Land of Plenty." *Observer (London)*, February 19, 2006.

Henwood, Doug. "Leaking Bubble." *The Nation*, March 27, 2006.

Hsu, Spenser S. "U.S. Tells D.C. to Pay Inaugural Expenses." *Washington Post*, January 11, 2005.

Huffington, Arianna. "Anatomy of a Crushing Defeat." *Arianna Online*, November 3, 2004. http://www.ariannaonline.com/columns/printer_friendly.php?id=742.

Ingram, Dale. "Drought-stricken Arkansas Farmers Only Wanted Food For Their Families. They Stirred America." *Arkansas Times*, January 19, 2006. http://www.arktimes.com/Articles/ArticleViewer.aspx.

International Monetary Fund. *World Economic Outlook*, September 2006. http://www.imf.org/external/pubs/ft/weo/2006/02/index.htm.

Irwin, Neal. "Family Savings Look Scary Across the Board." *Washington Post*, March 5, 2006.

Jefferson, Thomas. Thomas Jefferson to James Madison, October 28, 1785. *The Writings of Thomas Jefferson*. eds. Andrew A. Lipscomb and Albert Ellery Bergh, 19:17, Papers 8:682. Washington D.C.: The Thomas Jefferson Memorial Association, 1905.

Johnston, Day Cay. *Perfectly Legal: The Covert Campaign to Rig Our Tax System to Benefit the Super Rich—and Cheat Everybody Else*. New York: Portfolio, 2003.

Johnson, Hugh S. *The Blue Eagle from Egg to Earth*. Garden City, N.Y.: Doubleday, Doran, 1935.

Kennedy, Paul. *The Rise and Fall of the Great Powers: Economic Change and Military Conflict from 1500 to 2000*. New York: Vintage, 1989.

Krugman, Paul. "Graduate versus Oligarchs." *New York Times*, February 27, 2006.

Kuznets, Simon. *National Income and its Composition, 1919–1938*. New York: National Bureau of Economic Research, 1941.

Left Business Observer, nos. 107, 114.

Leuchtenburg, William E. *The Perils of Prosperity, 1914–1932*. 2nd ed. Chicago: University of Chicago Press, 1993.

Liu, Henry C.K. "America's Untested Management Team." *Asia Times Online*, June 17, 2006. http://www.atimes.com/atimes/Global_Economy/HF17Dj01.html.

Maddison, Angus. "Growth and Slowdown in Advanced Capitalist Economies: Techniques of Quantitative Assessment." *The Journal of Economic Literature* 25, no.2 (June 1987).

Madrick, Jeff. "Goodbye, Horatio Alger." *The Nation*, February 5, 2007.

Mason, John, Pierre Soulé, and James Buchanan. "The Ostend Manifesto." In *The Annals of America* (Chicago: Encyclopaedia Britannica, 1968) 8: 289–293.

Means, Gardiner. "The Consumer and the New Deal." *Annals of the American Academy of Political Social Sciences* 173 (May 1934): 11.

Moley, Raymond. *After Seven Years*. Harper and Brothers, 1939.

———. *The First New Deal*. New York: Harcourt, Brace and World, 1966.

Murray, Robert K. *The 103rd Ballot: Democrats and the Disaster in Madison Square Garden*. New York: Harper and Row, 1976.

McCarty, Harold Hull. *The Geographical Basis of American Economic Life*. 2 vols. Port Washington, N.Y.: Kennikat Press, 1970.

Nelson, Richard R., and Gavin Wright. "The Rise and Fall of American Technological Leadership: The Postwar Era in Historical Perspective." *Journal of Economic Literature* 30, no. 4 (December 1992.

Newman, Alan. "The Importance of 'Qs.'" *Crosscurrents*, November 6, 2004. http://crosscurrents.net/archives/nov04.htm.

Obama, Sen. Barack. "Moving Forward in Iraq." *Chicago Tribune*, November 22, 2005.

Olbermann, Keith. "The 'City' of Louisiana." *MSNBC Countdown*, September 5, 2005.

Parker, William N. ed. *The Structure of the Cotton Economy of the Antebellum South.* Vol. 44. Washington D.C.: The Agriculture History Society, 1970.

Perelman, Michael. *The Pathology of the U.S. Economy: The Cost of a Low-Wage System.* Houndsmills, England: MacMillan, 1993.

Picketty, Thomas, and Emmanuel Saez. "Income Inequality in the United States 1913–1998." *NBER Working Paper no. 8467* (September 2001).

Primack, Martin L., and James F. Willis. *An Economic History of the United States.* Menlo Park, CA: Benjamin Cummings, 1980.

Ransom, Roger L., and Richard Sutch. "Growth and Welfare in the American South in the Nineteenth Century." In *Market Institutions and Economic Progress in the New South 1865–1900*, eds. Walton and Shepard.

Republican Study Committee. "Highlights from the 2007 Social Security and Medicare Trustees Report." Washington D.C., 2000. http://www.house.gov/hensarling/rsc/PB_042407_SSMedicareTrustees.doc.

Robbins, Lionel. *The Great Depression.* London: Macmillan, 1934.

Robertson, Ross W., and Gary M. Walton. *History of the American Economy.* 4ᵗʰ ed. New York: Harcourt, Brace and Jovanovich, 1979.

Rosenman, Samuel I. *Working With Roosevelt.* New York: Harper and Brothers, 1952.

Rothstein, Morton. "The Cotton Frontier of the Antebellum United States: A Methodological Battleground." In *The Structure of the Cotton Economy of the Antebellum South*, ed. Parker.

San Francisco Chronicle. "Gov. Schwarzenegger to Stay the Course." October 18, 2006.

Saunders, Norman C. " A Summary of BLS Projections to 2014." *Monthly Labor Review Online*, November 2005. vol. 128, no. 11.

Schlesinger, Arthur M., Jr. *The Coming of the New Deal.* Boston: Houghton Mifflin, 1958.

Shannon, Fred A. *The Farmers Last Frontier: Agriculture 1980–1897.* Armonk, N.Y.: M.E. Sharpe, 1989.

Social Security Administration. "2007 Social Security Trustees Report." Table IV.B6.

Soule, George. *Prosperity Decade from War to Depression, 1917–1929.* 1947. Reprint, New York: Harper and Row, 1968.

Stoneman, William E. *A History of Economic Analysis of the Great Depression in America.* New York: Garland, 1979.

Tugwell, Rex. "The Price Also Rises." *Fortune* 9 (January 1934): 71–72.

UNCTAD. *World Investment Report 2006.* http://www.unctad.org/sections/dite_dir/docs/wir2006top100_en.pdf.

U.S. Department of Health and Human Services, Center for Medicare and Medicaid Services. "2007 Medicare Trustees Report." Tables III. B10, B11, C23.

U.S. Treasury Department. "Debt to the Penny and Who Holds It." *Treasury Direct.* http://www.treasurydirect.gov/NP/BPDLogin?application=np.

————. *Financial Statements of the United States Government. Statement of Operations and Changes of Net Position*. Washington D.C.: 2006. http://fms.treas.gov/fr/06Frusg/06stml.pdf.

VandeHei, Jim. "Old-School Team to Sell Kerry as Modern Centrist." *Washington Post*, April 21, 2004.

Walsh, John V. "The War Loses, Voters Win, Rahm's Loser." *Counterpunch*, November 11, 2006. http://counterpunch.com/walsh11112006.html.

Walton, Gary M., and James E. Shepard, eds. *Market Institutions and Economic Progress in the New South 1865–1900*. New York: Academia Press, 1991.

Wessel, David. "As Rich–Poor Gap Widens in U.S, Class Mobility Stalls." *Wall Street Journal*, May 13, 2005.

Wighton, David. "Morgan Stanley Taps China for $5bn." *FT.com*, December 19, 2007. http://www.ft.com/cms/s/o/294ed78a-ae3a-11dc-97aa-0000779fd2ac.html.

World Economic Forum. *Global Competitiveness Report*. http://www.weforum.org/en/initiatives/gcp/Global%20Competitiveness%20Report/index.htm.

Wright, Gavin. "Economic Democracy and the Concentration of Agricultural Wealth in the Cotton States, 1850–1860." In *The Structure of the Cotton Economy of the Antebellum South*, ed. Parker.

————. *Old South, New South: Revolution in the Southern Economy since the Civil War*. New York: Basic Books, 1986.

————. "The Origins of American Industrial Success 1879–1940." *American Economic Review* 80, no. 4 (September 1990).

INDEX

C